REVISED EDITION

ILLINOIS

Gardener's Guide

Published by Cool Springs Press, a Division of Thomas Nelson, Inc., P. O. Box 141000, Nashville, Tennessee, 37214.

Fizzell, James A. (James Alfred), 1935-
    Illinois gardener's guide / by James A. Fizzell.-- Rev. ed.
       p. cm.
    Includes bibliographical references (p.   ).
    ISBN: 1-888608-99-4 (pbk. : alk. paper)
    1. Landscape plants--Illinois. 2. Landscape gardening--Illinois.
    I. Title.
  SB407 .F384 2002
  635.9'09773--dc21

                                                    2001006793

First printing 2002
Printed in the United States of America
10 9 8 7 6 5 4

Managing Editor: Angela Reiner Downing
Horticulture Editor: Dr. Willard Witte, Assoc. Prof., University of Tennessee (retired)
Horticultural Copyeditor: Diana Maranhao
Copyeditor: Sara Goodrum
Designer: Sheri Ferguson
Production Artist: S.E. Anderson

On the cover: White Coneflower photographed by Dency Kane

Visit the Thomas Nelson website at www.ThomasNelson.com

REVISED EDITION

ILLINOIS
Gardener's Guide

JAMES A. FIZZELL

COOL
SPRINGS
PRESS

Nashville, Tennessee
A Division of Thomas Nelson, Inc.
www.ThomasNelson.com

Dedication

This book is dedicated to our adult children, Michael, Lori, Susan, and John, all of whom have gardened since they were children, and are teaching their children to love gardening as well.

Acknowledgments

No one who writes a book can claim credit for everything in it. It takes the efforts of lots of people who are kind enough to provide time and expertise to help make it a reality. *The Illinois Gardener's Guide* is no exception. The following friends have been especially helpful in preparation of this book:

Most important is (Adrienne) Jane Fizzell, my wife and business partner. The hours and hours it takes to write a book are hours that we could have spent together. Without any thought for her own time, she has read copy, edited, researched, fended off impatient clients, and offered to help in any way she could to make this book possible. Matt Turney, Pastor and good friend, always has a helpful suggestion—especially when things begin to pile up. He always sees the bright light at the end of the tunnel. Gregory R. Stack, Horticulturist, University of Illinois, Matteson, my friend and fellow horticulturist, shared an office for years at the University of Illinois. Greg is an outstanding horticulturist and provided resources and moral support. Kathy Judge, librarian at the Chicago Botanic Garden in Glencoe, willingly searches out and finds answers to perplexing questions. Special thanks goes to the late Dr. Floyd Swink, botanist of international reputation and friend, for editing the manuscript for the first edition of the *Illinois Gardener's Guide,* and for technical advice. His cheery demeanor and incomparable expertise are sorely missed. A sincere thank you to all of my wonderful friends.

Also, sincere thanks is due to the good people at Cool Springs Press. Roger Waynick for making the book possible; Hank McBride and Angela Downing for the many hours they have spent on the editing, layout, and production; and to Cindy Games for her tireless efforts in the distribution of this book.

God Bless You All!

Table of Contents

The Joy of
Illinois Gardening

Welcome to Illinois gardening, where horticulture is an art—an art that is learned by doing! We make our mistakes, and we have our successes. We correct our mistakes and go on. As I work with the folks who grow gardens and care for landscape plantings, and as fellow gardeners tell us of their problems at shows and on the air during my radio programs, I realize what tremendous interest there is in plants and how they grow. The questions we were asked a decade or two ago can now be answered by nearly every gardener. The questions today are complicated, showing a high level of expertise by Illinois gardeners.

But don't let that discourage you if you are a beginner. Plant people are different! Instead of trying to keep their secrets, they will go out of their way to tell them to you. Just because a gardener isn't "schooled" doesn't mean you can ignore the information. Those of us who have been at it a long time have made many mistakes and have profited from them. If the comments in this book are helpful to you, it is because I, along with my friends who helped put it together, have been where you are. We have had the question and found the answer. I thank all those unselfish gardeners who taught me, and I hope you can profit from our collective knowledge.

Illinois Gardening: History and Traditions

Settlers found flatlands and prairies when they reached Illinois. The land was quite a change from the hills and dense forests through which they had cut trails, and in which they had carved out farms. There were tall grasses as far as the eye could see, as high as a horse's head. The soil was flat and fertile, and there was enough wood from forests bordering rivers and streams to build their homes. The rivers provided good transportation to other settlements, to the Mississippi on the West and to the shores of Lake Michigan and the little community of Chicago up north.

Farming consisted of trying to grow some row crops and enough feed for the horses and livestock. That was man's work. The garden was next to the house, and women were in charge there. The garden was easily accessible to the kitchen and fenced to keep out wandering livestock.

The fifty years between the Civil War and World War I were a time of tremendous change. Illinois grew from a strictly rural state to an industrialized state, with Chicago, Peoria, Galena, and Decatur developing a privileged class who had the time and resources for landscaping and gardening. At the same time, the nation was experiencing a gardening revolution that led to burgeoning seed companies, nurseries, and horticulturists. Explorers were bringing in all kinds of plants from every part of the temperate world. The Orient was a particularly fruitful source, and many of the plants we grow today were introduced during those fertile years.

There were scores of gardening books published, and horticultural societies were founded. Landscape architects, among them Frederick Law Olmsted, who was the first to use that title, were busily planning the great gardens and conservatories. Daniel Burnham was planning the 1893 World Colombian Exposition in Chicago, and convincing the people there to preserve some of the rapidly diminishing vacant land. He enlisted Olmsted to plan the grounds for the Exposition, and many of those gardens and parks along the shores of Lake Michigan are still there. The forest preserves of the northern Illinois counties, the great estate gardens, and the Chicago motto, *Urbs in Horto* (City in a Garden) are all results of the inspiration of these two "plant people."

What Makes Gardening Unique in Illinois?

Illinois has a moist, temperate, continental climate. Spring is often cool and wet, with snow common until mid-April. Spring can be so wet that planting is delayed, and so cool that the emergence of leaves can be delayed until the end of April. In addition to the normal weather patterns, the nearness of Lake Michigan keeps areas in the northeast corner of the state cool.

Summers are warm with temperatures in the 80s and 90s, reaching 100 degrees Fahrenheit on occasion. A succession of low and high pressure systems produces alternating warm and cool weather and provides summer rains, mostly as thunderstorms as the lows pull humid air northward from the Gulf of Mexico. Rainfall averages about three inches per month throughout the summer.

Fall can be the most beautiful season of the year in Illinois. Temperatures are generally moderate, in the 60s and 70s in early fall, with daytime highs falling to the upper 30s by late November. October days can be clear and bright. Rainfall generally becomes more frequent, although extended drought is not uncommon. Late fall, from mid-November on, can be dark and cloudy. The first measurable snow can appear by mid-October. The first 3-inch snowfall can be expected by Thanksgiving.

Winter weather is often quite variable. Some years there is little snow, and temperatures remain moderate. Normally, however, there are about three feet of snow, and temperatures will fall to as low as minus 10 degrees Fahrenheit at least once during the season. Extreme low temperatures of minus 25 to minus 30 degrees have been recorded.

The growing season is from about 150 days in the northern part of the state to about 205 days far south. The average date of last frost is around April 5 near the Ohio River, May 5 in the Chicago area, and may be as late as May 10 farther northwest. The average date of first frost is October 20. The earliest frost has occurred around Labor Day, the latest usually around Halloween.

Weather and Plant Hardiness

Plant hardiness is affected by several factors, including low temperatures. The ability of a species or cultivar to tolerate the lowest temperatures it will experience in its location is usually what is meant by "plant hardiness." But hardiness is also affected by high temperatures, how fast the temperatures change, wind, shade, humidity, and soil conditions. And plants are often found growing well outside their suggested hardiness range where they are protected, or where extra care is provided.

There are two hardiness rating maps in general use. These zones are based on the average minimum temperatures that can be expected in a particular part of the continent. According to the United States Department of Agriculture (USDA) (see page 15), Illinois is in Plant Hardiness Zones 4b, 5, and 6. The Arnold Arboretum map indicates Illinois is in Zones 4, 5, and 6. Be sure to notice which rating system is being used for any plants you purchase. We follow the USDA system in this book.

Plants can be protected from adverse temperatures or weather for short periods. In spring or fall, tender plants can be covered with blankets until temperatures moderate. Plants on the south side of a building may be warmer because of the "Dutch Oven" effect. The effect may even last overnight, protecting otherwise sensitive plants. In summer, plants can be moved into the shade on particularly hot days, or some kind of shade cover can be provided.

Mulches can protect roots from temporary high or low temperatures. Water helps plants tolerate high or low temperatures. Water loss (transpiration) cools plant tissues, and water, as long as it doesn't freeze, can keep plant tissues from freezing. Be sure plants entering stressful periods are well watered. Wilted plants are much more sensitive to extreme temperatures.

Microclimates can affect the survival of plants. These effects can be regional or localized. Bodies of water affect plants near them, the larger the body, the larger the affected area. The moderating effect of Lake Michigan is mentioned above. Temperatures in urbanized areas tend to stay above those in surrounding areas; buildings and pavement warm up in the sun and keep the heat all night.

Wooded areas tend to stay cooler in summer and warmer in winter. Drive into a forest preserve on a hot summer day, and the change will be apparent. Shade and transpiration from leaves of the trees are responsible for most of this natural air-conditioning.

There can be big differences in microclimates within a garden. The shaded north side of the home may be cooler and moister than the south side. Trees provide shade and air conditioning the same as

those in the forest preserve. A fence can direct summer breezes and moderate winter winds. The south side of a building will stay warmer in winter, and plants like spring bulbs will bloom earlier than those planted elsewhere.

Deciduous trees planted on the south side will shade the home in summer but allow the sun to warm it in winter. Evergreens on the south side will provide summer shade but will shade the home in winter, preventing warming by the sun, keeping snow from melting from walks, steps, or roof. It is best to plan carefully before planting trees so they serve the purposes intended for them.

Understanding Soils

Soils are formed by the weathering of rock. They can form in place, or they may be moved by water or wind from their original locations. About 80 percent of the soils in Illinois are loess. This is material that was formed by the grinding down of rock by glaciers, deposited in river beds as glaciers retreated, then picked up by winds and carried east. Most of our soil material came from the Mississippi/Missouri River valleys. The soils tend to be coarser near those rivers, finer to the east. Loess soils are mostly loams.

Soils are made of solids (mineral and organic), air, and water. Productive soils are about 50 percent solids and 50 percent pore space. Ideally, half the pore space will be filled with air, half with water. In reality, this pore space is full of water following rainfall or watering and full of air when soils are dry.

Soils are named according to the kinds of solids in them: sands, silts, or clays. The names describe the soils and identify their characteristics.

Sands have large particles; their grains are big enough to be seen without a hand lens. Spaces between the grains are relatively large, too. Water moves easily through sandy soils, so they are described as well drained.

The particles of silts are small, and you can't see them individually. Spaces between the particles are tiny and easily filled by capillary water, leaving no room for air. Silts drain poorly and are hard to handle.

Clay particles are very tiny, molecular in size, and visible only with an electron microscope. Clays can be very productive if handled right, or they can be impossible. The structure determines whether they will support plants or not. With good structure, clays are friable and well aerated, with enough water for plants. If structure is poor, they are like modeling clay, saturated when wet, hard and cracked when dry.

Loams are soils that have the correct amounts of sand, silt, and clay. Loams are the best garden soils because they have the good features of each kind of soil. In Illinois the soils are mostly loams.

The Value of Organic Matter

Organic matter comes from things that were alive: grass clippings, dead garden plants, leaves, peat moss, straw, compost, manure . . . and lots of other things. The microorganisms in the soil break down organic matter and release the nutrients so plants can reuse them. They also help cement soil particles together to make aggregates.

Coarse organic matter opens the soil so air can get in. This is beneficial in heavy clay soils. Organic matter pieces are like sponges and hold lots of water, so they improve light sandy soils, too.

Lots of organic matter is essential for a healthy, productive garden soil. Try to add as much organic matter as you can to your soils. There is no need to throw any away.

Soil Acidity/Alkalinity (pH)

The soil pH measures soil acidity or alkalinity. At a pH of 7.0, the soil is neutral. Most plants prefer acidic conditions; a pH of 6.0 to 7.0 is ideal. Soils throughout Illinois, however, are often quite alkaline; a pH of 8.0 is not rare. Thus it is important to select plant material that will tolerate alkalinity (soils with a high pH are notoriously difficult to change).

Applications of lime (calcium carbonate) and gypsum (calcium sulfate) are often recommended for garden soils. You must test Illinois soils before adding lime or gypsum. Excess calcium adds to alkalinity and to the deficiency of other nutrient elements. Sulfur that lowers the pH is sometimes better in our soils.

Understanding Fertilizers

Fertilizers provide essential elements for plants. The elements used in the greatest amounts by plants are nitrogen, phosphorus, and potassium. Fertilizers usually contain some or all of these elements; the amounts of each in the particular fertilizer material are shown in the analysis on the label.

The analysis shows the amounts by weight of the Nitrogen (N), Phosphate (P), and Potash (K), always in that order. A fertilizer with an analysis of 10-6-4 contains 10 percent nitrogen, 6 percent phosphate, and 4 percent potash. This is a complete fertilizer containing all three of the major elements. A complete fertilizer containing all three elements in equal amounts is called a balanced fertilizer. An analysis of 16-16-16 is balanced.

Generally, unless a soil test has been done and specific recommendations are made, garden fertilizers are used based on the amount of nitrogen in them. The standard rate is 1 pound of actual nitrogen per 1000 square feet of lawn or garden. If you use the 10-6-4 fertilizer, with its 10 percent nitrogen, you will need 10 pounds of fertilizer to apply a pound of nitrogen. If you use a 16-16-16, you will need to spread

6$^1/_4$ pounds over 1000 square feet. The phosphorus and potassium go along for the ride, usually just for insurance in case there is a deficiency of either one.

Soil Preparation

The first step in preparing soil is to make sure the surface is graded so water runs off in the direction you want it to go. It must run away from the house or any other structure, and away from the garden.

Second, take the time to get rid of all vegetation. Spraying with a non-selective herbicide such as glyphosate according to label directions kills all existing vegetation, including underground parts, but it will not kill seeds that might germinate the next day. So let the soil lie dormant for a couple of weeks, and treat anything else that grows. For a perennial garden or ground cover bed, a third treatment may be worthwhile.

Next, check the drainage. Dig a hole a foot wide and deep and fill it with water. After it drains, fill it again. Do it a third time. If the hole drains out in 12 hours, the drainage is good. If it does not, install tiles or build raised beds. Some plants will tolerate slow drainage; other plants will deteriorate and eventually die.

Rototilling the soil is fine for annuals, and for some shallowly rooted perennials and ground covers. For deeply rooted plants, especially some perennials, spading to two or three spade depths is necessary. These procedures are called double-digging and trenching.

To double-dig the garden, remove the soil one spade deep across part of the garden. I try to start with an area two or three rows across and 5 or 6 feet wide. Stack the soil up to be used later. Add organic matter to the second layer, and spade it over. Move to an adjacent area of the garden, cover it with organic matter, and turn it into the area first vacated. This will open the second level for another few rows. Add organic matter and turn over. Work your way down the garden to the end. This will leave an open area into which you can dump the soil from the first rows you opened. Trenching is the same type of procedure, but 3 spades deep. This is a lot of work, but it is essential for plants like Delphiniums and

Lupines. You do not need to do the whole garden, just the places where you intend to put these demanding plants. Take your time. You don't need to complete the job all at once.

Soil Mechanics

Where two different soil materials meet abruptly, they cause an interface that prevents the movement of air or water, and the development of roots. Planting a sand-grown shrub in a clay soil, peat-grown sod over clay soil, or a light, artificial soil mix in garden soil creates interfaces. Prevent them by buying plants grown in the same kind of soil as you have in your garden, or mixing the two kinds of soil going back into the planting hole to cause a gradual change from one to the other. Soil incompatibility is the most common problem preventing successful transplanting of garden plants.

Insect and Disease Problems

Most plants are affected by some pests.

Sooner or later the pest problem will arise, and you will scramble to find out what to do about it. The first step is to identify the problem; until you know what it is, you won't know if it is necessary to treat it or whether it will go away on its own. When certain problems are common in a particular plant, we have tried to identify them in the plant descriptions.

The next line of defense is your neighborhood garden center. Often the folks there will have a troubleshooting guide on hand. If that is not sufficient help, there are University of Illinois Extension Offices in many counties where horticulturists or master gardeners are available to help. Community colleges and any of the four-year universities teaching horticulture courses have horticulturists on staff who are knowledgeable and helpful, and the Chicago Botanic Garden, Morton Arboretum, and the Klehm Arboretum have plant information offices to provide these kinds of services.

Don't overlook consulting an experienced gardener in your neighborhood. Such people have seen most of the neighborhood gardening problems before. Even if they can't exactly identify a particular problem, they may have found a way to contend with it.

It's all a process of discovery—understanding your own backyard while exploring what your region has to offer, learning about new plants and appreciating the tried and true. Enjoy the process, and enjoy your Illinois garden!

How to Use This Book

Each entry in the *Illinois Gardener's Guide: Revised Edition* provides you with information about a plant's particular characteristics, habits and basic requirements for active growth. I include the information you need to help you realize each plant's potential. Only when a plant performs at its best can one appreciate it fully. You will find such pertinent information as mature height and spread, bloom period and colors (if any), sun and soil preferences, water requirements, fertilizing needs, pruning and care, and pest information.

Sun Preferences

Symbols represent the range of sunlight suitable for each plant. The icon representing "Full Sun" means the plant needs to be sited in a full sun (8-10 hours of sun daily) location. "Mostly Sun" means the plant likes full sun, but may appreciate a few hours of protection from harsh, late afternoon sun. "Partial Sun/Shade" means the plant can be situated where it receives partial sun all day or morning sun, or dappled shade. "Full Shade" means the plant needs a shady location protected from direct sunlight. Some plants can be grown in more than one range of sun, so you will sometimes see more than one sun symbol.

Full Sun   **Mostly Sun**   **Partial Sun/Shade**   **Full Shade**

Additional Benefits

Many plants offer benefits that further enhance their appeal. The following symbols indicate some of the more notable additional benefits:

 Attracts Butterflies

 Attracts Hummingbirds

 Produces Edible Fruit

 Has Fragrance

 Produces Food for Birds and Wildlife

 Drought Resistant

 Suitable for Cut Flowers or Arrangements

 Long Bloom Period

 Native Plant

 Supports Bees

 Provides Shelter for Birds

 Good Fall Color

Companion Planting and Design

In the Companion Planting and Design sections, I provide landscape design ideas as well as suggestions for companion plants to help you achieve striking and personal results from your garden. I specify many kinds of plants that make gardening exciting in Illinois, and provide suggestions on how you can get the most enjoyment from them.

Did You Know

The Did You Know portions of the text provide interesting information about nomenclature and history, as well as little known facts about the featured plants. Share these facts with your neighbors and friends who stop by to admire your landscape!

USDA Cold Hardiness Zone Map

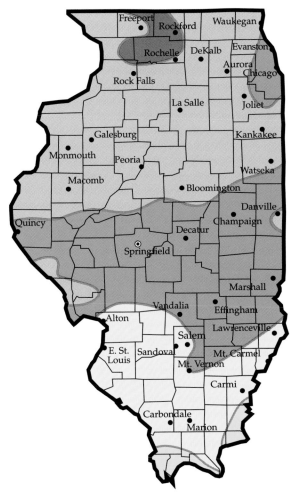

ZONE	Average Annual Minimum Temperature (°F)
4b	-20 to -25
5a	-15 to -20
5b	-10 to -15
6a	-5 to -10
6b	0 to -5

Hardiness Zones

Cold-hardiness zone designations were developed by the United States Department of Agriculture (USDA) to indicate the minimum average temperature for an area. A zone assigned to an individual plant indicates the lowest temperature at which the plant can be expected to survive over the winter. Illinois has zones ranging from 4b to 6b. Though a plant may grow (and grow well) in zones colder than its recommended cold-hardiness zone, it is a good indication of which plants to consider for your landscape. Unless otherwise indicated, the plants in this book are suitable for all hardiness zones in Illinois.

Annuals *for Illinois*

If you want color and excitement in your garden, nothing can beat annuals—their flowers provide immediate color, and they last all season long.

An annual is a plant that completes its life cycle in one season. It germinates from seed, grows, flowers, ripens new seed, and dies, all in one year. Garden flowers are not the only annuals—two other very familiar annuals are corn and soybeans. The seed from these plants is sown in spring, the plants flower in early summer, and the crop (seed) is harvested and in the bin by late fall.

Some plants grown as annuals in Illinois are actually tender perennials, plants that grow from seed one year and then live and flower for years. In truly mild climates with no frost these plants can go on year after year. Geraniums, for example, grow into huge plants in California; Begonias can be kept as houseplants for years here in Illinois, but we usually let such plants freeze in fall, then start them over the next spring.

In addition to their season-long display of color, annuals have another distinct advantage: they begin the season in an empty garden, making it easy to till and improve the soil. Weeds can be eliminated before planting, using herbicides if necessary, as there will be no damage to flowers.

You can grow new annuals every year—no need to plant the same thing until bored stiff with it! And annuals are inexpensive. If they don't look good during the season, you can pull them out and plant something else.

Starting Annuals

You can buy annuals at garden centers, supermarkets, hardware stores . . . any place that plants are sold. But if you find the choices too limited, try starting your own seeds indoors under lights. You will need a plant stand with fluorescent lights—a stand 4 feet long and 2 feet wide will accommodate four standard 10-inch by 20-inch flats. The lights can be a pair of shoplight fixtures, each holding two

40-watt cool white tubes. Attach the lights to chains or to ropes, pulleys, and weights so they can be adjusted above the plants. Use one of the commercial artificial soil mixes for the propagating soil. Buy a mix such as Jiffy Mix, Pro Mix, or any other brand composed of shredded brown peat and polystyrene beads or perlite. (Black "potting soil" is not satisfactory for starting annuals.) The seed may be sown in the 20-row seed-starting inserts sold to fit the 10-inch by 20-inch flats. Moisten the soil mix, sow the seeds, label them, and cover the container with clear plastic wrap to keep it from drying out. Set it on the plant stand and lower the lights to an inch or so above the surface. This will provide all the heat and light needed. We have indicated in the following plant profiles whether the seed needs light or dark to germinate. If a seed needs light, don't cover it with soil or propagating mix.

When the seedlings are big enough to handle, transplant them into plastic cell-packs, the kind commercial growers use, or into any other convenient container. Keep the lights just above the plant tops and fertilize the plants with liquid fertilizer after they start to grow. Set in the garden when there is no danger of frost.

Using Annuals in the Garden

Annuals can be used in many ways. The shorter ones can be used for edging or bedding, and the taller ones may be placed in the back of the garden. Use annuals as fillers in perennial beds where the flowers have died down, or in a cutting garden. Annuals also can be used in pots, windowboxes, or planters, and they can be plugged into any bare spot in the yard. Check the descriptions in this chapter to see which will grow in the shade and which require full sun.

Some of the best annuals are chosen each year by All-America Selections for special awards. The Fleuroselect awards are selections made by European judges. Such awards are given to varieties that have been tested and found to be superior in all respects.

Annuals are wonderful plants. Don't be afraid to try them in new and different ways. Enjoy them. Let your imagination run wild—and most of all, have fun!

Ageratum

Ageratum houstonianum

Blue flowers with a long season of good show are difficult to find, but Ageratum is one of the best. Clusters of tiny, fluffy blooms cover mound-shaped plants that are well suited for borders, edging, or masses of color. If you are looking for the blue for a red, white, and blue border, Ageratum is perfect in combination with white Petunias and red Salvia. 'Adriatic', 'Blue Blazer', 'Blue Lagoon', and 'Blue Ribbon' are reliable and have compact low form. 'Fine Wine' is burgundy in color and has a good compact habit. The 'Hawaii Hybrid' series includes blue, white, and royal colors and good low form. Flowers of 'Bavaria' and 'Capri' are blue with white centers. 'Blue Tango', which grows to 12 inches, is good for cutting.

Other Name
Floss Flower

Bloom Period and Color
May blooms in blue, pink, white, lavender.

Mature Height × Spread
6 to 15 inches × 6 to 15 inches

When, Where, and How to Plant

Seeds are small, but they can be germinated easily indoors at 70°F under lights. Sow in late February for nice-sized plants by May 15. Broadcast the seeds on the soil surface, or sow them in the 20-row seeding inserts. Moisten the mix and cover the container with clear plastic wrap. Transplant seedlings and continue to grow them at 60°F. Cuttings root without much trouble. Set out started plants when danger of frost has passed. Ageratum does best in full sun; in partial shade it may become leggy. In the southern part of the state, however, protection from full sun during the hottest part of the day is desirable. Ageratums are usually sold as bedding plants, as blooming seedlings, or in 3- or 4-inch pots. Work up the soil by tilling or cultivating. Set the smaller, bedding types on 6- to 8-inch centers. Taller cultivars and plants for the cutting garden may be set up to 12 inches apart.

Growing Tips

Ageratum is adapted to a wide range of soils as long as you provide enough drainage and adequate water. Small plants are easily damaged by excess fertilizer, so fertilize with restraint until the plants are well established. If plants become a little tired and leggy in mid-season, they can be cut back to about half their height. Water when the plants wilt: apply an inch of water, then don't water again until the plants begin to wilt again.

Care and Maintenance

Aphids and mildew are occasionally troublesome. Overfertilization and overwatering can result in plants rotting off at the soil line.

Companion Planting and Design

Ageratum is an excellent edging or bedding plant and combines well with many other bedding plants. It is also excellent in containers and windowboxes. Use it where the true blue colors and low habit are needed.

Did You Know

The name Ageratum is derived from the Greek, *a,* not, and *geras,* meaning old, in reference to the flowers which are long-lasting, not quickly fading.

Alyssum
Lobularia maritima

When, Where, and How to Plant

In Illinois, Alyssum is strictly annual and eliminated by winter. Its vigorous habit is an asset. In especially favorable spots, Alyssum will reseed itself faithfully. In the hottest weather, flowering may be stalled; the plants will resume flowering with the return of cooler temperatures. Seeds are easily germinated at 70°F in the light. Broadcast them on the soil surface or sow them in the 20-row seeding inserts. Moisten the propagating mix and cover the container with clear plastic wrap. Alyssum does well in full sun or partial shade, and is tolerant of light frost. Purple cultivars do better in cooler spots or in partial shade. Because Alyssum does well in light shade, it is one of the annuals that can be recommended for shady gardens in the inner city. It does best in soils with good drainage. Plant on 6- to 8-inch centers. Set the plants shallowly, covering only the roots. Water in the plants, then hold off further watering until they are near wilting. Deep planting and overwatering can result in damping off. Sow seed directly in the border after the danger of a hard freeze is past. Scatter the seed evenly.

Growing Tips

Alyssum is basically free of troubles. If the plants become leggy, they can be sheared back; they will respond with renewed growth and blooms. Syringing with a light spray of water in the hottest weather may keep them blooming—in other words, it may prevent them from taking a summer vacation.

Care and Maintenance

Damping off can be troublesome, so be careful when watering. Plants may be set out after the average date of last frost.

Companion Planting and Design

Sweet Alyssum is a good edging plant for annual or perennial borders. It works well to hide the foliage of spring flowering bulbs. The tiny clusters of blooms cover the plants and blend well with Lobelias, Geraniums, Marigolds, Zinnias, or with Miniature Roses.

Did You Know

There are several kinds of Alyssums, all from the Mediterranean. True Alyssums are yellow-flowered perennials.

Alyssum is one of the most reliable edging plants and is at home in borders, masses, or rock gardens. Use it to hide the foliage of spring bulbs. In containers or hanging baskets, Alyssum will develop into cascades of fragrant blooms. Plant it in a windowbox or a raised planter next to your deck, and you will be able to enjoy it effortlessly. Little has been done (or maybe little can be done) to improve this popular plant. The 'Easter Basket' strain comes in Easter colors: white, pink, lavender, rose, and deep purple, as well as a mixture. The functional plants 'New Carpet of Snow' and 'Royal Carpet' do indeed have a carpet-like effect. 'Snow Crystals' seems to have better heat tolerance than the others.

Other Name
Sweet Alyssum

Bloom Period and Color
Spring blooms in white, lavender, pink.

Mature Height × Spread
4 to 8 inches × 12 to 18 inches

Begonia

Begonia semperflorens-cultorum

Begonias are among the most reliable annuals in the garden, relatively trouble-free and blooming faithfully from spring until fall, even continuing to bloom after light frost. Leaves are glossy (waxy) in many shades of green to dark bronze-red, or in variegated green-white. The better cultivars hold their blooms well above the foliage and produce masses of color in the garden. The 'Ambassador' and 'Senate' series advertises the newest colors. 'Cocktail Hybrid' is sun-resistant; 'Pizzazz Hybrid' is recommended for potting in the fall. Tuberous Begonias, Begonia × tuberhybrida, are tender perennials growing from tubers and may be saved over winter. Their flowers are huge, from 3 inches to more than 7 inches in diameter, are brightly colored and are borne in clusters. (See the Bulb section for a complete discussion of Tuberous Begonias.)

Other Name
Wax Begonia

Bloom Period and Color
Spring until frost, can be brought indoors for the winter. Blooms in white to shades of pink or red.

Mature Height × Spread
6 to 16 inches × 6 to 16 inches

When, Where, and How to Plant
The tiny, dust-like Begonia seeds are sown indoors under lights in January. Grow the plants in pots or packs at 70°F. Set them in the garden at the average date of last frost, usually about mid-May. Begonias are tolerant of many soils as long as there is good drainage and enough moisture. Plant in full sun to fairly dense shade. In the southern part of the state, the plants may sunburn if set in full sun without adequate hardening off. Move them gradually into full sun or protect with light shade until they are acclimated. Begonias are sold as bedding plants, or in 3- or 4-inch pots. Set smaller cultivars on 9- to 12-inch centers. Large-leaf cultivars can be set 15 to 18 inches apart. If the plants are potbound, slice the ball vertically on two or three sides to encourage roots to grow into the surrounding soil. Set the plants at the same depth they grew in the containers. You may lift the garden plants, wash the soil from their roots, and pot them with soil mix for indoor bloom all winter. Cuttings root easily for additional plants. Let the kids root some cuttings during the winter, pot them, and give them as gifts for Mother's Day.

Growing Tips
Begonias require little care other than watering when needed.

Care and Maintenance
The flowers of Wax Begonia are tiny, so there is no need to deadhead the plants. If the plants become leggy in midseason, they can be cut back and restarted. Botrytis blight, mildew, leaf spots, and thrips are Begonia's main pests, but they usually require no special treatment. During especially wet seasons, stem rot may result in some plant losses.

Companion Planting and Design
Begonias are excellent for shady places where almost no other annual will grow. Yet in full sun, they do not wilt the way Impatiens usually do.

Did You Know
Begonias are some of the few plants that can be propagated from leaves. Another common plant propagated this way is African Violet.

Browallia
Browallia speciosa

When, Where, and How to Plant

Sow seed under lights in February. Hold the temperature at 75°F until germination occurs. Transplant to packs or pots, and pinch when about 4 inches tall to encourage branching. Cuttings taken in spring or fall root easily. These tender annuals cannot stand any frost, so don't be too hasty to get them out in spring. Memorial Day is fine for planting. Equally at home in sun or shade, Browallia does best when protected from afternoon sun. It is best in light shade, but it will stand full sun if kept watered. Browallia blooms faithfully from early until late summer. In dense shade it will bloom poorly and become leggy. Plants are available as bedding plants, in 3-inch pots, or in hanging baskets. Prepare the soil well, making sure there is good drainage. Space plants 10 inches apart, or plant singly for accent. Set the plants at the same depth they were growing in their containers; too-deep planting can result in rotting of the plants at the soil line. If you want to try Browallia as a houseplant, dig and pot up plants before the first frost, or take cuttings and bring them indoors for the winter. Set the plants on a bed of moist pea gravel and mist daily, especially during the heating season, to maintain humidity.

Growing Tips

These plants need warm, moist conditions, but they resent wet soils. Good drainage is essential. Overwatering and overfertilizing will produce big, healthy plants, but few flowers. Potted plants and hanging baskets will benefit from daily misting to increase humidity.

Care and Maintenance

Few pests bother these plants, though whiteflies may become a serious problem.

Companion Planting and Design

Use Browallia in beds, borders, hanging baskets or windowboxes. The bright blue flowers go well with pink or white flowers or with the silver foliage of Dusty Miller.

Did You Know

Browallia comes from the rain forests, so it does not like hot, dry weather.

Masses of star-shaped flowers are borne on well-branched plants with attractive foliage. The neatly rounded form makes these plants ideal for planters, hanging baskets, urns, or for the border. Tolerance for shade makes them good as flowering houseplants all winter. Browallia prefers a rich, well-drained soil. It is a native of the rain forest and needs plenty of water and humidity in the hottest weather. Most hybridizing has been done to improve form and compactness. 'Blue Bells Improved' is a dwarf strain that needs no pinching. Some white cultivars are available—'Silver Bells' and 'White Troll' have pure white blooms on compact plants—but there are plenty of other white flowers to choose, so I prefer the intense blues such as 'Blue Troll' or 'Marine Bells'.

Other Name
Sapphire Flower

Bloom Period and Color
Early to late summer blooms in blue, lavender, or white.

Mature Height × Spread
12 to 18 inches × 12 to 18 inches

Celosia

Celosia sp.

Celosias are especially notable for their intense colors. The blooms are of three types: Crested, Plume, and Candle. The Crested type, C. cristata, look like large convoluted rooster's comb. Plume types, C. plumosa, are softer and have been infused with some pastel colors. New are the Candle types, C. argentea spicata. 'Fireglow' is a Crested type with outstanding, 6-inch, scarlet-orange blooms. 'Prestige Scarlet', is one of the most floriferous in masses. The 'Castle' series of Plume types includes scarlet, yellow, and a mixture, as well as 'Castle Pink' and 'Castle Orange'. Bright orange 'Apricot Brandy' was an AAS winner. Candle (or wheat) types 'Purple Flamingo' and 'Pink Candle' are two of the hottest new flowers for commercial florists and for amateur flower arrangers.

Other Name
Cockscomb

Bloom Period and Color
Summer blooms in red, pink, yellow, orange, gold.

Mature Height × Spread
6 to 30 inches × 6 to 24 inches

When, Where, and How to Plant

Sow indoors under lights eight weeks before the latest date of last frost. Cover the seeds lightly with soil, and hold at 75°F until they germinate. Grow the plants under bright light, at no lower than 65°F. Celosias need full sun, and they can take the heat. Don't plant them in the shade unless you have no choice. Celosia can be direct-seeded in the garden after danger of frost is past and the soil is warm. If the soil feels warm to the touch, it is at about 75°F, the right temperature for germination. Celosias are available as bedding plants or potted from garden centers. Set plants or thin seedlings of smaller cultivars to about a foot apart, taller cultivars to about 2 feet.

Growing Tips

Celosias are natives of Equatorial Africa, Asia, and America. The name Celosia means "hot" in Greek. This word can describe both the color of the flowers and the ability of these plants to stand the heat. Celosias are able to stand a light frost, but nothing is gained by setting them out while the soil is still cold. If the roots are chilled, the plants stop growing and take a long time to get started again.

Care and Maintenance

Tall cultivars may need staking. Deadheading as flowers fade will prolong bloom, especially for the tall varieties. Mites can be a problem, as can stem rot if the plants are kept too wet.

Companion Planting and Design

The Crested types are difficult to use with other kinds of plants, but the colors are outstanding. The Plumosa and Candle types are easier to use where some vertical effect is wanted. Use shorter cultivars in borders or edgings. Tall cultivars are best at the back of the garden or as accents in urns.

Did You Know

Celosias are excellent for cutting. They are long-lasting as fresh flowers, and can be dried for permanent flower arrangements.

Cleome

Cleome hassleriana

When, Where, and How to Plant

Cleome grows true to form from collected seed. Chill at near freezing for a week before sowing. Germinate at 80°F. Set plants out after the frost-free date, about mid-May in central Illinois. Cleome will reseed itself with abundant seedlings. These can be picked out and transplanted or hoed or easily pulled. If the volunteer plants are not allowed to flower, no seed will be produced for the next season. Started seedlings, not usually in bloom, are sold at most garden centers. Thin seedlings or set out started plants at least 2 feet apart. They prefer full sun, but they can stand partial shade. These are large plants that need room. If crowded, they will become leggy and weak. The plants also become leggy when grown in the shade and will need support.

Growing Tips

Little needs to be done to grow these plants. They prefer moist, well-drained soil, but they will tolerate drought.

Care and Maintenance

These plants are native to Brazil and Argentina. No diseases or insects bother them.

Companion Planting and Design

Cleomes are so spectacular and tall that they are hard to combine with other annuals. They are large plants. They can be used in the middles of beds or at the backs of the borders where they will not overwhelm smaller plants and they will have room to grow. The flowers are borne on indeterminate heads that keep elongating all season, leaving pods of seeds below. The dense plants and thorny stems make excellent temporary hedges and the blooms are attractive all summer long.

Did You Know

Cleomes make excellent cut flowers. Be very careful. The stems have thorns.

Cleome is a wonderful plant for use in hot areas. I have seen it along the south side of houses next to blacktop driveways where it gets baked by the sun, and with a little water it continues to thrive and bloom faithfully all summer. Yet it does well enough in partial shade to be on our list of shade-tolerant plants. Airy, spider-like, 6-inch heads of delicate blooms are borne on large 4-foot-tall and -wide plants. The name "Spider Flower" describes the individual blooms, which have abnormally long, 2-inch stamens. Leaves of the Cleome are palmately compound. Older stems will develop thorns. There are few named cultivars. The 'Queen' series includes pink, white, cherry, violet, and a mixture. 'Helen Campbell' is white.

Other Name
Spider Flower

Bloom Period and Color
Summer blooms in pink, rose, cherry, lavender, white.

Mature Height × Spread
4 feet × 4 feet

Coleus
Coleus hybrids

Coleus is grown for the wonderful foliage colors it brings to the shady part of the garden. Individual leaves may be a solid color with a contrasting border, or they may have several colors spreading out from the middle of the leaf. The leaves may be wide or narrow, smooth, scalloped, or toothed. Coleus is vigorous, but it is not invasive in the garden. Plants are usually upright mounds, but some trailing kinds will cascade from hanging baskets. The 'Carefree' and 'Fiji' series are self-branching and will cascade quite nicely. 'Fairway' and 'Jazz' strains are dwarf, about 8 inches tall, and they will spread; they do well as edging. The 'Wizard' series is taller, 12 to 14 inches, and has large leaves. The 'Solar' series was developed especially for planting in full sun locations.

Other Name
Solenostemon

Bloom Period and Color
Foliage in combinations of green, white, yellow, chartreuse, maroon, pink, or red. Flowers, borne in spikes, are inconspicuous.

Mature Height × Spread
9 to 16 inches × 9 to 16 inches

When, Where, and How to Plant
Seed germinates easily when uncovered under lights at 70°, but seedlings develop slowly. Sow in March for nice-sized plants by Memorial Day. Cuttings root easily any time. Cuttings can be rooted in a glass of water at room temperature or in containers of propagating mix. Don't rush these plants into the garden. Coleus is a tender annual and cannot stand frost. Plants will not grow much until the soil warms up anyway. Coleus prefers well-drained, moist soil. It tolerates full sun, but it does best in light shade where the colors develop most intensely. Plants are available as bedding plants or in pots from garden centers. Set plants with large leaves on 12-inch centers; smaller-leaved cultivars may be set closer together. Set plants shallowly in a well-prepared moist soil, covering only the roots to avoid damping off.

Growing Tips
Once established, the plants require little care other than watering in dry weather and removing flowers to prolong the season of color.

Care and Maintenance
Coleus is nearly maintenance-free. If plants become leggy, pinching will renew them and keep new foliage developing. In unusually wet weather, leaf spots may develop. Several kinds of insects—whitefly, aphids, mealybugs, and mites—can become troublesome. Propagation of these plants from cuttings is so easy that this can be a great first lesson in horticulture for children. As cold weather approaches in fall, lift a stock plant and have youngsters take cuttings, root them in water, and pot them up for holiday gift plants.

Companion Planting and Design
Use in edgings, borders, pots, planters, and hanging baskets. Uniform, single-color selections are well suited for floral carpets. The bright colors of Coleuses simply overwhelm anything planted with them. Use them in the shade or sun.

Did You Know
Coleus is one of the easiest plants to propagate. Stick a stem in water and in a few days roots will emerge.

Cosmos
Cosmos sp.

When, Where, and How to Plant

Seeds germinate easily at 70°F under lights. Sow eight weeks before the last frost date, covering lightly with soil. Transplant, then grow on at 65°. Started plants are available from garden centers. Sow seed directly in the garden, or set plants when all danger of frost is past. Thin seedlings to 12 inches apart. The extras can be transplanted if care is used to avoid breaking off tiny roots. Set started plants 12 inches apart as well. This is closer than would normally be recommended for plants of this size, but the close spacing allows the plants to weave together, which helps them to support each other. They reseed easily enough to assure plants for the following year, but not so much as to be a nuisance. Smaller, seed-eating birds will be seen after a fall frost trying to get the last seeds from the old dry stems—so don't be too hasty to cut down the old plants in the fall!

Growing Tips

Cosmos plants are virtually maintenance-free. They tolerate drought, and they resent overwatering and overfertilizing.

Care and Maintenance

Few insects or diseases bother them. Too much fertilizer and water will mean extra-floppy plants and fewer blooms.

Companion Planting and Design

Cosmos plants need plenty of room to grow. Put them at the back of a border or along a fence in full sun. Plant a row in the cutting garden if you want a ready source of blooms all summer long. These compound flowers are attractive to butterflies. They lend an informal look to the garden. Popular in cottage gardens, they are light and lacy, tolerating heat and drought.

Did You Know

Seeds of Cosmos are large and germinate quite fast. These are excellent plants for children just learning about how plants grow. Easy-to-handle seeds, quick growth, and few pests to contend with keep the youngsters interested until the flowers have a chance to develop.

Cosmos is an old-fashioned flower, much loved by Grandmother, who scattered seeds around the old water pump on the farm to add a bit of color. The warm pink shades were the colors of late summer. The plants were untidy, falling over if not supported, but they bloomed tirelessly. A tiny bouquet thoughtfully picked by small hands often graced the dinner table. These are large, feathery plants with daisy-like blooms, though newer selections are more tidy. The introduction of the sunny colors of C. sulphureus in the middle of the last century has greatly improved this favorite. Cosmos needs full sun, but it isn't particular about soil. C. bipinnatus types, in the old-fashioned warm colors, have been bred to reduce height and increase flower size.

Bloom Period and Color

Summer blooms in pastel, reddish, pink, rose, white, yellow, orange, or crimson.

Mature Height × Spread

18 to 36 inches × 9 to 18 inches

Dusty Miller
Senecio cineraria

Dusty Miller is so interesting that it automatically quali-fies for any list of annuals. Dusty Miller is a common name for several different plants, and it refers to the looks of the foliage of these plants rather than to any taxonomic similarity among them. All are dusty-white, many with lace-like foliage. They are grown for the color and texture of their leaves rather than for their flowers. Flowers are yellow and borne in clusters above the foliage, but most gardeners interested in the silver-white mass remove the flower stalks. Dusty Miller is adapted to edging, borders, bedding, and containers. 'Cirrus' is small, 6 to 8 inches, and silver. 'New Look' has white leaves, more oak-like than cut. 'Silver Lace' has the most delicately cut foliage.

Other Names
Chrysanthemum ptarmicaeflorum, Cineraria maritima

Bloom Period and Color
Summer foliage.

Mature Height × Spread
8 to 15 inches × 8 to 15 inches

When, Where, and How to Plant
Seed is easily germinated uncovered under lights at 75°. ('Silver Lace' is better at 65°.) Sow seed about the first of March. Damping off can be trouble-some. Transplant into pots or cell-packs as soon as the plants are large enough to handle. Continue to grow at 60 to 65°F, and set started plants in the garden after danger of frost is past. Dusty Miller does best in full sun. In shade it will become lanky and lose its characteristic compact form and rounded habit. It prefers dry soils rather than wet places, making it one of the more tolerant con-tainer plants. Dusty Miller plants are always available in spring at garden centers or any other place bedding plants are sold. Most of these outlets don't really know which "Dusty Miller" they are selling. If you want to be sure you know which one you are growing, you will have to grow your own from seed. Plant Dusty Miller about 6 inches apart in the border or bed, closer together in containers. Set the plants no deeper than they grew in the con-tainer. Water in.

Growing Tips
Constant application of small amounts of water will result in damping off of the plants. Remember to water thoroughly, then allow the plants to dry to the point of wilt before watering again.

Care and Maintenance
Dusty Miller is nearly trouble-free once it is established. Stem and root rot can be problems, but these are due to improper watering practices. Overgrown plants can be sheared back about halfway and will respond with a flush of new growth.

Companion Planting and Design
Use as edging, in beds, in rock gardens, in flower boxes or other containers. The silver white of Dusty Millers is perfect to set off the vibrant reds, pinks, purples, or blues of Geraniums, Impatiens, Petunias, Lobelias, or Pinks.

Did You Know
Dusty Miller foliage is excellent for fresh flower arrangements.

Flowering Tobacco
Nicotiana alata

When, Where, and How to Plant

Seeds germinate at 70° in the light. Don't cover them with propagating mix. Sow about ten weeks before the frost-free date, then set out in the garden when all danger of frost has passed. Nicotiana thrives in full sun, but it will stand some shade. Flowering Tobacco is available from garden centers as bedding plants, in pots, or in containers. Space plants of compact cultivars about 15 inches apart in the garden. Taller varieties such as *N. sylvestris* will need to be spaced about 2 feet apart. Drainage is essential. Improved cultivars of Nicotiana tolerate heat quite well.

Growing Tips

Once planted, Nicotiana requires very little care. Apply a balanced liquid fertilizer about mid-season if the foliage begins to go off color. Water if the plants stay wilted overnight, but never overwater.

Care and Maintenance

Insects that affect Tomatoes will sometimes invade Nicotiana. Tomato hornworm is easily picked off, but flea beetles can make leaves look like they were hit with buckshot. Try Sevin insecticide to control these pests. Nicotianas are also affected by the same diseases that affect tomatoes and peppers. To reduce these problems, plant them in a different part of the garden every few seasons and don't plant them where Tomatoes, Peppers, or Potatoes have been planted.

Companion Planting and Design

Large Nicotianas are loosely spreading plants and are difficult to mix with other annuals. The larger, more open plants work well in naturalized settings or in the cutting garden. The blooms are excellent for cut-flower arrangements. They are fragrant and long-lasting. The newer compact forms make excellent edging or borders, and are well suited for containers. They mix well with Dusty Millers, Lobelias, Alyssums, and other small-flowered, lacy kinds of annuals.

Did You Know

Much of the fragrance was lost in newer Nicotiana varieties. That has been largely corrected and more recent kinds have spectacular fragrance. These beautiful flowers are very attractive to hummingbirds and to hawk moths, making for entertaining viewing in the evening.

If you are interested in attracting hummingbirds or butterflies, there is nothing better than Flowering Tobacco. These plants, covered with trumpet-like blooms on upright stems, perfume the garden with a Tuberose-like fragrance; and their bright colors beckon. Some of the older hybrids were bred for form and color, and the fragrance was lost. Newer hybrids have regained some of the fragrance. Somewhat loose and lanky, Nicotiana is best used in a border or in the cutting garden where its untidy form won't be noticed. The 'Niki' series includes rose red, pink, white, and mixed colors. More compact and earlier blooming are the 'Domino' hybrids, which include pink with white eye, lime green, and mixtures. 'Heaven Scent Mix' has an improved habit and great fragrance.

Other Name
Nicotiana

Bloom Period and Color
Summer to fall blooms in red, white, pink, maroon, crimson, yellow, or green.

Mature Height × Spread
12 to 24 inches × 12 to 24 inches

Four-O'Clocks

Mirabilis jalapa

There are several things that make this otherwise unassuming plant worth growing in the annual garden; one, its flowers open at four o'clock in the afternoon (they may actually open before or after that, depending on the weather); two, they are very simple to grow; and three, there are flowers of various colors on the same plant, making them especially interesting to children. Four-O'Clocks, with their flowers that popped open late in the afternoon, were intriguing to me as a youngster. We did not grow them, but we had friends who did. It was a treat to go to see these neat plants in their garden. 'Jingles' cultivar is better branched than the species. Colors of the flowers are striped red, yellow, rose, white, and pink.

Bloom Period and Color
Summer to frost blooms in pink, white, yellow, red, or striped.

Mature Height × Spread
36 inches × 36 inches

When, Where, and How to Plant
Four-O'Clocks are undemanding. They can be planted in sun or shade and they tolerate just about any kind of soil. Places such as the narrow strip of ground between the house and driveway are fine for these plants. They are often used as temporary shrubs until permanent ones can be planted. These plants are well suited to an urban environment, as they tolerate dust, smoke, heat, and other kinds of pollution. They can stand hot, dry places in which other plants would die immediately. Four-O'Clocks are rarely available at garden centers. They are so easy to grow from collected seed that it is not profitable to try to grow them for sale. The seeds are large and easy for children to handle. They can be seeded into an artificial soil in any kind of container. Cover them about 1/2 inch deep. They will be ready for the garden in about a month. Set started plants in the garden when danger of frost has passed. Space about 2 feet apart. These plants are not particular, but are best set about as deep as they grew in the starter container. Seeding directly into the garden after danger of frost has passed will develop plants almost as fast as starting them ahead of time.

Growing Tips
Provide water if the plants do not recover from wilting overnight. Soak the ground, then don't water again until the plants wilt again.

Care and Maintenance
Few pests bother these plants. Four-O'Clocks will reseed vigorously. Hoe out the extra seedlings, or transplant them where they can be useful.

Companion Planting and Design
Use Four-O'Clocks in large borders, beds, or in containers. They are colorful and are curiosities as they open late in the day. Plant them where they can be watched from the patio in the evening as the flowers pop open.

Did You Know
Four-O'Clocks don't always open at four. Sometimes they are delayed. Nobody really knows why.

When, Where, and How to Plant

Gaillardia is a native North American plant. It is well adapted to our climate, especially our dry summers. It grows and produces colorful blooms in spots where nothing else seems to want to grow, and will reseed itself in some situations. About six weeks before the last frost date, sow Gaillardia seeds indoors on a moist planting medium; do not cover. The seeds need light and 70°F to germinate. Set seedlings in the garden when all danger of frost has passed. Gaillardia also grows well from seeds sown directly in the garden after the last frost; plants are available at garden centers in cell-packs or blooming in pots. Remember that Gaillardia is a plant for sunny, hot spots—if a spot is too hot and its soil too poor for most plants, Gaillardia will probably find it to its liking! Broadcast seed directly in the garden; thin seedlings to 12 inches apart. Home-grown or purchased plants should be set on 12- to 15-inch centers. Prepare poor soil by loosening it so the plants can get started.

Growing Tips

Once established, they require little care. Deep planting or overwatering can result in root rot.

Care and Maintenance

Gaillardia is essentially maintenance-free. Deadheading will prolong blooming, which continues until the plants are frozen off. Plants of taller cultivars may benefit from staking, but if closely planted, they will tend to support each other. Insects and diseases rarely cause problems.

Companion Planting and Design

Gailardias are well suited for edging beds or containers. They are compact and brilliantly colored. The intensity of their hot colors makes them tough to blend with other flowers. Try to balance them with flower colors of blue or silver. Blue Salvia or Dusty Miller would make a nice contrast.

Did You Know

Gaillardias are native plants of the southwestern tall grass prairie. They tolerate the heat and drought of that region, making them nearly trouble-free in the garden. Gaillardia is the state flower of Oklahoma.

Gaillardia is a bright addition to the annual garden. Its composite blooms, often multi-colored with yellow tips on the petals, resemble Indian blankets—thus the common name. Best planted in mass plantings or borders, these flowers will also adapt to naturalized areas, and breeders have developed more compact kinds that are suited to containers and bedding. Longer-stemmed cultivars are excellent for cutting. Gaillardia will stand hot, dry conditions. Tolerant of poor soils, it needs little fertilizer. It may become weak and overly vegetative if it receives too much nitrogen. Species Gaillardias are still offered in wildflower mixes, but most commercial offerings for the garden trade are hybrids. 'Red Plume' (AAS winner) and 'Yellow Plume' are fully double on compact, 12-inch plants. They are fine for bedding or containers.

Other Name
Annual Blanket Flower

Bloom Period and Color
Summer and fall blooms in combinations of red, bronze, orange, and yellow.

Mature Height × Spread
18 to 24 inches × 18 to 24 inches

Garden Pink
Dianthus chinensis

Pinks are delightful little flowers that have again become very popular. Several have achieved All-American status because of their reliability and bright colors. The Pinks are related to the florist's Carnations, and have the same, delicious, clove-like fragrance. Pinks derive their name not from the color, although some Pinks are pink, but from the edges of the petals which look as though they were cut with pinking shears. Pinks prefer cooler weather and may take a vacation when weather warms. They will resume blooming as soon as cooler weather returns. In the hotter parts of the state, planting in partial shade will prolong the blooming period by keeping them cooler. With some protection, they may survive the winter and flower the next season as well.

Other Names
Annual Pink, China Pink

Bloom Period and Color
Late spring and early summer, fall. Rose, pink, white, raspberry, and bi-colors.

Mature Height × Spread
10 to 12 inches tall × twice as wide.

When, Where, and How to Plant
Seeds and plants of Pinks are available at garden centers in early spring. Sow seeds indoors under lights at 70° about ten weeks before the frost-free date. Transplants can be set in the garden while there is still a threat of frost because they will stand freezing if hardened off sufficiently. Set the plants at the same depth they grew in the containers. For fall, seeds may be sown directly in the garden about July 15. A sunny to partially shaded location is ideal for Pinks. An eastern exposure that protects them from the hottest sun works well. Good drainage is essential to keep them from rotting off at the soil line. They are quite tolerant of alkaline soils, making them especially well adapted to foundation plantings where limey soils are common. Pinks are well suited for bedding, borders, containers, and windowboxes. Taller varieties are excellent for cutting.

Growing Tips
Keep Pinks well watered during hot weather. Light mulch will aid in keeping the soil moist and cool. Go lightly with the fertilizer. Excess nitrogen stimulates lots of leaves but few flowers, and can burn tips of the leaves.

Care and Maintenance
Cut the plants back halfway in midsummer to keep them from getting so ungainly. When cool weather arrives, they will be bushier and full of flowers. The small flowers normally require no deadheading, but keeping faded flowers picked off will stimulate quicker reblooming. Pinks are susceptible to aphids and mites. Use insecticidal soap to keep them under control.

Companion Planting and Design
Use with Ageratum, Lobelia, or Alyssum, which will not overpower these delicate flowers.

Did You Know
The name *Dianthus* is derived from the Greek *dios* (divine) and *anthos* (flower) thus the meaning, "divine flower." The florist Carnation is *D. caryophyllus*, *Caryophyllus* being the botanical name for Cloves, and makes reference to the wonderful fragrance of these flowers. The Sweet William, *D. barbatus,* is a biennial, and tends to be much taller than the Pinks.

Geranium
Pelargonium × hortorum

When, Where, and How to Plant
Start seed Geraniums under lights in January. Germination takes about two weeks at 75°F. Transplant seedlings to pots or packs. Today most Geraniums are grown from seed and sold, in bloom, as bedding plants or in 4- or 6-inch pots. Cuttings from older plants root easily; they can be rooted directly in pots. Plants can be set out after the threat of a freeze is past. Bring plants indoors for the winter. Lift entire plants, trim them back, pot, and grow indoors. Or take cuttings from plants before they freeze and grow them through the winter. A third way is Grandma's way: lift the plants, shake off the soil, and hang them upside down in brown paper bags in the basement. In spring, pot the plants, cutting off the shriveled parts. After leaves appear, the plants are ready for setting out. Geraniums are best planted in a cool, moist soil, where they will develop the most intense colors. To avoid stem rot problems, make sure the soil is well drained. Most cultivars will tolerate light shade, but they tend to become leggy. If planting in beds, set them about 12 inches apart and only as deep as they were growing in the container. In containers, they are usually spaced plant-to-plant.

Growing Tips
Natural rainfall is seldom sufficient to keep containers watered, so check them daily. Water in hot dry weather when planted in beds.

Care and Maintenance
Remove large clusters of flowers and old, yellow leaves to keep the plants attractive and to stimulate continuing bloom. Expect mites, leaf spot, and gray mold in wet weather, as well as various caterpillars.

Companion Planting and Design
Geraniums have been mainstays of the bedding plant industry for generations. They are equally at home in borders, beds, or containers.

Did You Know
Martha Washington Geraniums, the large-flowered pot plants grown by florists for spring holiday gifts are a related species, *P. × domesticum.*

Two-inch flowers are carried well above the foliage in large round clusters. Leaves are large, 3 to 5 inches across, round and scalloped, many with interesting zones or variegation. Whether used with just a few plants in a pot next to the front door, or in extensive beds, the brilliant flower colors contrast beautifully with the bright-green leaves. Today the 'Sprinter' series of seed-grown cultivars is the standard. 'Freckles' was a 1991 AAS winner. 'Orange Appeal', a true orange, received a 1991 Fleuroselect award. Smooth- and Ivy-leaved Geranium, P. peltatum, is used exclusively for hanging baskets or other containers. Colors include intense lavenders and purples. Scented Geraniums are grown for their fragrance and foliage—a few common ones are 'Lemon', 'Nutmeg', 'Peppermint', and 'Citronella'.

Other Name
Zonal Geraniums

Bloom Period and Color
Summer blooms in red, pink, salmon, or white.

Mature Height × Spread
12 to 18 inches × 12 to 18 inches

Gerbera
Gerbera jamesonii

Gerberas have been grown as commercial cut flowers for many years, often in greenhouses. Large, brightly colored, daisy-like flowers, 4 inches across, are borne on straight, strong, 24-inch stems. The body of the plant is a rosette of long leaves as large as a foot and a half in diameter. 'Rainbow' Gerberas are compact plants sold in mixtures or by separate colors. Catalogs list scarlet, orange, pink, crimson, rose, yellow, and white selections. 'Happipot Mix' is selected for container use, and it is often grown in a greenhouse as a potted plant. Cut Gerberas after they have been open for a few days. After cutting, keep the flowers straight up or the stems will bend; once bent, they are impossible to get straight again.

Other Name
Transvaal Daisy

Bloom Period and Color
Summer and fall blooms in scarlet, orange, pink, crimson, rose, yellow, and white.

Mature Height × Spread
18 to 24 inches × 12 to 18 inches

When, Where, and How to Plant
Seeds are very expensive. They require light and germinate in two weeks at 70°F; sow them in early February. Seedlings take up to three months before they are large enough to plant outside. Pot them as soon as they are large enough to handle; they may require repotting into larger pots as they grow. Unless you have a greenhouse or sophisticated indoor lighting system, it is better to buy plants from a garden center. Lift the pots and plants in fall to be moved indoors for the winter. Since these are actually tender perennials, they can be kept over easily. Set started plants into the garden when frost danger has passed. Gerberas need a spot with full sun and excellent drainage. Plants are available for sale in pots, often in bloom. If you intend to grow these plants for cut flowers, construct raised beds of a soil mix to assure necessary drainage. If the soil is wet, flower production will be poor, and the plants will have a tendency to rot off at the base. Set the started plants on 12-inch centers to allow enough room for their large leaves to extend fully. Set them no deeper than they were growing in the pot; deep planting will result in rotting of the crown at the base.

Growing Tips
Water only when the plants have dried to the point of wilting, then water thoroughly.

Care and Maintenance
Once established, Gerberas are relatively trouble-free. The most damaging problem is crown rot, which is invariably due to poor drainage or improper watering. Cut the flowers as they open, or deadhead if allowed to "die on the vine."

Companion Planting and Design
These delightful flowers are probably best grown in the cutting garden for fresh cut flowers. Newer selections are more compact and good for bedding or containers, however. The colors of Gerberas are so brilliant that combining them with others is difficult.

Did You Know
The most envied gardeners at flower shows are the those who grow their own long-stemmed Gerberas.

Heliotrope
Heliotropium arborescens

When, Where, and How to Plant

Heliotrope can be started from seed indoors under lights about eight weeks before the latest date of last frost. The seed needs light to germinate, so do not cover it. Transplant seedlings to cell-packs or peat pots when they are large enough to handle. Grow on at 60° and set in the garden when danger of a freeze is past. If planted out too early, the cold will turn the plants a deep purple color. It doesn't hurt them, but it doesn't help them either. Heliotropes need a warm, sunny spot, and a well-drained but moist soil. Space them at 12 inches to allow them to bush out. If the plants have grown tall and spindly, pinch them as they are planted to force them to branch.

Growing Tips

Fertilize monthly with a complete liquid fertilizer to keep the plants vigorous and productive. If the plants get overly-tall and floppy, cut them back and let them regrow. They will need watering if the weather is hot and dry.

Care and Maintenance

These plants require little care once established. Remove the spent blooms when they turn brown. Aphids and two-spotted mites can be troublesome. Try knocking them off with a strong stream of water, or treat with insecticidal soap.

Companion Planting and Design

Heliotropes blend well with oranges, reds, and pinks, such as Lantanas, Verbenas, Fire Cracker Plants, or Petunias, and with the cool, light greens of Bells of Ireland, for instance. Plant them next to the patio or porch where the fragrance can be enjoyed on a warm summer evening.

Did You Know

The name, Heliotrope, is derived from *helios*, the sun, and *trope*, to turn towards. The flowers supposedly follow the sun as it traverses the heavens each day. Unusually cool spring weather will turn the leaves of these plants a deep purple. They turn green again as soon as temperatures warm.

Heliotropes made their way west from eastern gardens in the wagon trains. A favorite in the 1880s and 90s, these delightful flowers are making a return in popularity. The resurgence of interest in Victorian architecture and the accompanying gardens has brought Heliotropes back from obscurity. The flowers are borne in large upright-arching, scorpioid cymes, and can be delightfully fragrant. In past history, there were many more varieties, and they were even more fragrant, often described as like cherry pie. In fact one common name for Heliotrope is . . . Cherry Pie! Nowadays, the fragrance is more like vanilla. Heliotrope is grown in Europe for perfume. Heliotrope is well suited for containers, and for cutting gardens. It was formerly grown extensively for large pots and by florists for cutting.

Other Name
Cherry Pie

Bloom Period and Color
Blooms early summer to frost. Colors are cool blues, intense deep purple, and violet. A white cultivar is available in some localities.

Mature Height × Spread
12 to 18 inches × 15 inches

Impatiens
Impatiens walleriana

There is no question that Impatiens is the number-one bedding plant in Illinois. Formerly considered a shade plant only, newer selections tolerate shade or full sun equally well, growing into mounds of succulent leaves and becoming covered with brilliant flowers. Even tiny plants flower, and the plantings are covered with blooms from spring until frost. Impatiens is the most reliable and easiest to grow of all the common annuals. Plant it, water it, and forget it. All the plants of a series such as 'Super Elfin' will grow to about the same size. The 'Pride' series is large flowered. The related New Guinea Impatiens is a newcomer on the scene. The plants are large-flowered and brightly colored, and their foliage is colorful as well.

Other Name
Balsam

Bloom Period and Color
Early summer to frost blooms in red, salmon, pink, orange, lavender, white, and bicolors.

Mature Height × Spread
8 to 18 inches × 12 to 24 inches

When, Where, and How to Plant
Impatiens plants take a long time to start. If you want to set out plants in mid-May, you must sow seeds in late January. Do not cover them—the seeds need light to germinate. Germination takes about two weeks at 70°F. Set started plants in the garden after danger of frost has passed. Soils must be moist but well drained. Plants will wilt in full sun during the heat of the day, but they recover readily as the temperatures moderate. There should be no difficulty finding the colors and types to suit your needs. They are normally sold as bedding plants, in flats, or in hanging baskets. Flats hold fifty to seventy-five plants each. Space smaller cultivars 6 inches apart; taller cultivars can be spaced as much as 1 foot apart. Set the plants no deeper than they were growing in the container. Water the plants after planting to settle the soil around the roots.

Growing Tips
Water is essential for Impatiens. If allowed to dry out they will lose their leaves, and they will take their time about recovering. Fertilizer is generally not needed; overfertilization will result in lanky, tall plants that will fall over.

Care and Maintenance
If plants become leggy in midsummer, cut them back to about 6 inches. They will regrow quickly into shorter, more compact plants. Thrips can cause injury to the leaves and flowers, but normally no treatment is necessary. Root rot due to poor drainage or improper watering is the most common problem.

Companion Planting and Design
Impatiens plants are excellent in planters, pots, hanging baskets, and shade gardens, for edging or bedding, and around the bases of trees. The colors are so brilliant that they are difficult to combine with other flowers. Best used with the bright greens of ornamental grasses, or in front of evergreens such as Dwarf Spreading Yews.

Did You Know
Impatiens make good houseplants if humidity is kept high.

Lobelia
Lobelia erinus

When, Where, and How to Plant

Sow seeds indoors under lights about mid-January. The seeds need light to germinate, so do not cover them with the medium. Keep the germinating medium moist by covering the container with clear plastic wrap. Set started plants in the garden when danger of frost has passed. In the hotter parts of the state, Lobelia should be protected from full sun during the heat of the day. In the cooler areas, it can stand full sun as long as it has adequate water. It prefers soil with good drainage. Lobelias are available in garden centers in spring as bedding plants, in hanging baskets, and in planters. Set plants about 12 inches apart in a border, planting no deeper than the plants were growing in their containers. *Lobelia erinus* is native to the Cape of Good Hope in South Africa. It prefers a cooler climate, and it may stop blooming if the weather gets too hot; flowering will resume when temperatures moderate.

Growing Tips

Root rot will show up if the plants are overwatered or in poorly drained soil. Correct the conditions by providing well-drained soil or growing in raised beds, and water only when the plants wilt.

Care and Maintenance

There are no serious problems with Lobelia. If it gets too leggy, cut it back. It will regrow without difficulty.

Companion Planting and Design

Lobelias are excellent for edging or for containers. The colors are so subtle that care should be used not to overwhelm them. Use them with other subtle flowers like Heliotrope, or in front of beds of Periwinkle ground cover.

Did You Know

Lobelia, because it is a native of the Cape of Good Hope seashore in South Africa, prefers the cool ocean breezes, often taking a rest when weather is hot and dry. The plant was named for Matthias de l'Obel, Flemish botanist and physician to England's King James I. Lobelias contain a toxin, lobelia acid, so don't chew on them.

There are so few plants that have blue flowers. Lobelia is a lovely little plant that does well in borders and as edging. It is especially good in the partially shaded border and in containers. The strap-like leaves are green or bronze. This is one of those plants that I learned to appreciate early in my gardening experiences. I saw it used extensively in winter gardens in Southern California, where its color was particularly appreciated. It is equally at home here in the Illinois summer. 'Blue Moon' is a deep, cobalt blue. 'Crystal Palace' is dark blue with bronze foliage. 'Paper Moon' is white. 'Rosamund' is deep carmine. Pendula types include the 'Fountain' series with colors of crimson, lilac, rose, blue, white, and a mix.

Bloom Period and Color
Spring to frost blooms in crimson, lilac, rose, blue, white.

Mature Height × Spread
6 inches × 12 to 18 inches

Madagascar Periwinkle
Catharanthus roseus

Sometimes we need a plant that can stand the toughest situations and faithfully continue to flower. Madagascar Periwinkle, or Vinca, is one of the best. Heat, drought, wind, and pollution don't faze this plant. It blooms all summer with the 1¹/₂- to 2-inch flowers, each with a darker-colored eye in the center, set above the glossy green foliage. When we lost an older tree to age and disease, our once shaded front yard was bright and sunny. The standby Impatiens no longer tolerated the conditions. Vinca has been an excellent replacement. The colors and form are similar, and the reliability is appreciated. The National Garden Bureau designated 2002 as the Year of the Vinca.

Other Name
Vinca

Bloom Period and Color
All summer. Rose-pink, deep rose, orchid, pink, white, often with eyes of contrasting colors.

Mature Height × Spread
Spreading types 3 to 8 inches tall spreading to 18 inches. Upright types 8 to 18 inches tall and wide.

When, Where, and How to Plant
Sow seeds indoors under lights twelve to fourteen weeks before the latest date of last frost. The seeds germinate slowly, so be patient. Keep the temperatures at 70 to 75° until seeds geminate. Or, buy started plants. Full-to-partial sun and a well-drained soil are essential, as these plants need warmth. Set out in their permanent location after any danger of frost has passed. Don't rush the season. These plants are very susceptible to overwatering and cold soils, and will rot off if the season is delayed. Set the plants at the same depth they were growing in the containers, spaced 8 to 12 inches apart. Vinca can be grown from cuttings taken in late summer, rooted, and potted up to be moved indoors for the winter. Cuttings root easily in moist sand or peatmoss. If kept in a warm bright spot, the plants will bloom all winter. Cuttings can be taken in spring to start plants for moving outdoors for summer.

Growing Tips
Water as needed to keep the plants from wilting, but do not overwater. Excessively wet soils will result in stems rotting off at the soil line.

Care and Maintenance
Little care is needed to keep these plants growing and attractive. The plants keep their neat form throughout the season; they need no deadheading, and few pests bother them. Slugs may be troublesome if the season is wet. Control with slug bait while the pests are still small.

Companion Planting and Design
Vinca is suited for use in borders, as bedding and ground cover, and in containers or window boxes. The strong colors of these flowers overpower most other kinds, but the contrast of Dusty Miller or yellow Marigolds makes an outstanding combination. It is often used in place of Impatiens in hot sunny areas where the Impatiens will not stand the heat.

Did You Know
Known as Madagascar Periwinkle, or more commonly known now as Vinca, this delightful plant is native to hot regions of India and Madagascar.

When, Where, and How to Plant

Seeds germinate quickly under lights, in as short a time as twenty-four hours at 70°F. Seed sown in April will develop into plants of sufficient size to plant in the garden by mid-May. Set plants in the garden when all danger of a freeze is past. Marigolds can stand the heat and they tolerate rather droughty soils. Marigolds are sold as bedding plants, in flats, pots, planters, and hanging baskets. Plants of the shorter hybrids should be spaced about 12 inches apart. Tall American or African kinds should be spaced at 2 feet. Work up the soil by tilling or cultivating, and set the plants no deeper than they were growing in their containers.

Growing Tips

Apply water only when the soil is dry and the plants have started to wilt (overly wet soils will result in stem rot).

Care and Maintenance

There are pests that can wreak havoc on Marigolds. Earwigs will make lace of the foliage—these nocturnal insects can destroy a planting overnight. Apply Sevin insecticide when you set them out. Marigolds are also lightning rods for mites. Try insecticidal soap or just a hard shower from beneath to dislodge these pests. Aster yellows disease will turn the flowers green and prevent them from opening; pull out and destroy any infected plants immediately. Except for fighting these pests, Marigolds require little care. Deadhead the larger kinds to promote continuing bloom. Marigolds have acquired an undeserved reputation for discouraging pests with their odor. If they do discourage pests, it is not because of their odor, but because they can trap soil-borne nematodes, reducing the numbers of this type of pest.

Companion Planting and Design

Use dwarf Marigolds in beds or as edging by themselves, or in combination with Celosias, purple Salvias, or Dusty Millers. Taller types can be used to hide ripening foliage of spring flowering bulbs.

Did You Know

Marigolds were the favorite flowers of Illinois Sen. Everett Dirksen from Tazewell County, who lobbied long and hard to make them the national flower.

Marigolds are the workhorses of the flower garden. They are cheery flowers with bright colors and upturned faces. Once they begin blooming, they brighten any corner of the garden, and they seem to tolerate almost any situation. Marigold type distinctions have become blurred. The American (African) Marigolds are best used in masses or for cutting. Dwarf French Marigolds are shorter and have either single or double flowers in rust, mahogany, yellow, orange, or bicolors. They include one of my favorites, 'Janie', now in many colors, but still with the good compact form. Triploids such as 'Zenith' don't set seed, so they are less likely to stall in the hottest weather; they have big flowers on compact plants. 'Discovery' and 'Inca' American types are reliable, large-flowered, and not as tall as many of the others.

Other Name

African Marigold

Bloom Period and Color

Summer to frost blooms in yellow, gold, orange, mahogany, white.

Mature Height × Spread

8 to 36 inches × 18 to 24 inches

Melampodium

Melampodium paludosum

This easy-to-grow annual is so new that many gardeners are only recently becoming familiar with it. The first planting I noticed was at the Chicago Botanic Garden where it created quite a sensation next to the entrance. (I needed to ask what it was too.) Melampodium is so easy to grow that it is a natural for new gardeners. It is seldom seen in garden centers because it grows so easily from seed sown directly in the garden. While seed from the catalogs is relatively expensive, seed can be collected late in the season and kept for sowing the next spring. Or, Melampodium will reseed itself readily if seed is allowed to fall.

Bloom Period and Color
Bright, 1-inch, daisy-like blooms literally cover the plants from early summer to frost.

Mature Height × Spread
The flowers cover tidy plants 18 to 24 inches tall and wide. Dwarf selections are 1 foot tall and wide.

When, Where, and How to Plant
Sow seeds indoors under lights about eight weeks before the last frost. Grow under lights at 65 to 70 degrees. Set Melampodium plants out in well-prepared, well-drained soil as soon as danger of frost has passed. Neighborhood garden centers are sure to begin growing it if there is enough demand, however plants grown in the high humidity of a greenhouse will look pretty bad until they become established outdoors. Space the started plants about 12 inches apart. Sow seed directly in the garden at the average date of last frost. Thin to the proper spacing when the seedlings have two true leaves. Melampodium thrives in hot, tough places. It needs full sun for best performance.

Growing Tips
Well-drained soil is essential for these plants. Over-watering is probably the easiest way to kill them. In many years they need no supplemental watering at all. Water only when plants begin to wilt.

Care and Maintenance
There are no insects or diseases that affect these adaptable plants. The plants do not need staking and small flowers do not need to be deadheaded. If the plants are fertilized too vigorously, they become overly long and begin to fall over. Cut them back and they will quickly resume flowering.

Companion Planting and Design
Melampodium is an excellent replacement for dwarf Marigolds, and seems to resist the predations of earwigs, which can decimate Marigold plantings. The bright yellow flowers and pale green foliage mix well with reds and oranges, and are especially effective if set off with the purples of Russian Sage, Purple Salvia, Verbena, or dwarf Veronicas. Melampodium blooms are excellent for cutting. They are long-lasting and easily used in floral arrangements. They also are well adapted for growing in containers where their heat and drought tolerance are especially welcome.

Did You Know
Plains-blackfoot, *Melampodium cinereum,* is a native wild flower of the West, growing in dry, rocky places where little else can survive. It has white flowers with yellow centers.

Morning Glory
Ipomoea purpurea

When, Where, and How to Plant

Seeds can be started indoors; they will germinate in a week at 75°F. But the plants grow so fast that starting seed indoors is probably an unnecessary exercise. Sow seeds outdoors directly where you want the plants to grow. Morning Glory seed coats are tough. Soak them overnight before you plant them, or nick the seed coat with a file. Morning Glories will tolerate partial shade, but they will flower less. Plant them where they have room to grow and a strong support. Morning Glories are rarely offered for sale at garden centers or other plant outlets. Occasionally you will see them in containers growing up a small trellis. These plants can be set into the garden, but be careful not to disturb the roots or the plants will stop growing. Work up the soil by tilling or spading and sow seeds in groups of threes. Push the seeds into the loosened soil about 1/2 inch deep and cover them with the soil. These plants produce a lot of plant material that will need to be removed in the fall. They vine by encircling whatever they can find to grow on.

Growing Tips

Heavy watering or fertilization will stimulate lots of leaves and vines, but flowering will be reduced.

Care and Maintenance

Once they start growing, Morning Glories are just about trouble free. It is possible to underestimate the weight of the vines; if you provide supports that do not have sufficient strength, the whole thing can come tumbling down. Make sure the supports are well fastened. If the vines do fall, they can be reattached and will continue to grow.

Companion Planting and Design

Morning Glories can be used to cover undesirable features, or to serve as a backdrop for taller-growing annuals and perennials. Grow them on trellises or on the fence.

Did You Know

Ipomoea comes from the Greek word for bindworm, *Ips.*

Often a temporary screen is needed to cover a utility pole, the vacant side of a garage, or an unattractive fence. Morning Glories perform that job well, and they look beautiful while doing it. They quickly cover a trellis. The heart-shaped leaves of these attractive plants are bright green. Their flowers are trumpet-shaped, purple, blue, pink, or white. (I prefer the traditional purple ones that remind me of Grandma's garden.) 'Heavenly Blue' is the best of the cultivars. Seeds are available for red, white, blue, or mixed colors. 'Moon vine', I. alba, a related species, has large fragrant white flowers that pop open at sunset. 'Tie Dye' has large, 6-inch flowers that are sky-blue overlaid with swirls or stripes of navy.

Other Name
Convolvulus purpureus

Bloom Period and Color
Summer blooms in blue, pink, purple, white.

Mature Height × Spread
Vines to 10 feet × 24 inches

Moss Rose
Portulaca grandiflora

Moss Rose will probably thrive in a spot in your garden where it is too hot and dry for anything else to grow. Well suited to harsh environments, Moss Rose is often used for roadside plantings where rain will not fall for months at a time. This is a spreading plant with succulent narrow leaves, and it is covered with brilliant blooms. With just a little water, these plants will flower faithfully all summer long. The newer selections are covered with fully double flowers in bright colors. They are superior, and come in a great range of colors with continuous blooming. Try the 'Sundial' or 'Afternoon Delight' series. Colors range from red, rose, orange, and pink to white and a new fuchsia and mango.

Bloom Period and Color
Summer blooms in red, rose, orange, pink, white, and fuchsia.

Mature Height × Spread
6 to 8 inches × 12 inches

When, Where, and How to Plant
Moss Rose produces a lot of seed, and volunteer plants will come up every year where these plants are grown regularly. Unfortunately, since the better cultivars are hybrids, the seedlings may not be up to par. Rely on some of the seed, but also start new plants from seed or transplants every year. Moss Rose seed can be started indoors under lights, germinating quickly at 70°F. Seed sown directly in the garden germinates when soil temperatures have warmed sufficiently, usually about the middle of June. These tough little plants are suited for hot, dry, sunny places where other things refuse to grow. They are useful in a perennial bed where the foliage has died down and left a void. Moss Rose plants are available as bedding plants at garden centers. Sow seed or set plants out when soils have warmed. Seed can be broadcast and lightly raked into the soil. Set plants about 6 inches apart and plant them no deeper than they were growing in their containers. These plants need hot weather!

Growing Tips
Moss Roses are tidy and require no care other than a little watering during extended droughts.

Care and Maintenance
The foliage is a little thin on these plants as they are starting, and weeds, particularly purslane, can be troublesome. Pull the purslane and apply a little pre-emergent herbicide. Dacthal works fine for this purpose.

Companion Planting and Design
Moss Rose tolerates conditions few other plants can stand. Try combining it with Vinca (*Catharanthus roseus*), which also will stand adverse sites. We use this plant in an area between two garages where it gets the full beating sun and heat from the blacktop all day. The soil is dry and accumulates salt in the winter, yet the plants do well, and reseed themselves.

Did You Know
Portulaca is derived from the Latin *Porto*, to carry, and *lac*, milk, referring to the milky sap of some species.

Nasturtium
Tropaeolum majus

When, Where, and How to Plant
Sow seeds of Nasturtiums directly in the garden as soon as danger of a freeze is past. Or, sow seeds in peat pots indoors under lights six weeks before the frost-free date. Set the started plants 12 inches apart and thin the seedlings when they are about 3 inches tall to the same spacing.

Growing Tips
Nasturtiums take little care once they are established. Water them only when they begin to wilt, and use fertilizer sparingly if at all.

Care and Maintenance
These plants seem to be magnets for aphids. Check the soft new tips and either snip off infested ones or treat with insecticidal soap when aphids are present. Additional treatments will be necessary when the insects reappear during the season. Mites and cabbage worms are attracted to Nasturtiums too. Soap keeps mites under control. *Bacillus thuringiensis (B.t.)* handles the worms. Bush types need no support. Vining types will need help if you want them to climb. Tie them to trellises or twist them up strings.

Companion Planting and Design
Use Nasturtiums where other things don't seem to do well. These are tough little plants. Vines can be used on the west side of a porch or patio to provide some protection from late afternoon sun and heat. The happy colors work well with the blues of Ageratum and Purple Salvia.

Did You Know
Nasturtiums, because they are so easy and so fast to flower, make excellent flowers for children to grow. Give them a place to garden and some seeds. Help them scratch up a seedbed and sow the seeds. In a few days, the seeds will be up, and in weeks there will happy little flowers. . . a great way to get kids interested in gardening. The flowers can be cut for bouquets. What child doesn't enjoy picking a handful of flowers for Mom or for a friend? Nasturtiums are related to Watercress, *Nasturtium officinale,* and contain mustard oil. The flowers and leaves are edible and add a little bite to summer salads.

Nasturtiums are bright happy flowers that will thrive in hot places with poor soil. In fact too much fertility results in lots of leaves and few flowers. We like them for a spot between our garage and the neighbor's where it gets very hot and dry, and the soil is thin. Little else wants to grow there, but these plants do very well. It has been said that Nasturtiums got their name because they do best if you are a bit nasty to them. This isn't true, but they do thrive on neglect. Actually, the botanical name, Tropaeolum, comes from tropaion *meaning trophy, and refers to the shape of the flowers which resemble a helmet and the leaves which seem to resemble a buckler.*

Other Name
Indian Cress

Bloom Period and Color
Red, orange, yellow, mahogany, pink, and white flowers are produced from early summer until frost.

Mature Height × Spread
These adaptable plants can be bushy, low-growing 1 foot tall and wide, semi-dwarf to 2 feet, or vines up to 6 feet tall.

Pansy
Viola × wittrockiana

Who doesn't enjoy the smiling faces and cheery colors of Pansies? The bright splashes of color in the garden are certainly welcome after a long, dreary Illinois winter. Even before soils are workable, you can set out a few plants in pots, for these hardy little plants will stand a freeze and keep on blooming. They have been known to survive a Northern winter if they have adequate snow cover for protection. While not particularly fond of heat, some of the newer selections will bloom throughout the summer if protected from the midday sun. 'Majestic Giants' are large-flowered and early. For bedding plants, single-color cultivars with smaller flowers and no faces are preferred. They stand up better in rainstorms, and the colors are more uniform.

Bloom Period and Color
Spring, early summer, and fall blooms in tri-colored, purple, yellow, white, blue, dark red, brown, and apricot.

Mature Height × Spread
4 to 8 inches × 12 inches

When, Where, and How to Plant
Plant Pansies where late-developing perennials are expected, or in annual beds where they can be removed in time to plant the hot-weather kinds. Pansies can be planted in full sun or partial shade. In the shade, they will flower all summer; in full sun, they tend to stall out. Soils should be cool, fertile, moist, and well drained. Set plants on 6- to 8-inch centers for immediate effect. Plant them at the same depth they were growing in the containers, and water them in to settle the soil. Do not keep them constantly wet, or the stems will rot at the soil line. If you would like Pansy plants in March, the seed can be started indoors under lights at 60°F in late December or January. Moisten the seed, and chill it for a week in the refrigerator. When starting, cover the seeds lightly with the propagating mix—they must be in the dark in order to germinate. Transplant them, and grow on at 55°F. Set them out when the soils are dry enough to work in March.

Growing Tips
Water them if the weather is dry, and remove the spent blooms to keep the plants flowering.

Care and Maintenance
Pansies require little care. When the plants get long and straggly, cut them back; they will respond with renewed growth and flowering. Pansies are affected by the usual problems associated with plants grown in cool moist places. Slugs and earwigs will make lace out of the flowers. Use slug baits, and spray the plants with Sevin to control earwigs. Both pests are easily controlled while they are still small, so start early. Super hardy Icicle Pansies can be planted for fall color to replace summer annuals. They are hardy enough to stand late freezes and continue blooming, often surviving the winter to provide early color the next spring.

Companion Planting and Design
Combine Pansies with small spring flowering bulbs such as Squill or Muscari.

Did You Know
Pansies are the modern day "Hearts-ease" of Elizabethan times.

Petunia

Petunia × hybrida

When, Where, and How to Plant

Petunias can be started from seed, but this does take time. Sow the seed indoors under lights in February, covering lightly with the propagating mix. Germination takes five days at 70°F. Transplant, and continue to grow the seedlings at 60 to 70°. Set them into the garden when all danger of a freeze is past. They will stand a frost if they are hardened off properly. Petunias are sun-loving plants. They will tolerate some shade at the expense of flower production. Good drainage is necessary to avoid stem rot. Petunias are available as bedding plants, and in pots, hanging baskets, and planters. Space bedding types 12 inches apart; ground cover types should be spaced about 3 feet. Work up the soil by tilling or cultivating, and set the plants no deeper than they were grown in their containers. After planting, water the plants thoroughly to settle the soil.

Growing Tips

Stem rot can be a major problem that is aggravated by poor drainage or poor watering practices. Water thoroughly to soak the soil, but always allow the plants to wilt before watering again. Avoid heavy mulches and frequent, light, shallow watering. Stem rot will show up on the lighter colors first. If you see this happen, reduce the watering and drench the bed with Banrot or a similar product.

Care and Maintenance

Petunias have their share of problems. Slugs and earwigs can make lace of flowers and leaves; protect the plants with slug bait and Sevin insecticide. Deadhead spent blooms. Cut back overly-long, straggly plants about midsummer; they will respond with renewed growth and flowers.

Companion Planting and Design

Petunias will give you a riot of color all season. They go well with Salvias, Geraniums, Alyssum, and Ageratum. Use in beds, borders, or containers.

Did You Know

The name Petunia comes from the Brazilian *petun* for Tobacco. They are solanaceous plants native to South America and related to Tobacco.

For decades, Petunias were the bedding plants of choice. The new ground cover types of Petunias have renewed interest in these plants. For dependability and long season of bloom, nothing comes close to Petunias. Petunias are grouped according to flower form. Multifloras have lots of single, 2- to 3-inch flowers, and there are double Multifloras as well. Grandifloras have fewer, but larger, 5-inch blooms. Double Grandifloras are huge and spectacular, better used for containers and pots. The blooms of double Grandifloras are too heavy for the garden; with the first rain, they will end up in the mud. Cascade types have longer, trailing stems and are best used in hanging baskets. The ground cover types, such as 'Purple Wave' and 'Pink Wave' are extra-vigorous Cascade types that make 6-inch-high mats covered with blooms.

Bloom Period and Color
Summer blooms in red, white, purple, pink, salmon, yellow, and with stripes or star-like marks.

Mature Height × Spread
8 to 16 inches × 8 to 16 inches

Salvia
Salvia splendens

Bright-red Salvia is one of the flowers especially suited to red, white, and blue flower beds. Red is still the most popular Salvia color, but breeders have developed other colors as well, and plant form and size have also undergone some changes. The strictly upright forms are giving way to short, compact types covered with blooms and better suited to bedding. Dwarf selections include 'Firecracker', 'Hot Stuff', and 'St. John's Fire'. Taller 'America' grows to 20 inches, 'Splendens Tall' to 30. The 'Hotline' series is short, 10 inches, and includes red, white, violet, burgundy, and mixed selections. 'Salsa Mix' includes burgundy, bicolor scarlet, and bicolor salmon. A related species is the Blue Salvia, S. farinacea, which is less showy, but excellent as a dried flower.

Other Name
Scarlet Sage

Bloom Period and Color
Summer to frost blooms in red, white, violet, salmon, yellow, purple, burgundy.

Mature Height × Spread
6 to 30 inches × upright or mound shaped

When, Where, and How to Plant
Salvia can be started from seed indoors under lights. The seed does need light to germinate, so don't cover it with soil. Germination takes about five days at 70°F. Transplant the seedlings, then grow them at 60°. Salvias do best and develop their most intense color in full sun. They can take a lot of heat, and they prefer moist but well-drained soil. In partial shade the plants will become leggy and may begin to fall over. Salvia is available as bedding plants from local garden centers and other plant stores. Set the plants in the garden when all danger of frost has passed. Soil should be prepared by tilling or cultivating; set started plants on 10- to 12-inch centers, planting no deeper than the plants were growing in their containers. Water thoroughly after planting to settle the soil. Pinching will hasten branching of the taller varieties. Newer, compact forms do not require pinching; they will branch themselves.

Growing Tips
Stem rot can be a problem if the soil stays wet, or if the plants are watered too often. Soak the soil thoroughly, and let it dry until the plants begin to wilt before watering again. The tiny plants are easily injured by fertilizer, so use it sparingly. Try liquid fertilizers at 1/4 normal strength.

Care and Maintenance
Salvia is relatively trouble-free. Some of the shorter cultivars will continue to bloom without dead-heading. Taller cultivars should have spent flower spikes removed for continuing bloom.

Companion Planting and Design
Salvias are best massed in beds, although a clump of several plants as an accent in an empty spot on the perennial garden works too. Combine red Salvias with Geraniums, or with white Petunias and blue Ageratum for a red, white, and blue garden.

Did You Know
Salvia is from Latin *salveo,* which means "to heal." Writings of Pliny, an early Roman scientist, refer to its medicinal properties. Red Salvia is native to Brazil.

Snapdragon
Antirrhinum majus

When, Where, and How to Plant
When the seeds are placed under lights at 70°F, Snapdragons will germinate in about seven days. Sow the seed in early March. Transplant the seedlings, and grow them at 60°. Snaps are cool-weather plants. The newer cultivars will tolerate heat, but the tall types will often stall. They will grow again when temperatures moderate. Snaps will tolerate frost, but plant the started plants when freeze danger has passed. Seed can be sown directly in the garden as early as the soil can be worked. They need a moist but well-drained soil. Space started plants of tall cultivars 12 inches apart, bedding cultivars on 6- to 8-inch centers. Prepare the soil by tilling or cultivating, and set the plants at the same depth they were growing in the containers. Deep planting can result in stem rot.

Growing Tips
Stem rot can become serious from poor drainage or poor watering practices. Snaps would rather be dry than wet. Water them thoroughly, but do not water again until the plants begin to wilt. If plant losses remain severe, treat the soil with Banrot.

Care and Maintenance
Bedding Snaps need tending to assure continued flowering; remove the spent blooms. If the plants begin to get leggy in mid-season, cut them back to about 6 inches and they will respond with new growth. Tall Snapdragons need support. Stake them so the stems are straight for cutting. After removal of the first spike, tall Snaps will rebloom with shorter side shoots. Spider mites can be troublesome in hot weather. Syringe them off with a stream of water, or try insecticidal soap.

Companion Planting and Design
Tall Snaps are excellent for flower arrangements. Plant tall Snaps at the back of the garden or in the cutting garden. Use dwarf selections in beds, or as border or edging plants. In containers mix with dwarf Gerberas, Nasturtiums and Plume Cockscomb.

Did You Know
Snaps will "snap" at you if you lightly pinch the sides of the individual flowers.

Snapdragons were some of the first plants I grew. They did well even when I sowed them directly in the garden. As I recall, our gardens were usually pretty much in the shade, but the Snapdragons grew anyway. Snaps in those days were tall and narrow, with blooms held upright on 20- to 30-inch stems; they belonged in the cutting garden or at the back of the border. The newer, more versatile cultivars are short, with spikes of interesting, pastel-colored flowers borne on compact 6-inch plants. Bedding types include early-flowering, heat-tolerant 'Tahiti'. Medium-tall 'Lipstick Silver' has white flowers with red "lips." 'Rocket' hybrid is the most common tall Snap for cutting gardens. At its best, it rivals the greenhouse Snaps grown for the florist trade.

Other Name
Snaps

Bloom Period and Color
Summer to fall blooms in white, pink, yellow, orange, lavender.

Mature Height × Spread
6 to 30 inches × 6 to 24 inches

Sunflower
Helianthus annuus

The name Sunflower immediately brings to mind a huge, tree-like plant with a nodding head well beyond the reach of a child. Things have improved. Even the tall cultivars have better stand-ability, and they don't get as tall as they did years ago. Tall Sunflowers are still popular, but breeders have developed dwarf kinds that produce the same large heads and seeds, but on shorter plants. The bushy dwarfs are from 4 to 6 feet, still tall by most standards. 'Velvet Tapestry' offers a mixture of crimsons, golds, and bicolors. 'Sunspot' is a large-flowered dwarf with 12-inch flowers on 2-foot plants. 'Pacino' has large flowers on 20-inch plants. Five-foot 'Sunshine Mix' includes more colors: white, cream, lemon yellow, gold, orange, bronze, red, and burgundy.

Bloom Period and Color
Summer blooms in red to brown discs with yellow to orange rays.

Mature Height × Spread
2 to 10 or more feet × 2 to 4 feet

When, Where, and How to Plant
Sunflowers can be started indoors in peat pots about four weeks before the frost-free date, or seeded directly into the garden when danger of frost has passed. Sunflowers are seldom available as bedding plants. Sunflowers are for the sun; plant them where they get full sun all day long. They tolerate dry soils. Sow seed directly in the garden, or transplant started seedlings. Cover seed with 1/2 inch of soil, and thin seedlings to about 2 feet. Set plants on 2-foot centers.

Growing Tips
For best seed production, give them plenty of water when their flowers are developing.

Care and Maintenance
Sunflowers require very little care. Some overly tall plants may need support if you can find something tall enough. Birds and squirrels are the worst of the pests. To prevent them from stealing all the seed before it ripens, try covering the flowerheads with old pantyhose. It looks strange, but it works.

Companion Planting and Design
Sunflowers do not lend themselves well to planting in a small garden. They are usually grown as conversation pieces and for the seed they produce for birds. Dwarf kinds are not for the border but if there is space, they are attractive additions to the flower garden. The smaller kinds are excellent for cut flowers. The tall types make fun summertime activities for kids. They grow quickly from seed into tree-like plants. Our town has a biggest sunflower contest each year. Plant Pole Beans under each Sunflower and train them up the stalk, making double use of the space. Be sure to water so they don't dry out.

Did You Know
The name *Helianthus* comes from the Greek, *helios*, sun, and *anthos*, flower. Tall Sunflowers are grown commercially for seeds and oil. Jerusalem Artichoke is a Sunflower, *Helianthus tuberosa*.

When, Where, and How to Plant

Verbena germinates with difficulty. Chill the sown seed in the refrigerator for about ten days to break its dormancy, then set out at 70°F. Cover lightly with soil mix, as the seed germinates in the dark and is sensitive to moisture; keep it on the dry side. Germination will take five to fifteen days. As soon as the seed has germinated, lower the temperature to 60°. Transplant when large enough to handle. You may set the plants in the garden when threat of a freeze is past. The plants will stand a frost if they have been properly hardened off. Plant in well-drained soil in full sun. These plants can stand a drought better than they can a flood! During hot summers, Verbena does better in the northern parts of the state. When temperatures are in the 90s day after day, blooming may stop. Watering is helpful at these times, as it tends to cool the plants, but a return to temperate conditions promotes renewed blooming. Verbena is always available at garden centers and plant stores as bedding plants or in pots. Work up the soil by tilling or cultivating. If the area is poorly drained, raise it or provide drainage. Set started plants on 15-inch centers, no deeper than they were growing in their containers. Deep planting can result in damping off from stem rot.

Growing Tips

If the weather is hot and dry, watering will help to stimulate flowering.

Care and Maintenance

Verbena requires little care. Removal of spent blooms will prolong flowering. Damping off is the most serious problem, and this is due to excess moisture.

Companion Planting and Design

Cheery flowers brighten any garden. Use the low-growing types as edging. They blend well with the colors of Marigolds or Plumosa Cockscomb. 'Peaches & Cream' is exceptional next to purple Salvia or Lobelia.

Did You Know

Verbena comes from the Latin word for the Laurel branches carried by priests.

When I was a youngster working in a garden center after school hours, this cheery plant was fascinating to me. It was one of the first plants for which I learned the botanical name. It makes a good ground cover, appearing brighter than most with its happy little flowers. It works well in rock gardens, beds, windowboxes, planters, and as edging. Verbena needs a moist, well-drained soil. Blooms of the heat-tolerant cultivar 'Peaches and Cream' are an unusual blend of salmon and apricot. In 1992 it won both AAS and Fleuroselect awards. 'Imagination' has lacy foliage and deep, magenta-blue flowers. Related are the taller V. rigida, which is available only in purple, and V. bonariensis, which is 3 to 4 feet tall and has lavender blooms.

Other Name

Verbena × hortensis

Bloom Period and Color

Summer blooms in bright red, white, blue, lavender, or purple with distinct white or yellow centers.

Mature Height × Spread

12 inches × 18 to 24 inches

Zinnia
Zinnia elegans

Zinnias mean summertime! These cheery flowers have been favorites for generations, and they remain so today. Zinnias are well adapted to our Midwest climate and soils. They are tolerant of our heat and drought, thriving in weather that sends other flowers into senescence. Hybridizing has developed smaller, bushier plants with a greater color range and disease resistance. Small cultivars include 'Thumbelina', which is 6 inches tall and produces 1^1/$_2$-inch flowers. The medium-sized 'Peter Pan Hybrids' are about a foot tall and have large, upward-facing blooms. The large-flowered (3^1/$_2$ to 4 inches) 'Dreamland Mix' is improved with additional colors. 12-inch-tall 'Pinwheel' has large, upward-facing single flowers in pastel colors and mildew resistance. Tall, giant-flowered cultivars include 'Big Top', 'Tetra Hybrid', and 'Burpee's Zenith Hybrid'.

Bloom Period and Color
Summer blooms in rose, red, white, yellow, green, orange, and violet.

Mature Height × Spread
12 to 36 inches × 6 to 18 inches

When, Where, and How to Plant
Start Zinnia seeds indoors under lights about eight weeks before the last frost date. Seeds germinate quickly under lights, in as little as 24 hours at 75 to 80°F. Seed sown in early April will develop into plants of sufficient size to plant in the garden by Memorial Day. Don't rush Zinnias into the garden. These are hot-weather plants, and cold weather will set them back. Plant Zinnias in full sun. They do best in hot, dry locations. Seed can be sown directly in the garden, and this is the better way to grow the tall cultivars. Space the tall-growing kinds at 24 inches. Dwarf Zinnias are always available as bedding plants from garden centers; taller cultivars are harder to find. Set out started plants when soils have warmed. Space dwarf cultivars about a foot apart.

Growing Tips
They don't mind dry soil, but they will flower better if given water when they are dry. To avoid mildew, water them early in the day so that the leaves will dry off before dusk. If mildew appears late in the season, spray the plants with sulfur or triforine.

Care and Maintenance
Zinnias don't require a lot of care. Remove spent blossoms to keep the plants flowering. Zinnias make excellent cut flowers, so keeping them cut for arrangements accomplishes the deadheading task. Tall cultivars may need staking.

Companion Planting and Design
Dwarf Zinnias are excellent for edging and borders in hot places such as next to the driveway. They mix well with Alyssum, Ageratum, or Marigolds. Shallow roots make them excellent for planting among the ripening foliage of spring-flowering bulbs.

Did You Know
Zinnias are easy to grow. Give the children some space and some seeds. Help them scratch up a seedbed and sow the seeds. In a few days, the seeds will be up, and in weeks there will be masses of blooms . . . a great way to get kids interested in gardening.

Bulbs *for Illinois*

Bulbs play an important part in the flower garden pageantry of spring and summer, and they can even move indoors for the winter. Crocuses break forth before the snow is quite gone and are followed by Daffodils and majestic Tulips. Then the summer bulbs take over with Cannas, Tuberous Begonias, Gladiolus, and stately Lilies.

Plants that come from bulbs, tubers, or corms are among the easiest plants to grow. Their underground structures allow them to survive adverse conditions such as winter in the northern climates, excessive heat, or droughts. Bulbs are actually compressed underground buds, while tubers and corms are stems.

Growing Bulbs

Inside a bulb is an embryonic plant complete with roots, stem, leaves, and flowers. If you cut an Onion or a Daffodil bulb in half lengthwise, you will be able to see all its parts just waiting for the right time to begin growing. Bulbs do not even require soil to grow. Stick a Paper-White Narcissus bulb in a glass of water, and it will burst forth with a mass of blooms.

Types of Bulbs

A true bulb consists of concentric layers which are bases of modified leaves. (These are called tunicated bulbs.) Daffodil or Tulip bulbs are true bulbs. Lily bulbs consist of individual overlapping scales.

Tubers are swollen underground stems that store starch. The new plant-leaves, stems, and roots grow from a single bud. Potatoes are tubers, and their eyes are the buds. Dahlias and Tuberous Begonias grow from tubers too. A corm is a short stem that has leaves and more stems growing from its pointed end, and roots growing from its bottom.

Irises and Daylilies grow from rhizomes. Rhizomes are slender, root-like underground stems that store starch as well. We will talk about them in the chapter on perennials.

Now we have defined these terms, but are the definitions really important? For all practical purposes, these are all "bulbs," and we are most concerned with getting flowers from them.

Using Bulbs in the Garden

Bulbs may be hardy or tender in our Illinois climate. Hardy bulbs stay in the ground, perfectly able to survive the winter. Because they will stay in place for many years, it is wise to take some time to plan their location and to prepare the ground for them.

Spring-flowering bulbs provide the best display if naturalized or if planted in masses. Planting them in straight rows like toy soldiers may show a lack of imagination! Plant a dozen or so in a mass where they will make a statement. Then plant another mass on the other side of the yard. Even if there is nothing in a bed later in the spring but the old leaves, a full bed of color will have created an image that will not be forgotten. Naturalized plantings of hundreds of Squills or Daffodils also create memorable sites (and sights!). Just scatter the bulbs and plant them where they fall. Be sure not to remove the leaves before they die, and these plantings will increase in size and color each year. Lilies are the aristocrats of the garden. With a little attention, their gorgeous blooms will faithfully appear at a time when their beauty is really appreciated.

Tender summer bulbs take over where the hardy spring bulbs leave off. You can plant them in the very beds vacated by the spring bulbs, among the perennials, in the cutting garden, or in a mass display for a striking effect. Tender bulbs should be lifted and stored for the winter and planted the following spring.

Bulbs of all kinds are sold in garden centers at the right times for planting. The best way to know what you are getting is to look at the pictures on the store display. Try a few that look good. If you like them when they grow in your garden, buy more the following year. One of the joys of gardening is experimentation. You never know what you will discover.

Caladium
Caladium × hortulanum

Caladiums are unrivaled for creating a spectacular display in a shady, moist spot in the garden. These are tender tropical perennials, and they are not at all hardy in our state, requiring special care. In spite of the extra work, the tremendous display these plants provide makes the effort worthwhile. Their leaves are large, heart-shaped, and richly colored. They are suited for growing in containers or for setting out into the garden. It is best to select started plants so you can see the range of colors. Some selections are 'Carolyn Wharton', which is pink, red, and green; 'Frieda Hemple', which is solid red with green margins; 'Florida Sweetheart', which is white with red veins and green margins; and 'White Christmas', white with green veins.

Bloom Period and Color
Foliage in combinations of white, pink, red, and green, two or more colors in each leaf.

Mature Height × Spread
1 to 2 feet × 1 to 2 feet

When, Where, and How to Plant
Caladium tubers need to be started indoors about eight weeks before the last frost-free date. They should be potted and watered, and set in a warm (70°F) place to develop. After all danger of frost is over, they may be moved outdoors. Caladiums can stand full sun if the humidity is high, but they are best suited to a shade border or to massing in a shade garden. Protect them from strong winds, which will tear the delicate leaves. In a border or shade garden, started plants may be removed from their pots and planted on 12-inch centers in the garden, or the pots may be plunged. Plants grown for urns or planters may be handled either way as well, but they are usually set plant to plant.

Growing Tips
Though these plants need a lot of water, their roots need plenty of air. Eighty-degree temperatures and high humidity are ideal. If the humidity is low the plants will suffer, and misting might be necessary. Caladiums can handle temperatures in the 90s as long as they have adequate moisture. Lift the plants and move them indoors before a frost. Allowed to dry, they can be stored in their pots, or in boxes of peat moss. After a rest period of about 5 months, the plants can be started again. If new tubers have grown on the sides of the parent tuber, they may be removed to start additional plants.

Care and Maintenance
Caladiums need a moist but well-drained soil. If they stand in water, the tubers will rot. If there is a drainage problem, try raised beds. Caladiums have no serious pests.

Companion Planting and Design
Caladiums are so spectacular that they can stand on their own. They can be planted among other shade-loving plants such as Ferns, and can be used to hide ripening foliage of spring flowering wild-flowers such as Jack-in-the-Pulpit, Trilliums or Virginia Bluebells.

Did You Know
Caladiums are Arums, the same family as Jack-in-the-Pulpit and other familiar plants such as Philodendrons.

Canna
Canna sp.

When, Where, and How to Plant

Cannas are tender perennial plants that grow from fleshy rhizomes. Smaller cultivars may be handled as annuals and their seed sown indoors in January. Plant rhizomes or started plants in the garden after all danger of frost is past. Cannas prefer a deeply prepared soil that has good drainage. If you are planting the larger cultivars, make sure there is enough room. Work up the soil in the planting area by spading or tilling to a depth of 12 inches. Set started plants or rhizomes on 12-inch centers. The plants are unbranched and can be planted quite close together. Rhizomes should be planted at least 4 to 6 inches deep, while started plants should be set at the same depth they grew in their containers. Water thoroughly to settle the soil around the tubers.

Growing Tips

Cannas are large plants. They will need water if the weather is dry. About an inch a week is sufficient. Apply fertilizer as the plants begin to grow in spring, a pound of 10-10-10 per 100 square feet or the equivalent.

Care and Maintenance

Cannas require little care in the garden. The first fall freeze will kill back the foliage, and the tubers must be removed for storage indoors. Cut off the stems about 6 inches above ground; you will use them for handles to carry the clump. Store the clumps of rhizomes in damp peat moss in a dark room at 45 degrees Fahrenheit. In spring, separate the clumps into rhizomes, each with three eyes. Pot them or place them in a box of sand to start the plants growing before setting them back in the garden when danger of frost has passed.

Companion Planting and Design

Use Cannas in the middle of beds or at the back of the border with other large plants such as Cleomes, or with tall Marigolds or Zinnias.

Did You Know

One species of Canna, *C. edulis,* is the source of arrowroot commonly used to thicken fruit sauces because it remains clear.

If you're going for the spectacular, nothing can beat Cannas. Their 6-foot-tall spikes of blooms in masses are the centerpieces of summer floral gardens in Chicago's Lincoln Park each year; on that grand scale, anything less would be lost. If you have room, these plants can have the same magnificent effect in your garden. Strongly upright with banana-like foliage, these plants are topped with stalks of brightly colored gladiolus-like blooms from early summer until frost. If you have less room, try the shorter cultivars; they also provide a spectacular display. Giant Canna cultivars include 'Red King Humbert', with red foliage and orange blooms; 'Richard Wallace', with yellow flowers and green leaves; and 'Rosamund Cole', which has green leaves and red flowers tipped with yellow.

Bloom Period and Color
Summer blooms in red, orange, pink, salmon, yellow.

Mature Height × Spread
1 to 6 feet × 1 to 3 feet

Daffodil
Narcissus species and hybrids

Bright yellow Daffodils are universal spring favorites. There are so many types of Narcissus that they have been classified into eleven major divisions by the (British) Royal Horticultural Society. Most of the classifications are based on trumpet length and color. The Daffodil is only one of many Narcissus, and the name refers to the types that have large yellow trumpet-like flowers. There are over 10,000 named cultivars of Narcissus. One of the most popular is the Paper-White Narcissus that can be forced in a dish of water. This is a great project for children who are looking for an indoor activity in the fall. Other types of Narcissus can be forced as well, but they require a long period of cold to prepare them.

Bloom Period and Color
Spring blooms in bright yellow, white, orange, pink, green, or bicolor.

Mature Height × Spread
6 inches to 2 feet × 6 to 12 inches

When, Where, and How to Plant
Daffodils are hardy spring-flowering bulbs, and they must be planted in the fall. Starting in September, bulbs are available in garden centers or wherever plants are sold. Daffodils can be planted in masses in the perennial border or naturalized throughout the lawn, garden, or wooded area. They are equally at home in sun or partial shade. Like most bulbs, Daffodils need good drainage. Wet soils will cause the bulbs to rot. Prepare the soil in beds by spading or tilling and add organic matter if the soil is particularly heavy. Plant the bulbs 6 to 12 inches apart and 6 inches deep. In sand or other light soils, plant them as deep as 8 to 10 inches. To naturalize, randomly scatter the bulbs over the area to be planted. With a trowel or bulb digger, plant them where they fall. When the bulbs have multiplied for a few years, their blooming will cease, and they will have to be dug up and divided.

Growing Tips
Keep the leaves growing as long as possible in spring. Apply 1 pound of 10-10-10 fertilizer or the equivalent per 100 square feet of bed after the flowers have faded. Water if the weather is dry.

Care and Maintenance
Once they are planted, Daffodils require very little care. After the plants bloom in spring, their foliage should be left to replenish the bulbs for the following year. Remove the foliage after it begins to turn yellow. Annuals can be planted between the ripening leaves to hide them; these annuals will be well established by the time the Daffodil leaves are removed.

Companion Planting and Design
Mass with other spring blooming plants such as Virginia Bluebells, Squills, and Grape Hyacinths.

Did You Know
If deer decimate your Tulips, plant Daffodils. They contain oxalate crystals that are distasteful to deer, so deer won't eat them.

When, Where, and How to Plant

Dahlias can be grown from tubers and from potted plants or transplants. Tubers are available from garden centers, either dormant or potted up and growing. Plant dormant tubers in pots indoors in March to get an early start. Or, set tubers in the garden when danger of frost has passed. Each tuber has a bud at the tip. Be careful not to break it off or the tuber will not grow. Prepare the soil by spading 10 to 12 inches deep. Set tubers on their sides 4 inches deep with the bud pointing up, and cover with finely prepared soil. Dahlias need full sun and well-drained, deeply-prepared soil. Smaller kinds are used for borders and edging. The larger specimen types are for the cutting garden, and are usually planted in rows like corn for convenience. They need to be staked to keep them from falling over.

Growing Tips

Keep the plants well watered and fertilize regularly with dilute, liquid fertilizer. Pinch tips from smaller bedding types to force branching and more flowers. Grow specimen types single-stem and disbudded to produce one large central flower.

Care and Maintenance

Dahlias are subject to attack by aphids and mites, and corn and stalk borers. Protect plants by spraying with Sevin and Kelthane. Wilt diseases will kill plants. Remove and dispose of them, not in the compost pile. Tubers will be killed by the winter weather. In fall after leaves are frosted, cut stems to 10 or 12 inches and carefully lift the clumps of tubers. Dry and store as clumps in sand or vermiculite at 35 to 40 degrees. Check monthly to make sure tubers are not wilting or rotting. Air dry or moisten as needed.

Companion Planting and Design

Bedding types can be mixed into the border utilizing several sizes and types for contrast, or with grasses. Or, plant in containers.

Did You Know

Dahlias came from higher elevations in Mexico, but have been extensively hybridized, and the species is rarely seen in this country. Dahlias form tubers in response to shortening day length in late summer to early fall.

Dahlias are tender perennials that grow from tubers (fleshy underground stems), and come in a wide range of colors, sizes, and flower types. There is something for any garden. Plants vary in size from knee high to head high. Dwarf kinds are usually seed-grown, handled like annuals and sold in packs or pots. They are not as uniform and not as heat tolerant as the tuberous rooted kinds. Tuberous-rooted kinds are not hardy, but are vegetatively propagated, and completely uniform. They need to be dug up and stored indoors for the winter. Dormant tubers are divided for sale in spring by commercial producers. Tubers, potted plants, and transplants are available from garden centers later in spring when frost no longer threatens.

Other Name
Garden Dahlias

Bloom Period and Color
Midsummer until frost. Red, orange, yellow, pink, purple, and white.

Mature Height × Spread
1 to 5 feet, rounded or erect.

Flowering Onion
Allium sp.

There are at least half a dozen species of Ornamental Onions used as garden flowers. They range from the Giant Onion, 4 feet tall with a 6-inch ball of blooms, to Lily Leek, a foot tall with clusters of bright yellow blooms. Onion bulbs are fully hardy in Illinois. The bloom period is only about two weeks, but during that time these flowers make a memorable show. Most make excellent cut flowers. Persian Onion, A. aflatunense, makes a clump of wide, strap-shaped leaves. Its star-shaped flowers are purple in a 4-inch ball that is held held 2 feet above the leaves; it is good in the border and lasts two weeks as a cut flower. 'Purple Sensation' is dark purple and blooms in late spring.

Bloom Period and Color
Late spring to early summer blooms in purple, white, pink, or yellow.

Mature Height × Spread
1 to 5 feet × 6 to 12 inches

When, Where, and How to Plant
Flowering Onions are planted in fall. Plant in full sun in a well-drained soil. If planted in shade, the flower stalks will be weak and will fall over; poor drainage will result in bulb rot problems. Prepare the soil by spading or tilling to a depth of at least 6 inches. Set the bulbs with at least 3 inches of soil above the tops. The taller kinds must be relegated to the back of the garden, and they may need to be supported in windy areas.

Growing Tips
As soon as the flowers die down, apply a complete fertilizer such as 10-10-10 at the rate of one pound per 100 square feet of bed. Keep the leaves growing as long as possible to replenish the bulbs. When the leaves begin to turn yellow, cut them off at the ground level.

Care and Maintenance
Once established, Flowering Onions require little care. Remove the flower stalk after the blooms have faded. Flowering Onions are nearly pest-free. Thrips sometimes damage foliage. Bulb rot is a problem only in wet locations. Plants may become crowded; they may be lifted after the foliage dies down and the bulblets that develop at the bases of larger bulbs can be removed. The large bulbs and the larger of these bulblets will flower the following year. Discard the small bulblets or give them to friends.

Companion Planting and Design
Flowering Onions come in many sizes. The flowering dates also vary, so check both when buying bulbs. Shorter types can be planted in the border; relegate taller types to the back of the border or to the cutting garden. Some make excellent cut flowers.

Did You Know
The Flowering Onions are all related to the culinary Onions, Chives, Leeks, and Garlic. Each has its own distinctive aroma if bruised. While not grown as ornamentals, Chives are attractive if allowed to go to bloom. *Allium* is the Latin name for Garlic.

Gladiolus
Gladiolus sp. and hybrids

When, Where, and How to Plant
With successive plantings Glads can be enjoyed from early summer until frost. These are summer-flowering tender perennials that grow from corms. Glads are tender and will not stand a freeze. Set corms out starting at the average date of last frost. Plant additional corms every week to ten days until August for continuous bloom. Glads do best in full sun. The soil should be well drained. Prepare the soil by spading or tilling to a depth of at least 6 inches. Plant individual corms pointed side up, 4 inches deep and about 6 inches apart. The corms must be dug before a hard freeze. Cut the tops to an inch or so, and spread out the corms to dry in a warm place. After drying, remove the fresh new corms from the old top and mother corm, and store at just above freezing temperature in onion bags. Large corms will flower the next year. Tiny cormels will not bloom for several years and are best discarded. Discard any corms that show signs of rotting.

Growing Tips
Provide 1 inch of water per week if the season is dry. Water early in the day so plants dry quickly to avoid diseases that may damage opening blooms.

Care and Maintenance
Glads require very little care as they grow. Thrips can be troublesome in some years, marking the blooms with tiny white trails. Use Orthene, insecticidal soap, or neem to control them.

Companion Planting and Design
Glads are strongly upright. In the border, plant them near the back to provide accents without hiding smaller plants. Remember, each corm produces a single stalk and a single spike of blooms, so plant them in clumps. In the cutting garden, plant them 6 inches apart in rows.

Did You Know
Cut Glads in early morning when bottom flowers are just beginning to open, keeping as many leaves as possible on the plants to replenish the corms for the next year.

Glads are favorites of the florist trade, used extensively as cut flowers. They are garden favorites as well, easy and rewarding to grow. Above sword-shaped upright foliage, the spikes of lovely flowers, some 4 inches across, are spectacular. While the large-flowered types are the most popular, there are dwarf forms as well. The tall, large-flowered hybrid Glads are vigorous growers, and they come in many colors. Buy the colors and kinds that appeal to you when you look at the pictures on the bulb displays or in the catalogs. G. primulinus hybrids are somewhat less vigorous than the taller kinds, but they are more graceful, especially for use in arrangements. (The larger-flowered types are often too big for use in most homes.)

Other Name
Glads

Bloom Period and Color
Summer blooms in red, yellow, orange, purple, green, white, some with contrasting colored markings.

Mature Height × Spread
2 to 4 feet × 1 to 2 feet

Lily
Lilium sp.

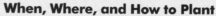

Lilies are the undisputed aristocrats of flowers. The traditional Easter Lily, L. longiflorum, is the most familiar one, and it can be grown in gardens throughout Illinois. There are, however, many better Lilies of varying colors and forms. Some are very easy to grow: plant them and forget them. Others require special care. Virtually all modern garden Lilies are hybrids. They have been developed from species Lilies collected all over the world. Species Lily bulbs are still available, and many of these plants are quite unusual. There are far too many kinds of Lilies to list them here. For a rather long listing and for other information on growing these magnificent plants, contact the North American Lily Society, Box 476, Waukee, IA 50263.

Bloom Period and Color
Early to late summer blooms in white, orange, yellow, rose, red, maroon, and bicolors.

Mature Height × Spread
2 to 8 feet × 1 to 2 feet

When, Where, and How to Plant
Plant Lilies in the fall when bulbs are available. Set potted Lilies in the garden any time during the growing season. Tiger Lilies will grow in full shade, and will even bloom well, but they will be tall and weak. Good drainage is always a must. Lilies do best when the bulbs are deeply planted in deeply prepared soil. The plants make roots from the underground stems and from the bottoms of the bulbs. Spade the soil a foot deep, making sure there is good drainage. If drainage is poor, construct raised beds or install tiles. Plant the bulbs twice as deep as they are tall; for example, a 3-inch bulb should be planted 6 inches deep. Make an exception to this rule when you plant Madonna Lilies—plant them 1 inch deep.

Growing Tips
Apply a balanced fertilizer in spring as the plants begin to grow. Keep the fertilizer away from developing foliage. Remove spent tops in the fall. Lilies grow from hardy bulbs, although some Lily varieties are marginally hardy in northern Illinois. These marginally hardy plants will benefit from mulching with straw to prevent freezing and thawing.

Care and Maintenance
Most Lilies require some care. Taller ones need support. Deadheading keeps the plants looking attractive as remaining buds open. The soil needs to be moist and cool; shade from other lower-growing plants or mulch is helpful. Aphids and slugs can be troublesome. Insecticidal soap will keep aphids at bay. Use slug bait around the plants, starting early while the slugs are still small. Repeated baiting will be necessary. Buy bulbs from reliable dealers to reduce the virus problem. If plants begin to show symptoms (malformed or spotted leaves), destroy them.

Companion Planting and Design
The best Lilies in our garden are: Regal (*L. regale*) for overall use and cutting, Tiger Lily (*L. tigrinum*) for naturalizing and tough situations, and the many new hybrids for borders and bedding.

Did You Know
Plant your Easter Lily in the garden when weather warms. It will flower the next year in June.

Spring-Flowering Bulbs
Chionodoxa luciliae, Crocus vernus, Scilla sibirica, others

When, Where, and How to Plant

Plant spring-flowering bulbs in the fall. You can find them in garden centers shortly after Labor Day. The earlier you get them in the ground, the better they will flower the next spring. These small plants prefer full sun but will be quite happy in the partial shade of leafless, deciduous trees or full shade at the north side of the house. They can stand moist soils, but they don't want to be drowned all spring. There is no need for any special soil preparation. These bulbs will grow in any garden soil where shrubs are growing, in natural areas, or where annuals will be planted. Plant them about 2 inches deep, using a trowel or bulb planter. In borders, plant them in groups of half a dozen, spaced 3 to 6 inches apart. For naturalizing in a lawn or a wooded area, scatter the bulbs at random and plant them where they fall.

Growing Tips

Water 1 inch per week if weather is dry, especially in fall if you are growing newly planted bulbs. Fertilize after flowers fade with 10-10-10 or similar, 1 pound per 100 square feet of bed.

Care and Maintenance

Once they are growing, these plants need virtually no care. Squirrels and mice will try to dig up the bulbs. If this is a problem, cover with chicken wire after planting. The wire can be removed in spring as new leaves arise. To replenish the bulbs, keep the foliage on as long as possible after the blooms die down. If these bulbs are planted in the lawn, mowing may need to be delayed until the leaves have ripened. Your alternative is to be prepared to replant each fall. If some plants do survive, all the better.

Companion Planting and Design

After flowers fade, interplant small spring bulbs with annuals. The annuals will hide the foliage until it has replenished the bulbs.

Did You Know

Many small bulbs are wonderful for cutting, and are fragrant as well. Some can be forced indoors for early bloom.

The many kinds of spring-flowering bulbs are delightful harbingers of the season, reminding us that even after the toughest winter, there will be flowers. Tulips and Daffodils are the most familiar, but there are many other kinds. Glory of the Snow, Chionodoxa luciliae, *has blue star-shaped flowers with white centers above a cluster of ribbon-like leaves. You may see Crocuses,* Crocus vernus, *blooming sometimes before the snow has melted. Squills,* Scilla sibirica, *are woodland plants that will tolerate quite a bit of shade. Their flowers are blue or white in clusters of five or six per stem, growing from a rosette of strap-shaped leaves. Other spring bulbs include: Trout Lilies,* Erythronium, *Grape Hyacinth,* Muscari, *Snowdrops,* Galanthus, *growing to 6 inches tall, and Winter Aconite,* Eranthis.

Bloom Period and Color
March, April, May blooms in white, purple, pink, yellow, striped.

Mature Height × Spread
6 to 12 inches × 6 to 12 inches

Tuberous Begonia
Begonia × tuberhybrida

If you want color in shaded situations, the Tuberous Begonia is spectacular. It has huge, exquisite 6-inch Camellia-like blooms in all colors except blues. While the newer cultivars are advertised to tolerate full sun, these are in reality shade plants. They are perfect for the patio or porch in containers or hanging baskets, and for shady spots in the garden, they can't be matched. Today the most popular cultivars are started from seed, and they perform well. There are many named cultivars of Tuberous Begonias. Started plants are usually in bloom so you will be able to see what you are buying. The exception to this is the 'Non-Stop' strain of seed-started plants. These are available in single colors or in a mix.

Bloom Period and Color
Summer blooms in white, orange, yellow, pink, and red.

Mature Height × Spread
12 inches × 12 inches

When, Where, and How to Plant
Plant tubers in the garden after danger of a freeze is past, setting them hollow side up so that the tip is an inch below the soil surface. Set started plants at the same depth they grew in the pots and about 12 inches apart. Sow the dust-like seed in December under lights at 70°F, scattering it on moist propagating medium. Transplant the seedlings into pots when large enough to handle. Set out when all danger of frost has passed. Plant Tuberous Begonias where they will get filtered shade at least during the middle of the day. Prepare the soil by spading or tilling to a depth of 6 inches. Good drainage is essential. Potted Begonias can be moved in for the winter—or the garden plants can be lifted, the soil washed off roots, and potted with soil mix for indoor bloom. The first freeze will kill the tops, after which the tubers must be dug up if the plants are to be saved. Allow the soil to dry, and shake the tubers loose. Store them in boxes of dry peat at about 45°F for the winter.

Growing Tips
Water Tuberous Begonias thoroughly and let them dry so the crowns and roots have a chance to get some air before watering again. Watering too much or too frequently will result in crown rot.

Care and Maintenance
The large flowers must be removed when they have faded to stimulate more blooms, and to reduce the incidence of botrytis. Slugs can be troublesome, and earwigs may damage the blooms. Slug bait and Sevin insecticide are effective controls.

Companion Planting and Design
Tuberous Begonias are great for shady gardens, adding splashes of color to Caladiums, Ferns, and Hostas. Set them directly in the ground, or set pots wherever needed for bright accents. You can move the pots whenever you need a change.

Did You Know
You can move pots of Tuberous Begonias indoors for winter color.

Tulip
Tulipa hybrids

When, Where, and How to Plant

Tulips are fully hardy spring-flowering bulbs, and must be planted in the fall. Tulips do best in full sun, but they will tolerate the filtered shade of bare deciduous trees. They prefer soils that are heavier, but they do need good drainage or the bulbs will rot. Spade the soil to a depth of at least 12 inches. Plant the bulbs 6 inches deep and 8 to 12 inches apart. These flowers look best in masses, so don't be tempted to plant rows of them like wooden soldiers. Plant groups of half a dozen or a dozen in one place, or plant full beds of them. Soak the bulbs after planting. If planting is late, the bulbs may not have time to make roots before the ground freezes. Four inches of straw will insulate the ground so that it doesn't freeze up as fast. Force tulips in pots for winter bloom. Choose forcing cultivars and pot them in bulb pans, using a soil-less potting mix. Plant them bulb to bulb with the tips just exposed. Moisten the mix, and cover the pots with clear plastic wrap. Store in the refrigerator for 16 weeks to break their dormancy, and allow the infant flower buds to develop. Bring a few out into a bright 60°F place every week or so for continuous bloom.

Growing Tips

Fertilize in spring after flowers fade with 10-10-10 or similar, 1 pound per 100 square feet of bed.

Care and Maintenance

Tulips require very little care. Their major pests are mice, squirrels, and rabbits. If these become a problem, cover the planting with chicken wire. Remove the wire in the spring when leaves begin to grow through it. Remove spent blooms.

Companion Planting and Design

After flowers fade, interplant the Tulips with annuals. The annuals will hide the ripening foliage until it has replenished the bulbs.

Did You Know

Tulips are great for cut flowers. Plant any extra bulbs in the cutting garden.

Tulips are probably the best-known and loved of the garden flowers. These most colorful of spring flowers are almost indispensable parts of the landscape. Nearly anyone with a little ground has planted a few of these undemanding flowers and been rewarded. Holland is still the major producer of Tulips. The auction at Aalsmeer is the number-one wholesale market for the cut blooms. Tulips are classified according to their size, time of bloom, and flower form. Early-season types include most of the Species Tulips and some named varieties. Mid-season types include the 'Mendel', 'Triumph', and 'Darwin' hybrids, which have the largest flowers. Late-season types are the tallest: 'Cottage', 'Darwin', and 'Rembrandt'. Plant a selection of cultivars, and your blooming period can last from early spring until June.

Bloom Period and Color

March, April, May blooms in red, orange, yellow, purple, pink, white, green, and blends.

Mature Height × Spread

6 to 36 inches × 12 inches

Ground Covers *for Illinois*

Ground covers are low-growing plants that are normally found in shady glens, on the banks of streams, on the forest floor, or in open sunny meadows.

There is no question that a well-tended lawn sets off a landscape, but lawns have a big problem: they require a tremendous amount of consistent (and costly) maintenance. They must be mowed, edged, cultivated, fertilized, and watered. Bugs, weeds, and diseases must be controlled. Most gardeners are trying to find ways to avoid such maintenance chores. Another problem with grass is that it won't grow everywhere. I receive as many questions about what to plant in those shaded areas where grass won't grow as I do questions on any other single topic. Turfgrasses are not suitable in shade, on slopes, in soggy spots, in borders, and in areas beneath low trees or shrubs, and in these places maintenance is just about impossible.

There is a whole group of plants that are more suitable to such conditions than are the turfgrasses. Low woody plants, vines, and herbaceous species can be found growing in just these conditions: these are the ground covers.

Types of Ground Covers

The woody ground covers are often found at a forest edge where they are exposed to shade and light. Sometimes they seem to struggle for their existence. Others inhabit rocky outcroppings or areas at the seashore with its constant sun and wind. Herbaceous ground covers are often found in the open woodlands, where they get light at certain times of the year or of the day. They may flower beautifully early in the season while light still reaches the forest floor. The natural adaptations of all of these plants to variable conditions make them perfect for the ground cover uses our landscapes require.

Using Ground Covers in the Garden

We can plant ground covers in beds under trees where it is too dark for grass. We can use them as facer plants between grass and the shrub plantings. They may be planted at the tops of banks, over walls, and in places where it is too hot, too wet, or too small for anything else. Sometimes we plant them just so there won't be so much grass to mow. Most of the time we plant ground covers because they add charm to our plantings—they are interesting and nice to look at.

Many ground covers are capable of spreading. Some, such as Cotoneaster and Sumac, root where they touch the ground. The vines do the same. Herbaceous types, such as Lily of the Valley and Sweet Woodruff, spread by rhizomes. Ginger produces abundant seed and rhizomes, allowing it to survive in difficult circumstances. Most spreading ground covers are so well suited to their circumstances that they will keep out weeds when used properly—but you may need to keep the ground covers under control as well!

On the following pages are profiles of just a few of these delightful plants. To see other members of the group, visit one of the arboreta or botanic gardens. We are fortunate in our wonderful state to have several outstanding places where plants can be observed, including the University of Illinois at Urbana/Champaign; Southern Illinois University, Carbondale and Edwardsville; the Chicago Botanic Garden at Glencoe; Morton Arboretum in Lisle; and the Klehm Arboretum in Rockford. We also can visit the Missouri Botanical Garden in neighboring St. Louis.

Ajuga
Ajuga reptans

Ajuga is a fast-growing spreading ground cover, evergreen or semi-evergreen. It will grow in full sun, but it tends to die out in the hotter parts of the state. This ground cover is most attractive in spring when it is covered with flowers. At other times, it is rather unnoticeable. It is one of the lowest-growing ground covers and serves its function well. In the proper location it becomes aggressive and will compete with weeds. It will invade the lawn under shaded conditions. Where this aggressive trait is an advantage, Ajuga is an excellent plant. There are several cultivars of A. reptans. 'Braunherz' has deep bronze foliage. 'Jungle Beauty' has multicolored leaves, but reverts back to purple. The more aggressive 'Rainbow' has tricolored leaves. 'Silver Beauty' is cream and white.

Other Name
Bugleweed

Bloom Period and Color
Spring blooms in blue, red, white, purple.

Mature Height × Spread
6 to 10 inches × spreading

When, Where, and How to Plant

Ajuga is available from nurseries and garden centers in spring and is best planted at that time. Plant Ajuga in sun or shade. It will grow very well where it is too dark for grass, under trees, and on the north side of the house. It will tolerate moist areas if the soil drains well. Ajugas are sold like bedding plants in flats or pots. Prepare the soil by spading or tilling. Set the plants at the depth they grew in the container, spacing them 6 to 12 inches apart, depending upon how quickly you need cover. If the plants in the containers were grown in a light artificial soil mix, shake as much of it as you can off the roots before planting. If the mix is left on the roots, the plant may be unable to grow out of it into the surrounding soil. Plants in this condition will wilt easily, and they will never become established.

Growing Tips

Water well during extended droughty periods. A balanced fertilizer in spring will aid in recovery from winter damage, and will hasten filling-in before weeds have the chance to become problematic.

Care and Maintenance

Keep weeds out of the planting until the Ajuga has become established. Crown rot is the major problem with this plant; if the planting becomes too dense or too wet, plants will die from this fungal disease. Prevent reinfection by working PCNB fungicide into the top 3 inches of soil before replanting.

Companion Planting and Design

Ajuga is an excellent replacement for lawns in spots where there is insufficient light for the grasses. Inter-plant it with other shade plants such as Hosta, Jack-in-the-Pulpit, Vinca, or Purple Leaf Winter Creeper.

Did You Know

Ajuga does well in full sun, but is subject to winter kill if exposed to winter sun and wind. Protect it with a loose mulch of lightly laid straw.

Barren Strawberry
Waldsteinia ternata

When, Where, and How to Plant

As with most ground covers, Barren Strawberry is best planted in spring. This allows it to become established before it must face the rigors of winter. Barren Strawberries will grow in shade or full sun, and they tolerate most garden soils. Use them under trees, in front of shrub borders, as edging, or in beds to hide the ripening foliage of spring bulbs. Barren Strawberries are sold the same way as bedding plants, in flats or pots. Work the soil by tilling or cultivating, adding organic matter to hard, clay soils. Set the plants at the same depth they were grown in their containers, spacing them about a foot apart. If the plants in the containers were grown in a light artificial soil mix, shake as much of it off the roots as you can before planting. If it is left on the roots, the plant may be unable to grow out of the mix into the surrounding soil. Plants in such a condition will wilt easily, and they will never become established.

Growing Tips

Barren Strawberries benefit from watering in hot, dry weather. A balanced fertilizer in spring will help them recover from winter damage, as well as hasten filling-in before weeds can become problematic.

Care and Maintenance

These plants need very little attention. Weeds can start before Barren Strawberries become established. Clean-cultivate and apply a preemergent herbicide or a light mulch to prevent germination of weed seed.

Companion Planting and Design

This low-growing plant can be used as bedding, and as edging for the perennial garden or the shrub border. The glossy, bright green leaves are very similar to Strawberry leaves, and the flowers are bright yellow. Blue Squills or purple Grape Hyacinths flower at about the same time for pleasant color combination.

Did You Know

Barren Strawberries do produce fruit, but they are tiny, brown, and nutlike, similar to the seeds on the outsides of regular Strawberries.

Barren Strawberry looks just like Strawberry-producing plants. These evergreen plants have similar foliage in mats, but the flowers are yellow rather than white, and no fruits are produced. The leaves are glossy green, giving the plants a clean look, and flowers are produced in profusion. The plant spreads by short rhizomes, so it is not aggressive. It makes an excellent edging plant that stays where it belongs without much care. It is tolerant of a variety of soils as long as it doesn't stand in water. It does best in cooler parts of the state, as it stalls in hot, dry weather. A slightly larger species is W. fragarioides. W. ternata is more compact and better suited as a ground cover plant than W. fragarioides.

Bloom Period and Color
Late spring blooms in yellow.

Mature Height × Spread
4 to 6 inches × spreading

Common Periwinkle

Vinca minor

Common Periwinkle, or Vinca, is one of the most popular ground covers for planting in Illinois. It makes an attractive cover and blooms in the spring. Since it is slow to develop, weeds can become a problem before it is dense enough to keep them out. Weeds are less troublesome when Vinca is grown in the shade. Once established, Vinca will spread, its long shoots rooting where they touch the ground. There are many selections of Vinca available, some with blue, pink, or white flowers or variegated leaves. A garden center may carry a green with purple flowers, a variegated with white flowers, or another named cultivar. Most will do just fine. If you want a specific cultivar, you may be able to get it through a mail-order catalog.

Other Name
Vinca

Bloom Period and Color
Spring blooms in lavender, lilac, blue, burgundy, pink and white.

Mature Height × Spread
3 to 6 inches × creeping

When, Where, and How to Plant
Plant from containers in spring so the plants can become well established before they face the rigors of an Illinois winter. Well-drained but moist soil is important to avoid stem rot. Prepare the planting area by tilling or cultivating, incorporating organic matter if the soil is heavy. Consider raised beds or drain tiles if drainage is poor. Set plants at the same depth they grew in their containers. Space them 6 to 12 inches apart, depending upon how quickly you need cover. Plants on 12-inch centers will take two years to fill in. If the plants in the containers were grown in a light artificial soil mix, shake as much of it off the roots as you can before planting. If it is left on the roots, the plant may be unable to grow out of the mix into the surrounding soil. Plants in this condition will wilt easily, and they will never become established.

Growing Tips
During hot, dry weather, apply an inch of water early in the day, and don't water again until the soil is dry and plants begin to wilt.

Care and Maintenance
Inspect Vinca periodically for any weed invasion, and pull or hoe weeds immediately. Fusilade applied according to label directions will kill grasses without damage to the Vinca. Winter sun may damage exposed plants. Before the plants begin to grow in spring, mow the bed with the power mower set at 3 inches. Remove the clippings and new shoots will quickly fill in. Root and stem rot is Vinca's major problem. Cut out the diseased plants and drench with a copper fungicide such as Phyton 27 or Bordeaux mixture.

Companion Planting and Design
Plant under trees or in other shaded areas where turfgrasses won't grow. Interplant with Daffodils and spring bulbs. The Vinca will hide the ripening foliage.

Did You Know
Vinca comes from the Latin *vincio,* meaning to bind, referring to the plant's vining runners.

Common Wintercreeper

Euonymus fortunei cultivars

When, Where, and How to Plant

Wintercreeper is best transplanted in spring. This allows it to become established before contending with a tough Illinois winter. It isn't particular about soils as long as it doesn't stand in water. Euonymus plants are grown in quart-sized to 5-gallon-sized containers, and as balled-and-burlapped plants. The hole for planting should be no deeper than the depth of the ball of the plant, and at least twice as wide. Remove the plants from containers, and slice any circling roots. Set the plant in the planting hole and replace half the soil. Fill the hole with water. (Remove the burlap from a balled-and-burlapped plant and stuff it down in the hole.) Replace the remaining soil and fill the hole with water again. Make a saucer around the plant with any remaining soil. Space the plants at 1¹/₂ to 2 feet.

Growing Tips

To renew the planting, mow it in spring before the start of new growth with the lawn mower set at 3 to 6 inches. As the leaves begin to develop in spring, add a balanced fertilizer. To reduce foliar diseases, water early in the day so the foliage dries before nightfall.

Care and Maintenance

These plants are susceptible to several insects and diseases. Crown gall, which causes large growths on the stems and roots, can kill the plants. Mildew and anthracnose disfigure leaves. To reduce foliar diseases, water early in the day so the foliage dries before nightfall. Black vine weevils eat notches out of the margins of leaves and feed on the roots. Euonymus scale is the most damaging: spray with acephate about the time Catalpas are in bloom to control it. Repeat two or three times during the season.

Companion Planting and Design

The bright green cultivars contrast well with the dark greens of Taxus, and the purples of New Guinea Impatiens or Heliotrope. *E. coloratus* blends well with pink Impatiens or Petunias.

Did You Know

Euonymus is a large genus that includes trees, shrubs, and vines.

The Wintercreepers are semi-evergreen plants with varying habits from low and spreading to climbing vines. 'Coloratus' is one of the more commonly used ground cover plants in Illinois. It is low-growing and easy to keep under control. The color is deep green in summer; in fall it turns plum-colored for the winter. In spring, new growth develops a good green color, but quite often the overwintering foliage never turns green again; it is best removed. 'Vegetus' is larger and more aggressive. The color is medium green, and the leaves are larger. Unless there is sufficient room, this plant may be too much to handle. This species mutates continuously and easily. 'Coloratus' is probably the most reliably true to type. It is an attractive and serviceable ground cover.

Other Name

'Vegetus'

Bloom Period and Color

Semi-evergreen foliage in pale green, dark green with pale veins, variegated, or deep green turning purple.

Mature Height × Spread

6 to 12 inches × 3 feet or more

Creeping Cotoneaster
Cotoneaster adpressus

With glossy foliage and red fruits, Creeping Cotoneaster is one of the more attractive woody ground covers. Its branches, spreading herringbone-like, pile themselves on top of one another, creating a layered effect. Cotoneasters are large plants that need room. If planted too close together, they will require excessive pruning. With judicious pruning they can be kept in bounds and present a nice appearance. They are effective in rock gardens and cascading over walls. Two cultivars known as 'Tom Thumb', and 'Little Gem' are available in the nursery trade. They make dense mounds of shiny green foliage and bear no fruit. These plants achieve a height of about half a foot in ten years. Several other taller and shorter species and selections are listed in nursery catalogs.

Other Name
Cotoneaster

Bloom Period and Color
Spring blooms in pink.

Mature Height × Spread
18 inches × 4 to 6 feet

When, Where, and How to Plant

Plant Cotoneasters in either spring or fall. Though tolerant of some shade, these plants are at their best in full sun. They do well in almost any soil, but they don't like wet feet. Cotoneaster plants come in quart- to 5-gallon-sized containers, or balled and burlapped. The hole for planting should be no deeper than the depth of the ball of the plant, and at least twice as wide. Remove the plants from their containers, and slice any circling roots. Set the plant in the planting hole, and replace half the soil. Fill the hole with water. (Remove the burlap from a balled-and-burlapped plant and stuff it down in the hole.) Replace the remaining soil, and fill the hole with water again. Make a saucer around the plant with any remaining soil. Space the plants 2 to 3 feet apart.

Growing Tips

Cotoneasters do well in hot, dry situations as long as they are watered during extended dry periods.

Care and Maintenance

The shade produced by these somewhat open plants is not dense enough to keep out weeds. Pull or hoe the weeds; preemergent herbicides and grass preventers are also helpful. Cotoneaster plants only require a little pruning and watering. Don't shear them; head them back. Cut overly long branches to a side branch that is growing in the same direction, but shorter. Prune in spring before growth starts or as needed during the season. Cotoneasters are susceptible to leaf roller caterpillars, webworms, and mites, as well as fire blight disease. Control the caterpillars and webworms with *Bacillus thuringiensis*, the mites with insecticidal soap. Prune out fire blight-damaged stems.

Companion Planting and Design

Plant spring bulbs under the Cotoneasters. The bulbs will come up and flower before the Cotoneaster leafs out, but the ripening leaves will be hidden.

Did You Know

These plants will root anywhere a stem touches the ground. They eventually make a dense mat of stems, keeping out weeds.

English Ivy
Hedera helix

When, Where, and How to Plant
English Ivy is available from garden centers in pots. Plant in spring so the plants can become well established before they must stand the rigors of an Illinois winter. Growing best in shade, English Ivy especially needs protection from winter sun. It prefers a cool, rich, well-drained soil. It tolerates dry sites and slopes when well established. It tends to be shallowly rooted. Prepare the planting area by tilling or cultivating, incorporating organic matter if the soil is heavy. Set plants at the same depth they grew in their containers. Space them 12 inches or more apart, depending upon how quickly you need cover. Plants on 12-inch centers will take two years to fill in. If the plants were grown in a light artificial soil mix, shake as much of it as you can off the roots before planting. If it is left on the roots, the plant may be unable to grow out of the mix into the surrounding soil. Plants in this condition will wilt easily and never become established.

Growing Tips
Water thoroughly but infrequently. Plant losses can occur when Ivy plantings next to lawns are watered continuously.

Care and Maintenance
English Ivy needs annual pruning; heavily prune it in spring before growth begins. To keep the planting dense, mow every two years, using a rotary mower set as high as it will go. Rake out clippings. Tips can be cut back at any time during the season to keep the plant in bounds. Aphids and mites can be troublesome. Insecticidal soap will control both. Leaf spot diseases develop in wet seasons. Use Bordeaux mixture, triforine, or maneb fungicides where needed. Root rot will develop in wet sites. Provide adequate drainage.

Companion Planting and Design
English Ivy makes a wonderful carpet of green under shade trees and will climb the trunks if allowed to do so. Interplant with small spring bulbs and wild flowers such as Virginia Bluebells. The Ivy will hide the ripening leaves.

Did You Know
There are hundreds of varieties of English Ivy.

English Ivy is a beautiful plant with bright green leaves. It spreads easily as a ground cover, quickly providing cover. As it spreads, it roots at nodes, providing good stability to the soils. It does an excellent job of holding banks. Supported, this plant will climb as high as the support allows, reportedly 90 feet in some cases. English Ivy mutates freely. In Illinois, selections are made for both cold tolerance and summer heat tolerance. Many selections have been made for Illinois conditions. 'Bulgaria' was selected by the Missouri Botanical Garden for cold tolerance and for its ability to withstand drought. 'Thorndale' has larger leaves and will tolerate severe winters. Some small-leaved selections of English Ivy make excellent houseplants, pointing up the diversity of this species.

Bloom Period and Color
Evergreen foliage.

Mature Height × Spread
6 to 10 inches × trailing

European Ginger

Asarum europaeum

European Ginger is one of the most attractive ground covers. It is slow-growing, spreading by short rhizomes, and thus quite expensive. The glossy, kidney-shaped leaves are bright green and grow in neat mounds. This Ginger does best in shade, but will tolerate filtered light and even some direct sun for part of the day. The inconspicuous Ginger flowers are borne under the leaves. They produce lots of seeds which germinate in the planting, helping to fill in. The glossy leaves of this Ginger make it useful in shaded areas. There are other Gingers available as ground covers, but none is as refined as European Ginger. Canadian Wild Ginger, A. canadense, is coarser and taller. Its stems can be dried and used as a substitute for true Ginger.

Other Name
Shiny Ginger

Bloom Period and Color
Semi-evergreen foliage.

Mature Height × **Spread**
6- to 10-inch-tall clumps

When, Where, and How to Plant

Plant Ginger in spring in partial shade beneath overhanging trees or shrubs, or on the north side of a house. The soil must be moist and well supplied with organic matter. European Ginger is usually sold in 4-inch pots. Work the soil by tilling or cultivating. Set the plants only as deep as they grew in their containers, spacing them at 12 inches or closer. At 12 inches, they will take about two years to fill in. If the plants in the containers were grown in a light artificial soil mix, shake as much of it off the roots as you can before planting. If it is left on the roots, the plants will not grow out of the mix into the surrounding soil. Plants in such a condition wilt easily and will never become established.

Growing Tips

European Ginger needs a lot of water. It wilts readily when too dry, so do not let it dry out. Water early in the day to allow foliage to dry off before nightfall. If it seems impossible to keep the plants wet enough, check to make sure the soil mix is not interfering with the rooting of the plants.

Care and Maintenance

Little care is required once the plants have filled in. The cover is dense enough to keep weeds out. Pull or hoe weeds that start before the plants fill in. Protect the evergreen foliage with a 4-inch layer of straw applied in late November. Exposed leaves will dry up but the normal spring clean-up will remove them. Be careful to avoid damaging the shallow rhizomes. The plants quickly develop new, green leaves in spring.

Companion Planting and Design

Use as edging or beds in moist, shaded areas. European Ginger will not tolerate drought.

Did You Know

Ornamental Gingers got their names from the pungent odor of the leaves and stems. Canadian Wild Ginger can be ground as a substitute for true Ginger.

When, Where, and How to Plant

Plant Gro-Low Sumac any time from containers. Balled-and-burlapped plants are available in spring and fall. Use it as a ground cover on banks, terraces, and hills, and next to walks and drives where it will get salted. Use it in newly developed, compact soils where other plants have difficulty. Gro-Low Sumac plants are grown in 1- to 5-gallon containers, and as balled-and-burlapped plants. The hole for planting should be no deeper than the depth of the ball of the plant and at least twice as wide. Remove the plants from their containers and slice any circling roots. Set the plant in the planting hole, and replace half the soil. Fill the hole with water. (Remove the burlap from a balled-and-burlapped plant and stuff it down in the hole.) Replace the remaining soil, and fill the hole with water again. Make a saucer around the plant with any remaining soil. Space the plants 2 to 3 feet apart.

Growing Tips

Fall color is best on plants in full sun on dry sites. Withholding water late in the season may intensify the color.

Care and Maintenance

Gro-Low Sumac is relatively trouble-free. There are a few leaf spot diseases that will affect it, and occasionally insects may take up residence. None is worth treating. If it gets too tall, Gro-Low can be sheared to 6 inches in spring. It will take about two seasons to get back to full height. Cut out any dead branches that may have been broken by snow load. A twiggy plant, Gro-Low will accumulate tree leaves and trash over the winter. Rake them out, or have a landscape contractor vacuum them out in spring.

Companion Planting and Design

Annuals can be planted in front of Gro-Low Sumac. It is not so overpowering and blends well with Pansies in spring, and with Impatiens, Petunias, Marigolds, and Mums in fall.

Did You Know

Gro-Low is an Illinois nursery selection of Fragrant Sumac.

Gro-Low Sumac is a dwarf, suitable for ground cover plantings in tough places. It is salt tolerant and grows best in dry, poor soils. It is adapted to either full sun or shade. Gro-Low Sumac is well suited to urban plantings where it actually likes the conditions instead of simply tolerating them as do most other plants. The plant develops a low mass of tangled stems, rooting where they touch the ground. It is excellent for stabilizing soils. Gro-Low has glossy bluish green leaves. Bright, yellow flowers in April are followed by red, showy fruit in late summer. Fall color is a good orange-red. Leaves and stems of all the selections of fragrant Sumac are pungently aromatic when crushed. Gro-Low is the lowest-growing of the fragrant Sumac selections.

Bloom Period and Color
Spring blooms in yellow.

Mature Height × Spread
1 to 2 feet tall × 10 feet

Japanese Spurge
Pachysandra terminalis

When homeowners ask for an alternative to grass in a shaded garden, Japanese Spurge, or Pachysandra, is the one I recommend. Pachysandra will grow satisfactorily beneath trees and shrubs, but where it is exposed to too much sun or wind, it will develop a yellowish color. Under dense trees such as Norway Maples or Beech, these plants compete easily with the shallow tree roots, and they thrive in the cool darkness. White flowers appear in early spring just as new leaves begin. These flowers are otherwise not conspicuous, but because there is little else in bloom at the time, they are of interest. They are fragrant and seem to attract honeybees. 'Green Carpet' is more upright than the species and has foliage that is deeper green and waxy.

Other Name
Pachysandra

Bloom Period and Color
Spring blooms in yellow.

Mature Height × Spread
6 to 12 inches × 12 inches

When, Where, and How to Plant
Pachysandra is available in pots or flats at garden centers. It is probably best planted in spring. Dense to light shade is best. Soils should be well drained, but moist and cool. Prepare the planting area by tilling or cultivating. Be careful not to disturb roots if you are planting beneath shallow-rooted trees, and incorporate organic matter into the soil if it is heavy. Set plants at the same depth they grew in the containers. Space them 6 to 12 inches apart, depending on how quickly you need cover. Plants on 12-inch centers will take more than two years to fill in. If the plants were grown in a light artificial soil mix, shake as much of it as you can off the roots before planting. If it is left on the roots, the plant will not grow out of the mix into the surrounding soil. Plants in this condition wilt easily and will never become established.

Growing Tips
Water weekly during dry weather.

Care and Maintenance
Pachysandra will have to be mowed down each spring before new growth begins, using a rotary mower set as high as possible. Collect the clippings. During the season, the plants may be clipped back to keep them in bounds. Pachysandra is a rather tidy plant and requires little tending. Stem rot, a fungus disease caused by Volutella, can be serious. If the disease is brought into a planting, a fungicide drench will be necessary to rescue it. Mancozeb, Daconil 2787, or Zyban drenched into the soil every two weeks throughout the season, starting in spring, is effective. Be very selective about where you acquire plants for your garden.

Companion Planting and Design
Pachysandra contrasts well with the dark green of Yews or blue of Creeping Junipers. Interplant with masses of spring bulbs for early color.

Did You Know
Don't waste this plant in sunny spots; it doesn't like them.

Juniper

Juniperus sp.

When, Where, and How to Plant

Junipers can be planted anytime from containers. Balled-and-burlapped plants are available in spring and fall. Plant Junipers in full sun on a well-drained site. Junipers are grown in 1- to 5-gallon containers and as balled-and-burlapped plants. The hole for planting should be no deeper than the depth of the ball of the plant, and at least twice as wide. Remove the plant from its container and slice any circling roots. Set the plant in the planting hole and replace half the soil. Fill the hole with water. Be sure to remove the burlap from a balled-and-burlapped plant and stuff it down in the hole. Replace the remaining soil and fill the hole with water again. Make a saucer around the plant with any remaining soil. Space the plants at 2$^{1}/_{2}$ to 5 feet, depending on the cultivar.

Growing Tips

These plants tolerate drought. Soak thoroughly only during extended dry spells.

Care and Maintenance

Junipers require pruning. Winter-killed branches need to be cut out in spring, and overly long branches encroaching on walks or other plantings need to be headed back. Cut out entire branch to a vigorous side shoot growing in the same direction. Make the cut beneath an overhanging branch so it will not be exposed. Leave at least some green growth on the remaining branch or the plant will cease growing. Do not cut into the dead area in the center of the plant. Junipers are usually dense enough to keep weeds out. Hoe or pull weeds that do get started. Junipers are susceptible to mites, which can be controlled by insecticidal soap. Tip blight (Phomopsis) can be severe in wet weather; spray affected plants with benomyl or triforine according to label directions.

Companion Planting and Design

Use in front of larger shrubs for borders, massed in beds, creeping over walls or in rock gardens. Add annual Phlox for color.

Did You Know

It has been said: If you can't grow Junipers, don't bother growing anything at all.

Junipers are among the toughest of all evergreen plants. Juniper ground covers are especially tough, and there are several species and cultivars. They spread with long, horizontal stems that do not root where they touch the ground. Colors vary from bright green to blue. Junipers tolerate almost any well-drained soil. Some will grow in sand and endure droughty soils. They seem unaffected by soil pH. All Junipers prefer full sun. They grow in shade, but become sparse and leggy. Junipers have been overused in unsuitable situations and have received an undeserved bad reputation. When planted in the right conditions, they do very well. Dwarf Japanese Garden Juniper, J. procumbens 'Nana', is 1 foot tall and spreads 5 feet. Color is blue-green in summer, purplish in winter.

Bloom Period and Color
Evergreen foliage.

Mature Height × Spread
6 to 18 inches × 6 feet

Lily of the Valley
Convallaria majalis

The fragrance! The fragrance alone makes this different kind of flowering ground cover valuable. Just a few in a jelly glass on the kitchen table perfume the whole room. Lily of the Valley has attractive green foliage that comes up early. The flowers are tiny, bell-shaped, and borne between pairs of upright leaves along short stalks. They have been grown in greenhouses for centuries. These plants spread aggressively and will cover an area in a short time. Don't plant them where they can get away and invade the lawn or flower border. The berries are showy, but poisonous. Remove them! 'Flora Pleno' is a double with flowers larger than those of the species. 'Rosea' has blooms that are pale pink instead of the normal white.

Bloom Period and Color
Spring blooms in white, pink.

Mature Height × Spread
6 to 18 inches × 6 inches, but spreads by creeping

When, Where, and How to Plant
Starts of these plants are called "pips." These are short pieces of rhizome that have two or three buds. They are available from seed catalogs or at some garden centers. Occasionally a garden center will stock started pips in pots. Divisions may be made of existing plants. Plant in spring. Lily of the Valley is a shade plant; it is an excellent plant for a spot where nothing else will grow. It tolerates terrible soils and will grow in an alley if it has a chance. For best growth and flowering, however, a rich organic soil is preferred. Prepare the soil by tilling or cultivating. Plant single pips 3 to 4 inches apart, setting them so that the buds on the pips are just at the soil surface. Divisions can be spaced at 6 to 8 inches. Properly spaced and well fertilized, these plants will fill in the second year.

Growing Tips
If you are growing this plant for its flowers, apply fertilizer and organic mulch. While these plants will tolerate dry soils, they are best if they get an inch of water a week.

Care and Maintenance
Lily of the Valley dies down each fall, and the leaves should be raked out of the bed. In hot dry weather, plants may be damaged by spider mites. Insecticidal soap will help. In wet weather, slugs may be a problem. Baits are effective. When plants become crowded, lift them and select the plumpest pips for replanting.

Companion Planting and Design
Lily of the Valley is a tough plant and can become a weed if planted with less aggressive plants. The aggressive qualities are beneficial in tough spots where nothing else will grow. Small shaded areas between houses in the city, on dry slopes to prevent erosion, and beneath evergreen trees where it is too dark and the soil is too dry are places where this plant is at its best as a ground cover.

Did You Know
Lily of the Valley can be grown as a potted plant for indoor display.

When, Where, and How to Plant

Sweet Woodruff is best planted in spring so the plants can become well established before they must face the rigors of an Illinois winter. Plant in medium to deep shade. It grows best in a cool, moist, but well-drained soil. Sweet Woodruff plants are sold like bedding plants in flats or pots. Prepare the soil by spading or tilling. Set the plants at the depth they grew in the container and space them 6 to 12 inches apart, depending upon how quickly you need cover. If the plants in the containers were grown in a light artificial soil mix, shake as much of it as you can off the roots before planting. If it is left on the roots, the plant will not grow out of the mix into the surrounding soil. Plants in this condition wilt easily and may fail to become established. If conditions are good, the plants will fill in rapidly, and they may invade lawn or other border plantings.

Growing Tips

Fertilize lightly in spring for best flower production. Once established, Sweet Woodruff needs watering only in extended dry periods.

Care and Maintenance

Sweet Woodruff dies down to the ground in fall, later than Lily of the Valley. The dead tops should be raked out in fall or in spring. Shear during the season to keep in bounds. If the plants invade nearby plantings, hoe or pull them out. Sweet Woodruff is free of serious diseases and insect pests. If leaf spot becomes troublesome, treat with copper sulfate fungicide such as Bordeaux mixture.

Companion Planting and Design

The fragrance of these plants demands that they be planted where you will encounter them. Plant them next to the front door or around the patio where the fragrance can be enjoyed. Sweet Woodruff is excellent for edging if kept under control, or in a shady rock garden.

Did You Know

Sweet Woodruff is native to Europe and western Asia where it was used to curdle milk and for mattress stuffing.

This is an old-fashioned garden plant that has been used for ground covers, in naturalized areas, and in rock gardens for generations. Fragrant white flowers appear in late spring above whorls of six to eight leaves spaced along upright stems. The dried and crushed leaves are used for potpourris and have the fragrance of newly cut hay. As a ground cover, Sweet Woodruff is perfectly happy in the shade of overhanging trees. It tolerates the deep shade of Norway Maple and competes well with the tree's shallow roots. This is a plant that can be put in that spot under the Maple in the front yard where nothing else will grow. Sweet Woodruff combines well in less demanding situations with spring-flowering bulbs or with English Ivy.

Other Name
Bedstraw

Bloom Period and Color
May or June blooms in white.

Mature Height × Spread
6 to 18 inches × 6 to 18 inches

Ornamental Grasses *for Illinois*

Illinois is the Prairie State—the prairies that now produce corn were once covered by tall grasses. The most important tall grass was Big Bluestem, reaching ten feet high and extending as far as the horizon. There isn't much native tall prairie grass left, but interest in these plants has increased, and more and more people are planting prairies. The Illinois Department of Conservation has restored prairies in various places throughout the state, and some conservation districts are doing the same thing. The plantings include the Bluestems and other native grasses.

Using Ornamental Grasses in the Garden

Big Bluestem is only one of many ornamental and native grasses—in fact, there are hundreds. They have been gracing the natural landscapes throughout history, and now they are being planted to bring color and movement into the garden. They also bring sound and mass. The volume of grasses is one of their more interesting features. The plants grow from nothing in the spring to large masses of foliage and blooms by summer's end. Many stay through the winter, providing something to look at that is more interesting than snow-covered bare ground.

Ornamental grasses vary in height from a few inches to more than 10 feet tall. They can be used as edging, as border plants, in the perennial garden, for hedges, and for screens. They can be planted in containers, next to water features, or as specimens. Many are excellent for cutting and for dried flower arrangements. These grasses require so little care that they can be planted and forgotten until they enliven the landscape with their presence. They require no staking, pruning, or pest control. The native kinds will stand any weather that Illinois has to offer; they evolved with it.

Unheard of a decade ago, there are grass gardens being planted in which form, size, color, and texture create the interest. The grasses mix well with other flowers, too. The prairie was more than grass: Sunflowers, Joe-Pye Weed, Rattlesnake Master, and other taller kinds of plants shared the land with grasses. Today they fit together well in the garden.

Growing Ornamental Grasses

Ornamental grasses vary in hardiness. Those native to Illinois are hardy, most of them in all parts of the state. Exotic grasses may be partially hardy, or they may need to be handled like annuals and replanted each year. Some are worth trying even though they may be lost every few years. Some gardeners go to extremes to grow varieties that aren't recommended for Illinois—and make liars of us who say it can't be done! Tall Pampas Grass is not hardy in northern Illinois, but there are people who protect it and get it through winter so that it will later grace their gardens with magic plumes on 15-foot stems.

If you have never grown ornamental grasses in your garden, try one or two. Some of the smaller ones will fit in any garden. Some of these are described in the following pages. Most will grow in any good garden soil. If you are starting an ornamental grass garden, plant several of the kinds that interest you in a trial garden. Make note of the dates they begin to grow in spring, how tall the leaves become, and their color. Indicate when the flower arises, how tall it grows, and what color it is. Record how much the plant spreads and whether it stays presentable in winter or whether leaves and stalks need to be removed in fall.

Once you have the profile for each grass, seeing where it fits in the garden plan is easy. Be sure to draw your plan, to scale if possible, and try to follow it as best as you can. Even after you have the garden planted, you will find yourself looking at other kinds of grasses that show up in neighbors' gardens, at the conservatory, and in demonstration plantings at garden centers. Take a few home and try them. If they fit, buy more.

There is still a lot to be learned about ornamental grasses, especially grass gardens. If you begin to grow them, your garden will be different from anyone else's. No matter what anyone says, unless you try a grass in your garden, you won't know how it will grow there. That is part of the fun of gardening; every garden is different.

Here are some ornamental grasses worth trying in your garden. Plant some and enjoy them.

Blue Fescue

Festuca ovina var. glauca, Festuca glauca

Blue Fescue is a common inhabitant of perennial gardens, rock gardens, and borders. It forms a mound of thin, blue-green leaves. Flowers are produced well above the leaves on 2-foot high stems. The flower stalks are not very ornamental, and most gardeners remove them as they develop. The dense mounds of this plant do not spread well, so it is best used as an accent plant. For ground cover uses where complete cover is needed to keep out weeds, set individual plants very close together. In the border, use mulch between the plants to keep weeds under control. It has the appearance of a seashore plant, and is particularly attractive when used with rock mulches.

Other Name
Gray Fescue

Bloom Period and Color
Buff-colored spikes, early June to early July.

Mature Height × Spread
6 to 19 inches × 6 to 19 inches

When, Where, and How to Plant

Set out started plants or divisions in spring to allow time for the plants to become well established by winter. Full sun and good drainage are essential for the most intense blue color to develop. Wet soils result in clumps with dead centers. Plants are available in pots from nurseries and garden centers in spring. Set the plants in well-prepared soil at the same depth they grew in the pots. For specimen plants, space about a foot apart. For ground cover plantings, set the plants about 8 inches apart so they fill in.

Growing Tips

Blue Fescue is a low-maintenance plant. Do not over-water or over-fertilize.

Care and Maintenance

Try to keep these plants hardened off and growing slowly. Slow growing plants have much better color. If too vigorous, clumps will soon develop open centers and will need transplanting. Wet soils result in root rot. These plants are evergreen, but if exposed to sun and wind all winter, the leaves will burn. Trim the old leaves back in spring before new growth begins. Every three or four years, when the clumps become too crowded or the centers begin to open up, divide them and start the planting over. The best time to divide them is in early spring before new growth begins. Lift the clump and cut away the open, dead center. Divide the remaining part into four or five sections and replant. No diseases or insect pests seem to affect these plants.

Companion Planting and Design

Use Blue Fescues as border, edging or specimen plantings. They are so unique it is difficult to get them to blend with other plants. In the rock garden, they can be used as individuals for their unusual color and tidy form.

Did You Know

Blue Fescue is quite tolerant of salinity and can be used next to walks and drives where salt is spread for winter snow removal.

Dwarf Pampas Grass
Cortaderia selloana 'Pumila'

When, Where, and How to Plant
Set the started plants in the garden in mid-May in the southern part of the state, about Memorial Day in northern Illinois. Plant Dwarf Pampas Grass in a moist, well-prepared garden soil. Drainage must be good and fertility high. These plants will have to do a lot of growing in a short time. Prepare the soil as you would for a perennial garden. Turn the soil at least two spades deep, adding organic matter to each layer. If drainage is poor, consider forming raised beds. Dig the planting holes the same depth and twice as wide as the rootballs on the plants. Set started plants at the same depth they were growing in their containers. If the soil in the container is an artificial mix or much different from that in your garden, shake some of it off the roots and mix it with the soil that will go back in the planting holes. Water the plants thoroughly to settle the soil around the roots.

Growing Tips
Dwarf Pampas Grass will need watering if the weather is dry. Fertilize monthly with a balanced soluble fertilizer such as 20-20-20 (Peters, Miracle-Gro, etc.).

Care and Maintenance
In the southern part of the state, there is a good chance that the plants will overwinter. In the North, heavy snow cover or a mild winter may help the plants survive. Heavily mulching the crowns to prevent extreme temperature changes and heaving may provide enough protection to save them, but don't count on it.

Companion Planting and Design
Use this magnificent grass as an accent plant or at the back of the garden where it won't hide other plants. Marginally hardy, it is well suited for containers which could be moved into a protected place for the winter.

Did You Know
Dwarf Pampas Grass is a cultivar of the tall species that comes from the Pampas of Argentina which is grown commercially in California for the plumes.

The Tall Pampas Grass reaches up to 12 feet with swaying, puffy white plumes. It is not hardy in Illinois, although some gardeners try to winter it over by digging it up, putting it in a bushel basket, and bringing it indoors where it won't freeze. An alternative is to grow it in a tub that can be moved into a cold but frost-free place. Dwarf Pampas Grass is so vigorous that started plants can be set out after all danger of a freeze has passed, and they will flower before frost. The plants are not overly expensive, so it is a practical means of growing them. The leaves are attractive, gray-green, and about 3 feet tall. The plumes are carried well above the foliage.

Bloom Period and Color
Late summer blooms in ivory cream.

Mature Height × Spread
3 to 6 feet × 6 feet

Feather Reed Grass
Calamagrostis acutiflora

Feather Reed Grass is one of the best of the medium-height ornamental grasses. It grows easily in full sun or light shade, in any good garden soil. It is not particular about alkalinity and will grow in any soil as long as the drainage is adequate. Feather Reed Grass is an upright plant, forming tight orderly clumps. The stems are stiffly vertical, and foliage, flowers, and seedheads stand upright, with flowers and seedheads held well above the foliage. Leaves are about 3 feet long with pointed tips, dull green, and rough. Feather Reed Grass is a cool-season grass, but will tolerate the hottest summer days without looking tired. It stays attractive well into winter. It is one of the first grasses to begin growing in spring. C. acutiflora 'Karl Foerster' was The Perennial Plant Association 2001 Plant of The Year.

Bloom Period and Color
Midsummer into fall blooms in cream tinged with pink.

Mature Height × Spread
4 to 5 feet × 2 feet

When, Where, and How to Plant
Divide plants in spring before or as growth begins. Potted plants are available during the season from ornamental grass specialists. Plant in full sun. Although Feather Reed Grass will grow in light shade, it tends to become weak and may not stand upright. Use Feather Reed Grass as a specimen planting, as an accent at the end or back of the perennial border, around water features, by streams, or in masses. Soil should be moist but well drained. Plants are available in containers or they may be planted as divisions. Dig the planting holes as deep and twice as wide as the plant balls and set the plants in at the same depth they were growing in the nursery. Water them thoroughly to make sure the soil is settled around the roots. Space the plants about 2 feet apart; larger clumps may be planted slightly farther apart. These plants do not spread aggressively. They grow mostly within the clump.

Growing Tips
These plants will need watering in dry weather. Soak the clumps thoroughly and allow them to dry before watering again. If winter is dry, the plants risk desiccation, which will kill them. Make sure they go into winter well watered.

Care and Maintenance
As is true of most ornamental grasses, Feather Reed Grass requires little maintenance. Remove the old leaves and stems in spring.

Companion Planting and Design
Feather Reed Grass is strongly upright and is excellent as an accent in the center of a flower bed. Surround it with Russian Sage and Black-Eyed Susans. Since it is so narrowly upright and tolerates salt, it lends itself to planting in those narrow strips of ground next to the sidewalk where nothing else seems to do well.

Did You Know
Feather Reed Grass is excellent for cutting. It can be cut as the flower heads develop and when it turns richly straw colored. Use the flowers fresh, or cut them a little later and dry them for use either with fresh flowers or in dry arrangements.

Fountain Grass

Pennisetum alopecuroides

When, Where, and How to Plant

Divide plants in spring. Seed may be sown in spring or fall. Fountain Grass should be grown in a sunny, well-drained place. It will deteriorate in dry soils unless watered as needed; in shade, it will flower poorly or not at all. Fountain Grass is one of the best all-around grasses for the small home garden. Use it in the border, as an accent in the perennial garden, along walks, or next to water features. It tolerates moist soil and can be used near streams or ponds. Sow seed in a small nursery bed. Set the seedlings in the garden when large enough to handle. Dig planting holes for plants and divisions the same depth and twice as wide as the plant ball. Set container-grown plants and divisions at the same depth they were growing at the nursery. Each clump should have several old stems and some well-developed roots. Set individual plants at least 3 to 4 feet apart; they will spread. For masses, set the plants at $2^{1}/_{2}$ to 3 feet apart; the plants will grow into a meadow-like carpet.

Growing Tips

Water the plants in dry weather; these are plants of wet areas, and they will suffer in dry soils.

Care and Maintenance

Fountain Grass requires no special care. These ornamental grasses are usually free of insect and disease pests. In spring before growth begins, remove the overwintering foliage. Fountain Grass is a warm-weather species. It will begin growth in May, later than the cool-weather kinds. If you are growing a cultivar, remove all seedlings that develop—sometimes they do not come true from seed.

Companion Planting and Design

Fountain Grass blends well with 'Autumn Joy' Sedum, Russian Sage, and Coneflowers. The leaves turn to a warm gold before they turn almond for the winter. The loose fountain shape of the plant lends itself well to use around ponds. Caution: Cut the flowers before the seed ripens and falls into the pond.

Did You Know

Use fresh Fountain Grass flowers in summer flower arrangements.

Slow-growing Fountain Grass grows into a fountain-shaped plant about 2 feet high. Its soft arching stems bear bottlebrush-like clusters of flowers at the ends. Use its fresh flowers in floral arrangements. The flowers eventually shatter outdoors, with seeds dropping into the clump. The foliage form persists all winter, offering something of interest in the garden. As the foliage ripens in fall, it turns briefly to shades of rose and gold before turning its winter almond-tan. There are several species of Fountain Grass. Black-Seeded Fountain Grass is shorter with black flower heads and dark-green leaves. It is hardy to Zone 7, and it may winterkill north of that. Red Fountain Grass, P. setaceum 'Rubrum' ('Atro-sanguineum'), is an annual grass. It is spectacular, with dark-red leaves and flowers.

Bloom Period and Color
Midsummer blooms in green.

Mature Height × Spread
1 to 2 feet × 1 to 2 feet

Hakonechloa

Hakonechloa macra 'Aureola'

Many gardeners consider this the most beautiful of the ornamental grasses. That may be stretching things a bit. However, this interesting grass is one that tolerates shade and a moist soil, and is a bright addition to shaded gardens. The leaves are yellow with thin, green, longitudinal lines creating mounded clumps. Variegated Hakonechloa is a cultivar of Hakone Grass, a perennial Japanese forest grass. The species, Hakone Grass, has bright green foliage and is tougher and hardier than the variegated form. As forest grasses, these plants do stand the shade and blend well with other shade plants. Hakonechloa is slow-growing and is not invasive. It takes some time for it to become established. In the meantime, it needs extra care, watering in dry periods and protection for the winter.

Other Name
Golden Variegated Hakonechloa

Bloom Period and Color
Late Summer. Yellowish green, not showy.

Mature Height × Spread
A mound 12 to 18 inches tall and 2 feet wide, eventually developing into cascades of mounds as the plant spreads.

When, Where, and How to Plant

Hakonechloa plants in containers are available in spring from garden centers. Plant Hakonechloa in early spring so they have time to become well established before winter. Preferred is a shady spot with moist, but well-drained soil. Prepare the soil by spading it over and incorporating ample organic matter. Set the plants at the same depth they were growing in the containers. Space the plants 18 to 24 inches apart. These plants can be grown in containers as well. Plant using a potting mix or artificial soil mix. Water as needed to keep the plants from wilting. Add liquid fertilizer once a month. The plants will need to be removed from the containers, or the containers moved for the winter to a place where roots can be protected from severe cold. Sometimes setting the containers tightly against each other and mulching them in is sufficient. Or, bury the pots, and mulch. The alternative is to treat the plants as annuals, disposing of them each year and starting over the next.

Growing Tips

These are moderate maintenance plants. During the season, fertilize regularly with diluted liquid fertilizer. Follow directions on the package. Water as needed to keep the plants from wilting. Poor drainage and freezing and thawing during the winter will kill these plants. Covering them after they are frozen late in the fall will help.

Care and Maintenance

Cut back winter-damaged foliage in spring before new growth begins. Divide when plants become crowded or outgrow their location. Spring is best.

Companion Planting and Design

The bright colors blend well with the greens of Hostas and Ferns, and with summer annuals such as Impatiens. Cascading plantings of Hakonechloa down a shady slope among rocks beneath evergreen trees, for instance, makes an unforgettable picture.

Did You Know

These plants are natives of Japan. They turn a warm pink in fall, adding to their value in the garden.

Moor Grass
Molinia caerulea ssp. *arundinacea*

When, Where, and How to Plant
Divisions are best planted in early spring. Container-grown plants may be planted any time during the season. Moor Grasses may be planted as accents in the perennial border, though they are better as specimen plants or in beds or masses by themselves. These plants are too striking to be hidden among other plants. Moor Grasses do best in fertile, moist soils that have good drainage. They prefer full sun. In partial shade, their color is not as good, the plants may not be as strong, and the flower stalks tend to fall over. The soil must be moist and well drained. The soil should ideally be acidic, but the plants will grow in more alkaline soils too. High-pH soils are decidedly detrimental. If the soil is too alkaline, acidify it or import a more acidic soil. Acid peat will be helpful if there is good drainage. Aluminum sulfate or sulfur can be added to the soil to lower the pH. The pH should be at neutral or lower. Dig planting holes the same depth and twice as wide as the plant balls. Set divisions or containerized plants at the same depth they were growing in the nursery.

Growing Tips
In dry weather, provide an inch of water per week. Fertiliize lightly in spring as growth begins. Apply $1/2$ pound of 10-10-10 or the equivalent per 100 square feet of bed.

Care and Maintenance
Moor Grasses are warm-season grasses that grow and develop slowly. No insects or diseases affect Moor Grasses. In fall the flower stalks and leaves break off just above the crowns of the plants. These must be removed, or they will blow around. This is one of just a few grasses that develop abscission layers and lose their leaves in fall.

Companion Planting and Design
Plant Moor Grass against a dark background where the flower clusters can be seen as they sway in the breeze.

Did You Know
Moor Grass seedheads make excellent cut flowers.

Moor Grasses are interesting specimens in the garden. Each one seems to have a special feature that makes it fun, even exciting. Moor Grasses are warm-season plants that are slow to start in the spring. They have erect, arching leaves to about 2 feet tall. The delicate flower clusters appear above the foliage in early to mid summer. Cultivars of Purple Moor Grass, M. caerulea, may be short, as are 'Dauerstrahl' and 'Heather Bride' ('Heidebraut'). They have compact foliage and 2- to 3-foot flower stems. Tall Moor Grass is a small, 3-foot tall plant, but it sends up a 6-foot-tall flower stem. The stems are slender and the flower heads airy. The slightest breeze sets them swaying, giving rise to a common name, "Dancing Moor Grass."

Bloom Period and Color
Summer blooms in green.

Mature Height × Spread
4 to 7 feet × 2 feet

Northern Sea Oats
Chasmanthium latifolium

Northern Sea Oats are naturalized in some parts of Illinois. You might find them classified as Uniola latifolia. Northern Sea Oats are warm-season clump Grasses that grow very slowly from rhizomes and are not aggressive. With their stiff stems and horizontal leaves, they resemble small Bamboos. The flowers and seedheads are similar to those of Eastern Sea Oats or to Agronomic Oats. They are borne on slender stems (culms), which droop under the weight of the flowers. Northern Sea Oats are excellent for cutting and for use in dry arrangements. The flowers do not shatter even if picked when the seeds are mature; they will last all winter in the garden. The dried flower heads are collected and sold at wholesale florist outlets and craft shops.

Other Name
Spike Grass

Bloom Period and Color
Summer blooms in pale green.

Mature Height × Spread
2 to 3 feet × 1 1/2 to 2 feet

When, Where, and How to Plant

Northern Sea Oats are planted in spring. Seed may be sown in late fall or in spring. These plants are natives of flood plains and they do best in a deep, fertile, moist soil. They are suited for use in shade gardens, borders, in sunny naturalized areas, and around water features. They make good transition plants from the wooded areas to the lawn areas of a garden. They are interesting specimen plants which will be taller and may be weaker when growing in shaded locations. When planted densely, Northern Sea Oats make tall but satisfactory ground covers. Dig planting holes for divisions or container-grown plants the same depth and twice the width of the rootballs. Set the plants at the same depth they were growing at the nursery, spacing them 1 to 2 feet apart. The seeds may be sown in a small nursery bed. Set the seedlings in the garden when large enough to handle, or seed may be sown in naturalized plantings. Prepare the soil by tilling or disking. Broadcast the seed and drag to cover it lightly, or sow the seed with a conservation drill. Northern Sea Oats will reseed itself within the planting. Seed may be collected for seeding elsewhere, but germination percentages may be low because many of the flowers are sterile. These warm-season plants may be late to start if spring is cool.

Growing Tips

Water Northern Sea Oats during dry weather the first season after planting.

Care and Maintenance

This grass requires little care once it is established. Remove the old leaves and stems in spring before growth begins. There are no diseases or insect pests that affect these grasses.

Companion Planting and Design

Plant Northern Sea Oats in masses where the seedheads can be enjoyed waving in the breeze. Tolerant of shade and moist soils, they do well around ponds too.

Did You Know

The Sea Oats used to stabilize seashores in the southern U.S. is a related grass, *Uniola paniculata*.

Tufted Hair Grass

Deschampsia caespitosa

When, Where, and How to Plant

These cool-season plants may be divided in spring or fall. Container-grown plants may be set out anytime during the season. Plant these interesting Grasses in full sun or shade in a moist, humusy, well-drained soil. Hair Grasses should be used in the border, in naturalized areas, in shade gardens, as accents, or around water features. Plants are available in containers, sometimes in bloom. Divisions may be purchased, or they may be acquired from other gardeners when they divide their plants. Prepare the soil by digging or tilling, adding organic matter. The soil should drain well; if it does not, consider raising the planting areas. Dig planting holes the same depth and twice as wide as the rootball on the plants. Set the plants at the same depth they were growing at the nursery. Water after planting to settle the soil around the roots. Space the plants about 3 feet apart, or plug individual plants into nooks and crannies in the garden. These plants will grow in soil-filled pockets or cracks in a rock garden. Tufted Hair Grasses can be started from seeds. Sow them in a nursery bed in fall, and move the seedlings when they are large enough to handle.

Growing Tips

The plants must have water; soak them well in dry weather.

Care and Maintenance

No insect or disease problems affect Tufted Hair Grasses. Divide the plants if they become crowded.

Companion Planting and Design

Tufted Hair Grasses are cool-season evergreen plants. They provide early-season color as bulbs are coming up, and later hide the ripening foliage. The flowers are delicate, so mass them for best effect with Witchhazel, Purple Smoke Tree, Cornelian Cherry, or other shrubs. Set them against a darker background where the delicate flowers will show up. Excellent at the borders of woodlands.

Did You Know

Tufted Hair Grass is used in golf course roughs for color and interest.

Tufted Hair Grass is a cool-season grass that will stay green most winters. It does well in moist places and partial shade, and prefers places where water seeps into the ground, keeping it soft. It will grow in shaded locations, so it is well suited to gardens beneath deciduous trees where most ornamental grasses find conditions too dark. Since the shaded soil can be kept moist, the Hair Grasses will grow well and will even self-seed. These plants are grown mostly for the flower effects. The bloom period lasts all summer, and the flowers are borne in large dainty inflorescences. The clump of foliage is a mound, not much over a foot tall, but the flower stalk grows 2 feet or more above the leaves.

Bloom Period and Color
Summer blooms in light green.

Mature Height × Spread
1 to 4 feet × 4 feet

Perennials *for Illinois*

Growing perennials is a challenge to any gardener's skill and ingenuity. After several years of planting annuals and replanting them each year, many beginning gardeners decide that they will spend some money on perennials and save themselves a lot of work. The idea is that you simply plant the perennials, and every year they come up and burst into bloom.

Then reality sets in. After asking a few questions, the gardener will learn that perennial gardening is a whole new world, requiring special soil preparation and sometimes elaborate planning. But after the initial surprise, those who are serious will discover that this new world can provide a lifetime of pleasure, opening a door to a fascinating new group of plants with specific needs and challenges. The payoff is being able to grow a tremendous variety of plants with delightful flowers and surprising habits. There will be continuous change in the garden, day after day. Perennial flower growers can't wait to get out early in the morning to see what's new in the garden!

Using Perennials in the Garden

Getting started with perennials takes some thought and experimentation. The plant descriptions in this chapter will help you determine the perennials you would like to grow.

Because each garden is different, you will need to learn how your selections will grow in your garden. Soil, light, temperatures, water, and your attention will all affect how the plants behave. Plants that grow well in my garden (10 miles from Lake Michigan in a soil that has been tilled for a quarter of a century) may be utter failures in yours . . . and vice versa. The only way to find out is to plant some selections and see how they do. Start by setting out a dozen or so plants in a row. Label them so you can learn them by sight. Keep a record book, making observations such as where the plants were bought and when, planting date, flowering date, size, and any other information you think will be helpful. Some such as Peonies that don't like to be moved will have to planted in their permanent spots, so take these qualities into consideration when you do your planning.

Preparing the Soil

Because perennials stay put for several years, soil preparation is especially important. The soil will need to be turned, and organic matter should be incorporated into it. When preparing a perennial bed, the rototiller just won't do. Annuals have shallow root systems, and tilling their soil 3 or 4 inches deep is enough to get them through the season, but preparing a perennial garden requires a lot more. We usually recommend that the garden be double-dug. That means to dig to at least two spade depths: 12 to 15 inches. This is not as daunting a task as it sounds, because you don't need to do it all at once. Dig a little now and more next week, and eventually the job will be done. Begin collecting organic matter: leaves, grass clippings, plant tops, kitchen scraps-whatever you can get. Compost the material on the garden or in a compost pile, or just dig it directly into the garden.

Planning the Garden

The third step is planning your garden. Study the descriptions of the perennials that interest you. Note size, color, when the plants flower, and whether there is a dead time when the plants will disappear from the garden. Draw the garden to scale on graph paper and mark the plants in areas on the plan. Changing them on a paper plan is easier than digging them up and starting over in your real garden.

After these preliminaries are completed, it is time to start planting. It is not necessary to plant perennials everywhere in the garden all at once. Where there are voids, fill in with annuals. A perennial garden is a dynamic thing and will change from day to day. Some plants you thought you wanted will not work out. Some plants you are thinking about discarding will later become interesting to you. When growing perennials, you will never stop learning new things. Visit the gardens in your area. Take notes. Talk to other gardeners. You will find we are all on a journey. Some have been on it longer, but all will happily share their experiences. Plant people are some of the greatest people in the world, and we're glad you are part of the family.

Aster
Aster sp.

Asters are reliable flowers for late summer and fall gardens. They bloom in profusion at a time when there are few perennial flowers left in the garden. Wild Asters are in bloom at that time, but the hybrids have a wider range of colors, and larger and more prolific blooms. New England (Aster novae-angliae) and New York (Aster novi-belgii) Asters are most often grown in Illinois gardens. Many are tall, about 4 feet, and they should be relegated to the back of the garden where they will have room to spread. Dwarf cultivars are suitable for the border and edging. 'Alma Potschke', 36 inches tall, is bright pink. 'Harrington's Pink' is 4 feet tall and light pink. New York Aster 'Marie Ballard' is powder blue and 3 feet tall.

Bloom Period and Color
August to October blooms in purple, pink, white, blue.

Mature Height × Spread
1 to 4 feet × nearly as wide

When, Where, and How to Plant
Asters are planted in spring from started plants available from garden centers or mail-order houses. Some larger discount houses with garden departments are beginning to stock perennials. Plant Asters in the sun or partial shade. Often these adaptable plants can be found growing naturalized along the edges of woodlands or old pastures. They will grow in any soil as long as it has sufficient drainage. Plant in the border, cutting garden, or naturalized areas; dwarf kinds may also be planted in rock gardens. Work the soil by spading or tilling to a depth of 12 inches. Set the plants at the same depth they grew in their containers; space larger types 2 to 3 feet apart, smaller ones at 12 inches.

Growing Tips
These native prairie plants will be tall and floppy if they receive too much care. The plants should be fertilized in spring and watered to keep them from wilting. Taller kinds will need staking anyway.

Care and Maintenance
Asters require very little care, though you will probably have to stake the tall kinds. Pinching in July will reduce their height somewhat and increase the number of flowers. Clumps should be divided every two to three years in early spring. Few insects or diseases affect these plants.

Companion Planting and Design
These plants are suited for borders and for the back of the perennial garden. They need room, as much as 4 feet square for larger plants. They are fall-blooming and fill a spot in the bloom cycle where there are not too many other plants in bloom. Plant them behind Purple Coneflowers, Daylilies, and other perennials that bloom earlier in the season.

Did You Know
Asters are native North American plants, but they were not popular until they were taken to Europe where they quickly caught on. Then they returned home as welcome additions to the perennial garden. Aster is now the flower of the month of September.

Astilbe

Astilbe × arendsii

When, Where, and How to Plant

Astilbe can be planted in spring or fall. These are shade plants. Put them in filtered light beneath somewhat open trees. They can stand full sun in the morning before temperatures rise; most important is a moist, well-drained soil. Plants are available as divisions or potted seedlings from garden centers, nurseries, or wherever plants are sold. Mail-order catalogs list many cultivars. Prepare the soil by spading or tilling to at least a foot deep. These plants will stay put for several years, so good preparation is needed. Incorporate organic matter for improved structure and moisture retention. Set the plants at the depth they were growing in their containers. Water in thoroughly and mulch if the weather is hot.

Growing Tips

Once established, Astilbes require little care, though watering in hot, dry weather is essential. If allowed to dry out, they will quickly deteriorate and will be finished for the year. Fertilizer will often stimulate soft, floppy growth and fewer flowers. Eventually, dividing will be necessary; postpone it as long as you can.

Care and Maintenance

Divide when plants become crowded. Lift entire clumps in early spring, cut into smaller clumps, and replant. Keep track of the cultivar or at least the color when dividing the plants. Labels placed in fall are helpful. On darker-colored cultivars, the foliage is tinted red. It will stay attractive all season in protected, cooler sites. If growing in a hot location, it may deteriorate and need to be kept hidden behind other plants. Some cultivars make excellent long-lasting cut flowers. Slugs may be troublesome, as they are abundant in most damp locations. Baits are effective controls. These plants are affected by few other pests or diseases.

Companion Planting and Design

Use Astilbes in the shade garden in combination with Hostas and in front of large Ferns.

Did You Know

Astilbes bloom as Bleeding Hearts finish. Perennial gardens provide a succession of blooms through the season.

There is no shade garden that should be without at least a few Astilbes. Both the flowers and the foliage of these plants are delicate and feathery. Astilbes resent dry, hot weather. They can stand the heat, but they must have moist soil. The number of blooms and clumps will increase each year. Try 'Amethyst', with brilliant violet spikes that grow to 3 feet; or 'Deutschland', which is white, and 'Fanal', red (both are about 18 inches tall). A. chinensis 'Pumila' has mauve blooms in August and September, grows less than a foot tall, will stand dry spots, and may spread. The 4-foot 'Professor van der Wielen', white with arching plumes, and the coral-pink 'Ostrich Plume' are distinctive enough to be classified as specimen plants.

Bloom Period and Color

June, July blooms in pink, red, magenta, cream, white.

Mature Height × Spread

1 to 4 feet x 2 feet

Bearded Iris
Iris hybrids

Bearded Irises are the most popular of the large class of perennial flowers known as Iris. Some Irises grow from bulbs, but most, including the Bearded Iris, grow from rhizome systems. Bearded Irises are categorized according to height, as dwarf (under 15 inches), intermediate (15 to 28 inches), or tall (over 28 inches). Irises are simple to grow. Few flowers reward you so well for so little work. Drainage is important so the fleshy roots and rhizomes don't rot. There are literally hundreds of Iris cultivars, and there are many other Iris species. Japanese Iris, I. ensata, has gorgeous big flowers and is a plant of wet places, well adapted to pondside plantings. Blue Flag, I. virginica, is a native wildflower found throughout the tallgrass prairie.

Bloom Period and Color
Late spring to early summer blooms in blue, violet, purple, pink, yellow, white, red.

Mature Height × Spread
13 inches to 4 feet × 12 to 24 inches

When, Where, and How to Plant
Plant Irises in August after the blooms have died down. Plants in containers may be planted anytime during the season. They are sold in 1-, 2-, and 6-gallon cans, or as divisions. Plant Irises in a good, well-drained garden soil. Prepare the soil by tilling to a 6-inch depth, adding organic matter to improve the condition and drainage. Holes will have to be dug for container-grown plants, as deep and twice as wide as the plant ball. Set the plants at the same depth they were growing in the nursery, with the rhizomes at the soil surface. Space dwarfs 12 to 18 inches apart. Tall Irises can be set 2 to 3 feet apart. Soak the plants thoroughly following planting to settle the soil around the roots.

Growing Tips
Provide an inch of water per week; fertilize in early spring.

Care and Maintenance
Irises are relatively trouble-free. They have one pest that will destroy them if not controlled: iris borer, the larva of a night-flying moth. The borers tunnel through the edges of the leaves to the rhizomes, where they proceed to chew them to bits. A bacterial rot grows in the mess. Control the borers by spraying the plants in spring when leaves are 5 to 6 inches tall, using Cygon or Orthene. These systemic insecticides are absorbed by the leaves. Follow directions on the container very carefully. Tall Irises may tend to fall over, especially if growing in semi-shaded or windy areas. Stake the flower stalks, being careful not to injure the roots or rhizomes. Divide Irises when they become crowded. Lift the clumps in midsummer and cut away any damaged parts. Separate into segments, each with a fan of leaves, a piece of rhizome, and several feeder roots.

Companion Planting and Design
Irises bloom in early spring. Interplant with perennials blooming later such as Coneflowers, Coreopsis, or Daylilies. The foliage blends well with ornamental grasses.

Did You Know
There are literally hundreds of Irises, many native to the U.S.

Beebalm
Monarda didyma

When, Where, and How to Plant

Monarda can be planted in fall or early spring. Potted plants can be planted anytime during the season. Divisions or plants are available at garden centers in spring. Plant it where you can control it. The center of the clump tends to die out after a few years, but the plants around the edge will continue to grow. This makes it unwieldy, and it takes up a lot of room. In shade, it will grow taller and more floppy. Dig and divide in the spring. Gardeners usually have more than enough divisions to spare. Prepare the soil by spading or tilling to at least a foot deep. These plants will stay put for 2 or 3 years, so some preparation is needed. Even though they will grow in wet places, they prefer the soil a little on the dry side. Provide good drainage; if the soil is wet, the plants will be taller and weaker. Set the plants at the depth they were growing in their containers. Space them at least 4 feet apart; they will spread.

Growing Tips

Water only as needed to prevent wilting in dry weather.

Care and Maintenance

Beebalm requires only a little care. Tie up plants knocked down by storms and cut back tops after blooming. Most plants will make a new mound of leaves that stays attractive for the rest of the summer. Divide every two to three years. Few diseases or insects affect Beebalm. Mildew will cover the foliage with white dust in fall when the nights are cool and dew is heavy. There is little that needs to be done, since the leaves have just about completed their work for the season by then.

Companion Planting and Design

Beebalm makes a large plant. Set it at the back of the perennial garden.

Did You Know

Beebalm leaves are great for teas, but also for stuffings, salads, and potpourris.

Beebalm is a popular plant for attracting hummingbirds, butterflies, and bees. (If you are allergic to bees, plant these flowers where you can see them but where you won't be getting too close.) Beebalm is attractive in flower, covered with fluffy clusters of blooms, and after the flowers fall, the seedheads remain attractive. This native plant is perfectly at home in our Illinois conditions. It is a well-adapted, rather rambunctious plant; it will need room, and it may decide to spread. Try the shorter kinds for areas that receive less than full sun. Popular cultivars are 'Cambridge Scarlet', 'Croftway Pink', and 'Snow Queen'. 'Mahogany' is a little shorter, it blooms earlier and is advertised as being mildew-resistant. Lemon Mint, M. pectinata, flowers rose-pink on 2-foot stems.

Other Names
Oswego Tea, Monarda

Bloom Period and Color
July, August blooms in purple, red, pink, white.

Mature Height × Spread
2 to 3^1/$_2$ feet × 2 to 3^1/$_2$ feet

Bellflower
Campanula sp.

Bellflower is a diverse group of plants and includes some biennials. They are suitable for the border, rock gardens, and the cutting garden. Some more aggressive kinds are useful in the wild garden or woodlands. The flowers are characteristically bell-shaped. The most commonly grown Campanula, Carpathian Bellflower (C. carpatica), is an excellent edging plant, generally a foot or less tall. It bears blue or white flowers all summer. C. persicifolia, Peach-leaved Bellflower, is 2 to 3 feet tall and will naturalize in woodlands. Blue, lavender, or white flowers are cup-shaped and are borne above the leaves. Excellent for cutting, the flowers will last as long as two weeks. English Harebell, C. rotundifolia, with dainty blue flowers, will naturalize and at times may be too aggressive.

Bloom Period and Color
June to August blooms in blue, violet, white.

Mature Height × Spread
1 to 3^1/$_2$ feet × 1 to 3^1/$_2$ feet

When, Where, and How to Plant
Plant in spring or fall. Seeds of species may be sown in place in midsummer. Named cultivars are available only as divisions or plants. Plant Bellflowers in sun or light shade. The taller types prefer full sun, the shorter kinds partial shade. They prefer moist, well-drained soil. Carpathian Bellflower will stand drier soil than most. Prepare the soil by spading to a depth of 6 inches. Provide drainage if the area is wet. Plants are available from mail-order catalogs, garden centers, and nurseries in spring. Divisions and potted plants are available all season. Plant them in their permanent places in the garden in spring, summer, or fall. Set plants at the depth they were grown, spacing them 9 to 12 inches apart. Divide plants in early spring.

Growing Tips
Water only as needed to prevent wilting. Fertilize cautiously, especially with nitrogen. Overly vigorous plants will not flower well and will be long and floppy. Mulching will keep the soil moist and cool and will help hold down weeds.

Care and Maintenance
Campanulas require little care once they are established. Slugs can be troublesome in shaded, wet gardens, but baits will discourage them. English Harebell may need to be restrained if it decides to take off on its own. Deadheading will keep the Bellflowers blooming; flowering will cease if seeds are allowed to develop. Plan to divide the clumps every three to four years when plants become floppy and the centers die out.

Companion Planting and Design
Use shorter varieties as edging and in the shaded rock garden where the soil stays damp. Use taller kinds in the back of the perennial garden or border and in the cutting garden. Species can be used in informal or naturalized plantings.

Did You Know
Creeping Bellflower, *C. rapunculoides,* is a common shade plant, often considered a weed. In Europe it is known as Rampion and its leaves and roots are used in salads.

Bleeding Heart
Dicentra spectabilis

When, Where, and How to Plant

Bleeding Hearts can be planted in spring or fall. Potted plants can be planted all season. Partial to full shade is best. Direct sun early in the day before temperatures rise is acceptable. Full sun at midday will cause premature die-down of the foliage. A cool moist soil with good drainage is best. Plants are available, potted and in bloom in spring, at garden centers and nurseries. Divisions are available in fall or spring. Spade or till the soil to a depth of 12 inches. Set the plants at the same depth they were growing in their containers. Water thoroughly to settle the soil around the roots.

Growing Tips

Bleeding Hearts generally do not need to be watered unless the spring is very dry. Fertilize carefully to avoid overstimulating the plants. They will make lots of leaves and fewer flowers. A mulch to preserve moisture and keep the soil cool is helpful.

Care and Maintenance

Bleeding Hearts require very little care. When the foliage dies down, remove it; plants can be divided at that time. Bleeding Heart plants increase in size and should be divided every three to four years. They produce seed in abundance as well, which means there are always extra plants to give away. These plants are always greatly prized by those who receive them. They require so little care that they are no burden, even for the most casual gardener.

Companion Planting and Design

Plant Bleeding Hearts among other perennials so the empty space after the plants die back will be hidden or at the back of the garden so their absence won't be as noticeable. Or, plant annuals. We plant the Bleeding Hearts in the border, and plant Impatiens around and under them. They fill in quickly after the Bleeding Heart foliage dies down.

Did You Know

The related Fringed Bleeding Heart, *D. eximia,* is a smaller plant that blooms most of the summer. The delicate, lacy, leaves do not die down but persist all summer.

Bleeding Heart is a favorite garden flower, identifiable to even the youngest child because of its distinctive flowers. The blooms are heart-shaped and have teardrop-like petals dripping from them, making them appear as if they are bleeding. These flowers are borne drooping along arching stems above deeply cut foliage. Two North American Bleeding Hearts are suitable for rock gardens. D. eximia, Eastern Bleeding Heart, is smaller and will bloom all summer in shaded gardens. It is pink, and there is a white form as well. D. formosa, Pacific Bleeding Heart, is best in cool damp locations. 'Luxuriant' is superior in form, 2 feet tall, blooms all summer, and stands heat without stalling if there is adequate moisture. D. cucullaria is the cream-over-white-flowered Dutchman's Breeches.

Bloom Period and Color
May, June blooms in pink and white, or white.

Mature Height × Spread
12 inches to 2 feet × 2 feet

Broadleaf Purple Coneflower

Echinacea purpurea

Broadleaf Purple Coneflowers are native American wildflowers. They are gaining popularity for the perennial garden, partly because of their long season of bloom and improved cultivars. Broadleaf Purple Coneflower tolerates all the conditions that make gardening difficult in Illinois. It is fully hardy; it tolerates heavy soils and alkalinity; and it suffers through the summer dry periods and heat, continuing to bloom. After the ray flowers fall and the plants dry up, the seeds in the fruiting heads will attract birds that hang on to the swaying stems to find a seed. The flowers are excellent for cutting. The cones are good for dry arrangements. 'Alba' is creamy white; 'Crimson Star', deep crimson red; 'Magnus', deep rose; and 'White Swan' has creamy-white flowers and a copper cone.

Other Name
Purple Coneflower

Bloom Period and Color
Summer blooms in purple, pink, white, crimson-red, and rose.

Mature Height × Spread
2 to 4 feet × 2 to 4 feet

When, Where, and How to Plant
Broadleaf Purple Coneflowers may be planted in spring or fall. Plant containers at any time during the season. Broadleaf Purple Coneflowers prefer full sun and a well-drained soil. They will tolerate partial shade, though they may become tall and weak. In the southern part of the state, partial shade during the middle of the day will prevent fading of the flowers. Use these plants in the back, middle, or at the ends of the border, or plant them in naturalized areas or the cutting garden. Broadleaf Purple Coneflower plants are available in 1- and 6-gallon cans, and as divisions in spring or fall. Prepare the soil by tilling or spading to a 6-inch depth. Make sure the area is well drained, but there is no need to enrich the soil. Coneflowers tolerate heavy soils. Dig the planting hole the same depth and twice as wide as the plant ball and set divisions at the same depth they were growing in their containers. Space the plants 2 feet apart. If the containerized plants were growing in a light soil mix, shake some of it off the ball, and mix it with the soil going back into the planting hole. After planting, water to settle the soil around the roots.

Growing Tips
Water as needed to prevent wilting and scorching of the leaves. Fertilize in spring before growth begins.

Care and Maintenance
Broadleaf Purple Coneflower requires no special treatment. It the plants start to fall over, stake them up. Deadheading will prolong flowering, but it also removes the interesting cones. These plants will reseed themselves. If you are growing a hybrid selection, cut off the cones before they drop seeds; these plants do not come true from seed, and the seedlings will revert back to the species.

Companion Planting and Design
Broadleaf Purple Coneflowers fit well with most perennials blooming in late summer. Plant at the back or side of the garden.

Did You Know
Leave the last blooms on the plants to make seed for the birds but hoe out any seedlings that develop.

Columbine
Aquilegia hybrids

When, Where, and How to Plant
Started plants and divisions are available in spring. Set plants out when the soil is dry enough to till. Divisions may be made in fall. Plant Columbines in a well-drained, moist soil. Columbines will tolerate various soils as long as they are well drained and not allowed to become too dry. Full sun is fine, but flowering will be prolonged in light shade. Plant tall kinds at the back of the border; shorter kinds may be planted as edging. Columbines will lose their leaves in midsummer, creating a hole where there once was a plant. Tuck them in among other plants that will cover such bare spots, or plant annuals in place of them. Prepare the soil by tilling or spading to a 6-inch depth. Plants are available as potted seedlings or divisions from garden centers. Set the plants at the same depth they were growing in their containers. Space tall cultivars at 12 inches, dwarf cultivars at 6.

Growing Tips
Water as needed to keep the plants from wilting. Fertilize cautiously to prevent tall floppy plants.

Care and Maintenance
Columbines do require some care. The taller cultivars may need staking to keep them from being blown over in storms. Most cultivars are prolific seed producers and will reseed themselves very well. Some hybrids revert to their wild forms in the process. Deadhead to prevent seeding of hybrid cultivars which do not come true from seed. Leaf miners can disfigure the plants. Cut damaged foliage to the ground and destroy it. The plants will respond with a fresh mound of leaves. Columbines may be grown from seed sown under lights in December. Sow the seeds and chill them in the refrigerator for three weeks. Then germinate at 75°F.

Companion Planting and Design
Columbines are semi-tall plants, but they fit into the border nicely.

Did You Know
Columbine is the state flower of Colorado. It is protected. Picking it can be costly.

Whether they are a few tiny flowers blooming in an abandoned pasture or big hybrid flowers blooming in a garden, Columbines are immediately recognizable. The unique flowers with their trailing spurs make excellent cut flowers for arrangements. The parents of present-day long-spurred Columbines are native wildflowers of the Rocky Mountains. They are commonly seen in the thin forests at high elevations. There are both tall-growing and dwarf kinds, suitable for the border or edging. The tall, large-flowered hybrids provide a good range of colors. 'Crimson Star' is crimson and white; 'Maxistar' is primrose yellow. 'Blue Shades' provides many tints of blue. 'Biedermeier Strain' is short, 12 inches, with white, purple, or pink flowers. 'Nora Barlow' is double-flowered, pink and red, and tinged with green.

Bloom Period and Color
May to July blooms in red, white, yellow, blue, violet, and bicolors.

Mature Height × Spread
12 inches to 3 feet × 12 to 18 inches

Coneflower

Rudbeckia nitida

Coneflower is a native North American plant. It is hardy and reliable, easy to establish, and rewarding in bloom. Most of the newer selections are short enough for the border garden. All of the perennial Rudbeckias make excellent long-lasting cut flowers. They will spread and persist without care as long as there is a little water. These plants are attractive to butterflies. Most are daisy-like, yellow with dark centers. The species, R. nitida, is 2 to 4 feet tall. It needs to be at the back of the garden and staked. 'Herbstsonne' grows to 7 feet in some sites, but usually nearer to 5 feet. It is one of the finest Coneflowers, with sulfur-yellow flowers in late summer. 'Goldsturm' is a compact form of R. fulgida, growing to 2 or 3 feet. Two-foot 'Goldquelle' has fluffy double blooms.

Other Name
Black-Eyed Susan

Bloom Period and Color
August to October blooms in yellow.

Mature Height × Spread
2 to 4 or 7 feet × 2 feet wide

When, Where, and How to Plant
Coneflowers are best planted in the spring. Containerized plants may be planted any time during the season. Coneflowers are at home in the middle to back of the garden, and in open naturalized areas as well. Plant Coneflowers in the border, in the middle of large beds, or in natural areas. They prefer full sun, but they will tolerate light shade. Stems may become floppy if grown in shaded spots. A moderately moist soil with good drainage is best. Prepare the soil by tilling to a 12-inch depth. Any garden soil is satisfactory and there is no need to add organic matter. Plants are usually sold in 1-, 2-, or 5-gallon cans. Set the plants at the depth they were growing in their containers, spacing them 2 to 4 feet apart.

Growing Tips
Plants in overly fertile soil will be weak and will need dividing sooner than necessary. Avoid fertilizing unless the plants are obviously deficient in nutrients. These plants prefer drier rather than wetter soil.

Care and Maintenance
Coneflowers need no care once they are established. Weeds are either choked out or shaded out. After the Coneflower tops die down in fall, they can be cut down and composted; or they may be left for the birds who will try to get the last of the seeds in the flower heads. When the plants become overcrowded, they can be divided. Dividing either in fall, after blooming has ceased, or early spring is satisfactory. The earlier the plants are divided, the better their flowering will be the next summer.

Companion Planting and Design
These are native prairie plants and will tolerate any conditions except poor drainage. Combine them in the border with grasses. They are especially attractive with Purple Coneflowers and Butterfly Weed.

Did You Know
Some Rudbeckias were used by Native Americans and early settlers as tonics. Forest Potawatomi used the tea to cure colds.

Coreopsis
Coreopsis grandiflora

When, Where, and How to Plant

Plant in spring from started plants. Divide plants in spring or fall. Plant in dry soil and full sun. Coreopsis is best suited to the middle or front of the border, and is also well suited to naturalized areas. Coreopsis is a native prairie wildflower. It can be planted and left unattended in natural areas. It will grow happily and spread if conditions are favorable. Wildflower mixes that are used to establish natural areas usually contain Coreopsis seeds. Plants are available potted as started seedlings or divisions in spring. Prepare the soil by tilling or spading to a 6-inch depth. Set the plants no deeper than they were grown in their containers.

Growing Tips

Water only in extended droughts. Do not improve the soil with added compost or fertilizer. In moist, fertile soils the plants will be overly vigorous, with reduced flowering, and will not support themselves.

Care and Maintenance

These plants thrive on neglect. If plants are overly tall and begin to tumble, tie them to a stake. Deadhead the plants to keep them blooming; if you cut enough flowers for arrangements, there will be little need to deadhead. Several insects can find their ways into a Coreopsis planting, but they seldom do any damage. It is nice to have plants that do not want to be babied. The bright flowers attract butterflies.

Companion Planting and Design

These plants are well suited to the front of the border. They will tolerate heat and drought without complaint. Other plants that stand the same conditions include Coneflower, Purple Coneflower, and Butterfly Weed. Don't try to combine Coreopsis with plants that need watering and fertilizing. The Coreopsis will be floppy and will flower poorly.

Did You Know

Several Coreopsis varieties are native or naturalized in Illinois. *C. grandiflora* from states farther west seems most common where stockyards once stood. Could it be that animals carried the seeds on their coats? Seeds got the name "beggar's ticks" because they stuck to outerwear.

Modern Coreopsis deliver masses of yellow blooms from the end of June until Labor Day! These are long-stemmed flowers that are long-lasting in the garden and excellent for cut flowers. Coreopsis is just about the easiest garden perennial to grow. It grows in full sun and is not particular about the soil it grows in, doing its best with a slightly dry soil and low fertility. Thread-leaf Coreopsis, C. verticillata, makes an airy mound of foliage sprinkled with bright yellow, star-like flowers. It is a good border plant that does well in full sun. C. verticillata 'Moonbeam' has light-yellow flowers on 15-inch mounds of foliage. It blooms all season and has unusual heat tolerance. 'Golden Showers' is 3 feet tall and not quite as lacy.

Other Names
Tickweed, Tickseed

Bloom Period and Color
Early to late summer blooms in yellow with yellow or coffee-colored centers; sometimes rose-tinted flowers with yellow centers.

Mature Height × Spread
2 to 3 feet × 1 1/2 feet

Daylily
Hemerocallis sp.

There is no perfect perennial flowering plant, but Daylilies come close. They bloom faithfully with little care. They grow in any soil, sometimes doing better in poor soil. They grow in full sun or dense shade. They have no insect pests or diseases. Is it any wonder that these are the most popular and widely used of the perennials? These flowers last only one day, thus the name. But there are as many as 30 flowers on a stem, each opening for a full day, so the blooming period can be extended for weeks. There are evergreen cultivars, but they are usually not completely hardy in the north. Select cultivars that will grow in your area—these are the ones available from stores where you live.

Bloom Period and Color
May to October blooms in all colors except white.

Mature Height × Spread
1 to 4 feet × 2 feet

When, Where, and How to Plant
Daylilies can be planted in spring or late summer. Containerized plants can be planted anytime during the season. Plant in full sun or light shade for best bloom. Avoid wet or overly fertile soils. Use in masses, as borders, naturalized, to stabilize banks, around water features, or along roadsides. Potted plants are available all summer long. New divisions are made in August. Prepare the soil by tilling or spading to a depth of 6 inches. Set the plants or divisions at the depth they were growing in the containers. Space standard cultivars 24 inches apart, dwarf cultivars at 12 inches.

Growing Tips
Daylilies are efficient scavengers and don't need much fertilizer. Excess nitrogen causes unattractive growth, poor flowering. Water to prevent wilting of the plants. Drought during flowering can result in scorched leaves, and fewer flowers.

Care and Maintenance
Deadhead the plants to improve their appearance. When all the flowers on a stem have faded, remove it. The foliage of some cultivars may decline in late summer; mow it down. It may regrow before freeze-up. Divide the hybrid cultivars every three to five years. Species may never need dividing unless you want to obtain plants for another location.

Companion Planting and Design
Plant Daylilies in clumps or masses for best display. Colorful and attractive in bloom, once blossoms fade the foliage begins to dry up and they become rather unattractive. Setting them behind Coreopsis, Coneflowers, or taller annuals hides foliage until it renews itself.

Did You Know
Daylilies have been garden favorites for generations. I recall as a child, rolling around in beds of "tiger lilies," not really Tiger Lilies, but old tawny Daylilies. They are naturalized throughout the country, along roads, in long-forgotten gardens, alleys, anywhere they can take root. Common Lemon Lily is bright yellow and fragrant, and less aggressive. Modern Daylilies are hybrids of these and a few other species, having a less wild nature and vastly improved flowers.

Delphinium
Delphinium elatum

When, Where, and How to Plant

Delphiniums can be grown from seed sown directly in the garden in August. Transplant seedlings when they are big enough to handle in the fall or the following spring. Container-grown started plants are available in spring or fall. Spring planting is best. Plant Delphiniums in full sun, or partial shade in the hotter parts of the state. Soil must be moist, deep, and well drained. Prepare the soil by double-digging to a depth of at least 12 inches or 2 feet. Incorporate organic matter into the soil. Provide drainage if needed. Set the plants at the same depth they grew in their containers—deep planting would increase the likelihood of root or crown rotting. Space at 12 inches. Blend PCNB granules (Terraclor) into the soil or drench PCNB into the soil following planting. Follow the directions on the label every time you use this material. Water the plants to prevent wilting.

Growing Tips

Fertilize with a complete balanced fertilizer such as a soluble 20-20-20. Delphiniums need water; don't let them dry out, but don't keep the ground saturated either.

Care and Maintenance

Remove winter mulch in spring. Drench the soil with PCNB to prevent root rot and set stakes for plants that will need support. Apply snail bait every seven to ten days. Remove faded blooms, but leave as much foliage as you can. The plants will rebloom until frost. After frost has killed back the tops in fall, remove them. Lightly mulch the plants to prevent heaving. The most damaging problem affecting Delphiniums is the disease *Sclerotium rolfsii*. Keep it out of the planting, and treat the soil to prevent infection. Purchase only disease-free plants.

Companion Planting and Design

Use as a backdrop in the perennial garden, or in the cutting garden.

Did You Know

D. virescens, Prairie Larkspur, is one of the most handsome native prairie flowers, and is commonly grown in flower gardens.

When I was working my way through college in a California seed store, I was amazed by the California Giant Delphiniums that grew there. Some were nearly 10 feet tall. They don't get that large here in Illinois, but they are still the most majestic of the border flowers. Averaging close to 4 to 5 feet tall, they produce magnificent flower-covered spikes in pastel colors. The biggest Delphiniums are the 'Pacific Giants' with double flowers in purple, blue, pink, and white. Shorter hybrids include the 'Dwarf Pacifics', blue and 2 feet tall, and the D. belladonna and D. bellamosa hybrids. The latter are branched, 2 to 4 feet tall, and blue or white. 'Connecticut Yankee' is short (to 2½ feet), bushy, blue, lavender, and white.

Bloom Period and Color

June to September blooms in blue, white-and-violet, red, pink, yellow.

Mature Height × Spread

2 to 6 feet × 12 inches

Ferns

Many genera, species, and varieties

Ferns are plants for the cool, moist shade garden, grown for their magnificent foliage. Their soft texture brings another dimension to the garden. They grow from spores that drop, usually from the lower sides of the leaves, to grow on the ground. There they grow into structures that look like tiny leaves (prothallia), where fertilization takes place and from which new plants will grow. Moisture is needed for this process; Ferns belong to wet areas. The heavily shaded, moist areas in established neighborhoods with large trees and shrubs, or on the north side of a home where the sun rarely shines are often thought of as liabilities. Most plants won't grow in such places, but these are exactly the conditions in which Ferns do best.

Bloom Period and Color
Seasonal foliage.

Mature Height × Spread
6 inches to 2 feet × 1 to 3 feet

When, Where, and How to Plant

Ferns are best planted in spring so they can become established before the onset of winter. Light to dense shade and a moist but well-drained soil are essential requirements. The soil type is immaterial; a pH near neutral is best, but the plants will tolerate quite a variation in acidity. Ours grow at a pH near 7.5. Ferns are available in 1- to-5-gallon cans from garden centers and nurseries, or from catalogs in spring. Prepare the soil by tilling or spading to a depth of 6 to 12 inches. Incorporate organic matter to assure good soil structure and provide drainage if necessary. If the area is low, construct berms or raised beds. Set the plants no deeper than they were growing in their containers. Space larger kinds such as Ostrich Fern at 3 to 4 feet, smaller kinds such as Maidenhair at 1 to 1^1/2 feet.

Growing Tips

Ferns must have water. When the weather is dry, they should be thoroughly watered to prevent wilting and scorching of the fronds. Fertilize ferns cautiously. Use a complete liquid fertilizer mixed according to directions on the label. Apply to the soil beneath the plants as they start growth in spring. Keep the fertilizer off the foliage.

Care and Maintenance

Remove dead foliage in the fall. These are essentially trouble-free plants. Once Ferns are established and growing, little needs to be done to keep them going. Weeds don't grow well around them, and there are few insect or disease problems in heavy shade.

Companion Planting and Design

Interplant Ferns with spring flowering bulbs and Virginia Bluebells. They will finish blooming about the time the Ferns begin to grow. Smaller Ferns blend well with Hostas and Tuberous Begonias.

Did You Know

New fronds emerging from some Ferns are called *fiddleheads* and are springtime delicacies, especially on the Pacific Coast and in the Canadian Maritimes. Caution: Some are poisonous. Don't pick them unless you know they are safe.

Gay-Feather

Liatris spicata

When, Where, and How to Plant

Liatris is best planted in the spring before growth begins. Containerized plants may be planted in the garden anytime during the season. Plant in full sun or very light shade. Soil should be well drained, drier rather than wet; these prairie plants will decline in wet soils. Containerized plants are available at garden centers and nurseries, and at discount stores in spring. Prepare the soil by spading or tilling to at least a foot deep. These plants will be there for two or three years, so some preparation is needed. Set the plants at the depth they were growing in their containers. Space them about 2 feet apart, which is close enough to allow them to hold each other up.

Growing Tips

The plants will be stronger and better resist being blown over if fertility is low, and flowers will be larger and more abundant with a moderate level of fertility. Fertilize the plants when they are actively growing with a complete soluble fertilizer such as 20-20-20 (Peters, Miracle-Gro, or similar), following directions. Water to prevent wilting. These plants are not deeply rooted and can be shoved out of the ground; winter mulch will help prevent frost heaving.

Care and Maintenance

Liatris requires little care once established. Plants may need to be staked in windy locations.

Companion Planting and Design

Gay-Feathers are excellent in the border. They blend well with pale yellows and with the mauve of Monarda. The plants flower later than many perennials and are welcome for their addition to the flower garden. Plant a row in your cutting garden for a continuous supply from midsummer to frost. Let the last blooms go to seed to provide for the birds.

Did You Know

Gay-Feathers are members of the composite or Daisy family. The flowers are arranged in spikes and open from the top down, the opposite of most other flowers. They are excellent cut flowers and grown commercially for florists.

Gay-Feather is a North American native plant, often included in prairie restoration plantings. It has not been used to its full potential in the garden. The flowers, fifty or more, are borne along a tall vertical stalk. The blooms are soft and pastel pink or lavender, and they open from the top of the stem rather than the bottom. The blooms are excellent as cut flowers. Cultivars L. scariosa 'September Glory' (deep purple) and 'White Spire' bloom in late summer. L. pycnostachya is Kansas Gay-Feather, about 4 feet. L. spicata 'Kobold', listed in the trade as Spike Gay Feather, is short (24 inches) and blooms in an intense rose-lavender from July to September. 'Floristan White' produces white flowers in August and September.

Other Names
Blazing Star, Liatris

Bloom Period and Color
Midsummer to late fall blooms in lavender, white, rose.

Mature Height × Spread
3 to 4 feet × 2 feet

Hardy Chrysanthemum
Dendranthema × grandiflora

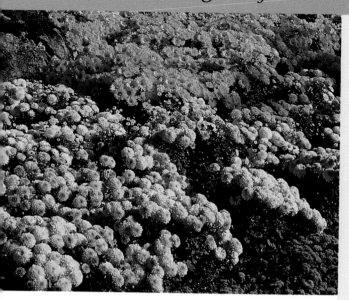

Hardy Mums take over where the annuals leave off in fall. The sturdy plants are covered with blooms of many colors and forms, including formal, ball-shaped pompons; daisy-like singles; spoons; and showy "football" types. These are the most colorful garden plants for flowering in late summer and fall. Mums are best planted in masses or in groups of 3 to 5 plants. Dwarf cushion types are suitable for edging; the tall kinds are best for the back of the border or for cutting garden. They are all excellent, long-lasting cut flowers. There are so many colors and forms that trying to buy Mums by cultivar name is impossible. Try to buy plants already in bloom so you can see their color and form.

Other Name
Hardy Mum

Bloom Period and Color
August to November blooms in white, yellow, pink, orange, bronze, red.

Mature Height × Spread
1 to 2 feet × 1 to 2 feet

When, Where, and How to Plant
Spring is the best time to plant Chrysanthemums. Full sun and well-drained soil are the keys to success with Mums. Poor drainage will lead to winter-kill. Plants may be started from cuttings or from potted plants in spring. Overwintered plants may be lifted and divided. Prepare the soil by tilling or spading to a depth of 6 inches, adding organic matter. Provide drainage if necessary with tiles or raised beds. Set container plants at the same depth they were growing in their containers. Plant rooted cuttings so the roots are just covered with soil. Space plants 18 inches apart. Mums are available in fall as potted plants to be planted as replacements for spent annuals. For fall planting, plants are sold in 1- or 2-gallon cans. Prepare the soil as above and dig a hole for each plant as deep and twice as wide as the ball of soil on the plant.

Growing Tips
Fertilize the plants when they are actively growing with a complete soluble fertilizer such as 20-20-20 (Peters, Miracle-Gro, or similar), following directions. Water to prevent wilting.

Care and Maintenance
To develop bushy plants, pinch to remove the growing tips. Make the first pinch when the plants are 6 inches tall, the second when the shoots have grown another 6 inches. Simply roll out the growing tip of each shoot. Do not pinch early cultivars after June 15; don't pinch later cultivars after mid-July. Control aphids and mites with insecticidal soap, earwigs with Sevin, and foliar diseases with captan or maneb, etc. Follow label directions carefully. When tops are frozen off, remove them and mulch the plants with 6 inches of straw.

Companion Planting and Design
Mums can be planted in fall to replace spent annuals, setting them over newly planted spring bulbs. Remove the Mums after they die down and heal them in elsewhere for the winter.

Did You Know
Florist Mums are the same as Garden Mums, but they bloom later.

Heuchera

Heuchera sp.

When, Where, and How to Plant

Potted plants are available in spring from nurseries and garden centers. Plants may be divided in early spring or fall. Seed may be sown in the garden in midsummer. Plant Heucheras in full sun or light shade. They prefer a moist, well-drained soil. Plant as facers for shrub plantings, or as edging for the perennial garden. Some of the showy kinds are suitable for the cutting garden. Prepare the soil by tilling or spading to a 6-inch depth. Add organic matter if possible, and make sure drainage is good (poor drainage will result in crown rot). Set the plants so that their crowns are buried up to the depth of the leaves. Space plants 12 to 15 inches apart.

Growing Tips

Watering during droughty periods will enhance flowering and will prevent scorching of the leaves. Fertilize cautiously in spring as growth is starting. Use a complete soluble fertilizer such as 20-20-20 (Peters, Miracle-Gro, or similar).

Care and Maintenance

These plants develop a bare, woody crown after a few years. Dig them up and remove and replant the shoots from around the woody part. Discard the old woody crown. Division will be necessary approximately every three years. Mulching or hilling up soil mix over the crowns will delay the need for division for a year or so. Be sure the plants are in a well-drained situation and that the soil used to hill them up is quite light. Otherwise crown rot may develop. Removal of the stalks will prolong flowering of the showy cultivars.

Companion Planting and Design

The plants with scalloped leaves often tinted with purple are excellent in rockeries and as edging. Their shade tolerance allows them to be used as woodland plants where their delightful flowers persist for weeks.

Did You Know

Heucheras are native to the Eastern U.S. and the Rockies. Hybrid Coral Bells crosses between *Heuchera* and *Tiarella*, Foam Flower, are called × *Heucherella*.

Heuchera is grown for its attractive foliage that may be marked with coppery or silver veins, or may be mahogany-colored. The form of the plant, a neat mound, makes it especially suitable for edging in front of shrubs or along the perennial border. (Coral Bells is larger, and its flowers are showy.) Heuchera and Coral Bells have been hybridized extensively to improve their flowering. Flowers of the species are tiny and ephemeral. Heucherella hybrids are crosses between Heuchera and Tiarella. Cultivars include 'Dale's Selection', with silver-blue leaves; 'Garnet', with bright garnet-colored leaves in spring; and 'Pewter Veil', with purplish, metallic-silver leaves. 'Palace Purple' has foliage that is purple-bronze on the upper surface and purplish-pink on the underside, and blooms white in July and August.

Other Names
Alumroot, Coral Bells

Bloom Period and Color
Late spring, early summer blooms in greenish-pink, red.

Mature Height × Spread
6 to 12 inches × 6 to 10 inches

Hosta

Hosta sp.

Hosta is a dependable perennial plant that requires little care. Its foliage has a regal character and is so distinctive that it can be mistaken for nothing else. Flowers are borne above the leaves in summer, but they are not the main reason for growing these plants; this is a shade plant grown for its foliage. Hosta comes in many forms, sizes, and colors. These plants can be various shades of green, from yellowish green to bright green, dark green, grayish green, or purple-green. Variegated cultivars can have white, gold, yellow, or cream-colored margins or other markings, or they may have various shades of green within each leaf. The leaves can be small or large. Some have wavy margins and others are smooth.

Other Name
Plantain Lily

Bloom Period and Color
Summer blooms in white or lavender.

Mature Height × Spread
1 to 2 feet × 2 to 4 feet

When, Where, and How to Plant
Divisions can be planted in spring or fall. Plant containers at any time during the season. Wavy-leaved Hostas can stand sun better than most kinds. Soil must be well drained but moist. Use Hostas in mass plantings under the shade of trees, around pools, in rock gardens, and in the border. They can be used in front of shrub plantings or interplanted around Azaleas or Rhododendrons in woodland settings. Hostas are sold in 1-, 2-, and 6-gallon cans, or as divisions. Prepare the soil by tilling or spading to a 6-inch depth. Add organic matter to improve water-holding and drainage. Holes will need to be dug for the larger, container-grown plants, as deep and twice as wide as the plant ball. Set the plants at the same depth they were growing in their containers. Space them about 18 inches apart; large-leaved cultivars can be set 2 feet apart. Soak the plants thoroughly following planting.

Growing Tips
Hostas need water. Soak them well during extended dry weather. Fertilizer is generally not necessary.

Care and Maintenance
There are several pests that can damage Hosta plantings. Slugs are the most damaging; control them with slug bait spread around the plants, keeping the bait away from the plants to draw out the slugs. Begin applications early in the season—the small slugs are much easier to kill than the adults. Slug bait must be moistened to be effective. Wet it if there is no rain or dew. An application lasts only a week or so. Re-treat every week as long as evidence of new feeding appears. Divide plants every five years or when overcrowded. The dense cover provided by Hostas will keep out weeds.

Companion Planting and Design
These are shade plants and do well where other perennials don't. Use them in the dark passageways between buildings, or in masses under trees.

Did You Know
Wavy-leaved Hostas will stand full sun if kept well watered.

Lavender, English
Lavandula angustifolia

When, Where, and How to Plant
Plant Lavender in spring after danger of frost is over so it has sufficient time to become well established before winter. Lavender needs full sun, adequate air movement to allow it to dry, and a well drained somewhat infertile soil. The alkaline soils of the Midwest are preferred. Plants are available from mail order catalogs, from some garden centers, and often are for sale at spring flower shows. Set the plants at the depth they grew in the container.

Growing Tips
They must have excellent drainage, but will need water if the weather is very dry. Do not fertilize these plants unless they are obviously deficient. Yellow leaves and lack of growth are symptomatic, but could also indicate excess watering. These plants thrive on somewhat dry infertile soils. If over-watered, they rapidly deteriorate. If soils are too fertile, the plants become rank and fall over. Flowering and fragrance are reduced.

Care and Maintenance
Lavender plants do not take a lot of care. Remove the flower stalks as soon as the flowers have faded. In severe climates, winter protection may be helpful. Use a light straw covering to moderate temperature changes and reduce the effect of drying winds. When the plants become old and ragged, replace them. Lavender is rarely affected by insects or diseases. Caterpillars sometimes show up, and leafspot diseases will affect leaves in wet weather. Pick off the offending creatures or damaged leaves.

Companion Planting and Design
These plants are great for borders and rock gardens. The fine grey-green foliage provides contrast to solid greens of most small shrubs. A row of Lavender in the cutting garden will provide flowers for drying. Sachets of them make prized gifts.

Did You Know
The name, Lavender, probably comes from the Latin *lavare*, to wash. Some fine soaps contain oil of Lavender. Lavender is more prized for its fragrance than nearly any other flower, second only to the Rose.

Lavender is a low-growing, semi-shrub grown for its wonderful fragrance. It has grey-green fragrant leaves that are partially evergreen, and the familiar spikes of deliciously fragrant flowers. The plants can be trimmed into formal shapes as low hedges, but are best used in masses where the fine foliage and flowers are striking. I often see Lavender planted in rows along the entrance walks where it looks like rows of wooden soldiers . . . not the best use, but the fragrance certainly welcomes visitors to the home. Lavender flowers can be cut and dried, with the fragrance lasting for years. English Lavender has been cultivated for centuries and is the source of oil of Lavender.

Other Name
Common Lavender

Bloom Period and Color
Lavender-purple, lilac, blue, pink, white flowers in June-July.

Mature Height × Spread
1 to 2 feet (sometimes 3 feet) high × 2 to 4 feet wide

Zones
5 to 6b

Oriental Poppy
Papaver orientale

As a child I was read the adventures of Dorothy and Toto in The Wizard of Oz. Enticed into a field of Poppies by the beautiful blooms, Dorothy and Toto are overcome by the vapors and lulled to sleep. Of course the story was about the Opium Poppy, but the gorgeous blooms of all Poppies are to be appreciated and enjoyed rather than feared. These brightly colored flowers are outstanding in the early-summer garden at a time when few things are blooming. Poppies are crepe-like and delicate, easily injured by storms. With their varied, brilliant colors, they are excellent for flower arrangements. Many Poppy cultivars are listed in catalogs. Many of these are seed strains; the trueness of type can't be assured.

Bloom Period and Color
June, July blooms in orange, pink, white, orange-red.

Mature Height × Spread
2 to 4 feet × 2 to 4 feet

When, Where, and How to Plant
Poppies are planted in spring, or divided in midsummer after leaves die down. Fall planting is more likely to result in flowers the first season. Plant these flowers in a sunny, well-drained spot in the garden. Poppies are sold as divisions, in pots, in 1- and 2-gallon cans, and in 6-gallon cans with plants in bloom. Prepare the soil by tilling or spading to a depth of 12 inches. Add organic matter to improve moisture-holding and aeration and be sure the area drains well. Set the plants at the same depth they were growing in their containers, spacing them about 2 feet apart. The fleshy roots are easily damaged, so handle the plants gently. Dig holes the depth of the plant ball and twice as wide. Set root divisions on their sides, and cover with soil. Water thoroughly to settle the soil. Poppies can be started from seed sown under lights at 55°F in March. If planted in the garden when large enough to handle, they will flower the second year.

Growing Tips
Water to keep the soil from drying, but do not keep dormant plants wet; they will tolerate relatively dry soil. Judicious watering while the plants are growing and flowering is important—do not overwater. Like most perennials, Poppies rarely need fertilizer. The added growth accelerates the need to divide the plants.

Care and Maintenance
Once planted, the thick, fleshy roots do not like to be disturbed. Leave them alone until it is time to divide them. They need to be divided and replanted every five years or so. Short root sections make new plants. Any sections left when clumps are lifted will grow. No diseases or insects are common to Poppies.

Companion Planting and Design
Poppies are so colorful, they need green foliage or more subtle flowers to set them off. Try Hostas or Daylilies.

Did You Know
Poppies die down after flowering, leaving a big hole. Fill in with annuals.

Peony
Paeonia hybrids

When, Where, and How to Plant

Plant Peony roots in fall. Plant containerized plants at any time. Soil must be deeply prepared and well drained. Allow enough room for the plants. Do not plant them where the roots of trees or shrubs will interfere with them. Prepare the soil by spading to a 12-inch depth. Incorporate organic matter and a low-nitrogen fertilizer such as 5-20-20 or similar. Use a handful for each plant (10 square feet). Peonies will stay in the same place, undisturbed, for as long as fifty years. Plant divisions with the small, pink buds exactly 1 inch below the soil surface; make sure the pointed ends are up. Set containerized plants at the same depth as they were growing in the containers and dig the planting hole the same depth and twice as wide as the plant ball. Allow at least 3 feet or more between plants. After planting, soak the soil to firm it around the roots.

Growing Tips

Fertilize in fall or in spring before growth begins with liquid 20-20-20 (Peters, Miracle-Gro, or similar). Water to provide an inch per week.

Care and Maintenance

Peonies require very little care once they are established, but controlling weeds, especially grasses, is important. Peony flowers are heavy, and if it rains while they are in full bloom, they will fall over. Install cages around the plants as they begin to grow in spring. After the petals have dropped, remove the flowers, but leave as much of the foliage as you can. A few diseases can damage Peonies. Removal of the old stems and care in keeping the plant tops dry will help avoid disease. Spraying may be necessary in wet seasons; use benomyl, maneb, or mancozeb.

Companion Planting and Design

Plant in the border or cutting garden.

Did You Know

Tree Peonies are shrubs, not trees.

The Peonies in Grandma's garden put forth their beautiful fragrant blooms just in time for Memorial Day. Pink and white, they were so special that one or two would be cut to bring indoors so the fragrance would fill the house. Peonies are magnificent flowers reserved for those of us who reside in the cold parts of the country. They are strictly for northern gardens, requiring extended cold weather during their dormancy period. The plants emerge as pink sprouts from massive underground root systems in early spring. By May, large bush-like plants have developed, with flower buds topping every stem. The flowers, in warm colors, are 6 inches or more in diameter, in single, anemone, or double cultivars. The plants remain attractive following blooming.

Bloom Period and Color
May, June blooms in white, pink, rose, red, some bicolors.

Mature Height × Spread
2 to 3 feet × 2 to 3 feet

Phlox

Phlox paniculata

Hillsides covered with waves of lavender, pink, and white . . .that is Phlox at its best. These lovely flowers are produced in clusters as much as a foot across on 2-foot stems. Planted in masses, they produce a solid blanket of color from midsummer until frost. They are the perennial flowers of summer and no garden should be without a few of them. Nurseries and garden centers offer many cultivars of Phlox. An even greater number are offered in seed catalogs. Worthy of mention are 'Blue Boy', true blue and 24 inches tall; 'Bright Eyes', pink with a red eye; and 'The King', deep purple. A related species with better mildew resistance, P. maculata, is Wild Sweet William. 'Miss Lingard' is pure white. Phlox 'David' is the 2002 Perennial Plant of The Year.

Bloom Period and Color
June to August blooms in white, pink, red, blue, purple.

Mature Height × Spread
2 to 3 feet × 2 to 3 feet

When, Where, and How to Plant
Phloxes should be planted in spring or fall, though containerized plants can be planted all season. Plant in masses in the back of the border. They need full sun and a moist, well-drained soil. Plants are available in 1-, 2-, and 6-gallon cans, and root cuttings are available from mail-order catalogs. Prepare the soil by tilling or spading to a 6-inch depth. Add organic matter to improve soil condition and moisture-holding. Set the plants at the same depth they were growing in their containers, setting them 12 to 15 inches apart. Dig the holes for containerized plants the same depth and twice as wide as the plant balls. Plant root cuttings 2 inches deep on their sides.

Growing Tips
Phloxes need water and fertilizer for best flowering. Apply a complete fertilizer such as 20-20-20 liquid (Peters, Miracle-Gro, or similar) as plants begin growth in spring, and every month during the season. Follow the mixing directions on the label.

Care and Maintenance
Mildew and mites may disfigure the leaves so that by late in the season they are quite unattractive. Control mites with insecticidal soap. Control mildew with triforine or sulfur and keep water off the leaves. Deadhead the plants without fail after blooms fade. Deadheading stimulates continued flowering. If allowed to go to seed, the hybrid cultivars revert to the species. (This gardening difficulty is actually what makes these plants so prolific along the roadsides.) Stake plants that have a tendency to fall over and divide the plants when they become crowded. The plants need to be divided regularly.

Companion Planting and Design
Phlox need to be planted in masses for best display. In the perennial garden, plant them in clumps near the back of the garden. Plant lower-growing kinds in front of them to hide the long stems.

Did You Know
Garden Phlox are hybrids of the common Prairie Phlox, and will revert back if the seedlings are allowed to grow. Cut the flowers before they produce seeds.

Russian Sage
Perovskia atriplicifolia

When, Where, and How to Plant
Russian Sage is planted from divisions or containerized plants. Divisions may be planted in either spring or fall. Containerized plants are often sold in bloom in 2- and 6-gallon cans, and can be planted at any time during the season. Plant in full sun in a well-drained soil. The only conditions Russian Sage will not tolerate are shade and soggy soil. Without proper drainage, it will decline and die from winter-kill. If planted in shade, this plant will decline and die out. Russian Sage is suitable as a filler plant in the border, as an accent plant, as a landscape plant, or in beds in difficult places. Prepare the soil by spading or tilling to a depth of 6 inches. If drainage is less than adequate, incorporate organic matter and sand to a 12-inch depth. Set the plants at the depth they were growing in their containers. Dig the hole for container-grown plants the same depth and twice the width of the plant ball. Soak the plants thoroughly to settle the soil. Do not water again unless the plants wilt.

Growing Tips
These plants thrive on neglect. If pampered they become floppy and bloom poorly. Water as needed to prevent wilting. Fertilize only if the plants show nutrient deficiencies.

Care and Maintenance
These plants require very little care. They are affected by no bugs or diseases. Their woody stems should be cut down to about 6 inches in spring before growth begins. This will keep the plants from becoming straggly and untidy.

Companion Planting and Design
The subtle lavender-blue spikes are easily lost if mixed with brighter colored flowers. Combine with the golds of Coneflowers or Goldenrod, oranges of Butterfly Weed, and rich tans of grasses such as 'Karl Foerster' Feather Reed Grass.

Did You Know
This plant is native of high Afghanistan deserts. It was introduced in the mid-1800s, but only recently has become popular in American gardens. It was the 1995 Perennial Plant of the Year.

Russian Sage, a semi-woody plant, is a relative newcomer on the perennial plant scene. It is attractive all-season and has the ability to grow where nothing else will. This perennial will grow in hot, dry parking lot islands, that strip between the south side of the house and the driveway, or a hot, dry parkway with cracked soil. The plant is attractive in leaf with aromatic gray-white leaves and stems. Flowers are borne in lavender-blue spikes that appear above the leaves. The spikes persist through winter. A few selections have been made of Russian Sage. Two of them are pale-blue 'Blue Haze', with leaves that have few notches, and 'Blue Spire', which has finely cut leaves and lavender flowers. 'Longin' is narrower with violet flowers.

Bloom Period and Color
July, August to winter blooms in lavender-blue.

Mature Height × Spread
3 to 4 feet × 4 feet

Salvia, Perennial
Salvia × superba

Perennial Salvia is a standard in the perennial garden and the border. It tends to keep its form well without staking, and flowers faithfully almost all summer. Most perennials have short periods of bloom, so plants with extended bloom periods are appreciated. Perennial Salvia is related to the red and blue Annual Salvias, and to the sages including the culinary Sage, S. officinalis. A couple of cultivars of Perennial Salvia are outstanding: 'Mainacht' ('May Night'), which is indigo-blue and was chosen to be Perennial Plant of the Year in 1997, is an older selection, but keeps its neat form throughout the season. 'Oestfriesland' ('East Friesland') is dark violet, dense and compact, and needs no staking. 'Rose Queen' is rose-pink.

Other Names
Violet Sage, Perennial Sage

Bloom Period and Color
June to September blooms in violet-blue, rose-pink.

Mature Height × Spread
2 to 3 feet tall and wide

When, Where, and How to Plant
The Salvias prefer full sun and well-drained soil. Plant container-grown or field-potted Salvias any time during the season. Seedlings are available from garden centers in spring. Prepare the soil by spading to a depth of a foot or so. Space the plants at about 18 inches apart. Set them at the same depth they grew in the containers.

Growing Tips
Water the plants as needed to keep them from wilting. Salvias do well without too much attention. They do well in well-drained and less fertile soils, so avoid over-fertilizing them. Excess care will result in floppy plants with lots of foliage and sparse blooming. Tall plants will need to be staked to keep them from falling over.

Care and Maintenance
Deadheading will prolong the blooming period. If the plants are floppy, cut them back instead of deadheading and they will come back shorter, sturdier, and full of blooms. Old plants become increasingly floppy and develop open centers. Divide them in spring. Lift the clumps and cut out the dead center. Separate the remaining pieces for replanting. Give extras to friends. Salvias are relatively pest-free. Mildew may affect the leaves late in the season. Insects that may appear generally do little damage and require no treatment.

Companion Planting and Design
Taller Salvias can be used as background plants for shorter perennials and annuals. The purples blend well with the warm yellows and oranges. The pinks are more subtle and blend with the purples and with whites. They also make excellent fillers for the perennial garden. They can be planted in naturalized settings, or in rows for fresh cut flowers or for drying. Combine them with orange Butterfly Weed and lavender Butterfly-Bush to attract butterflies to your garden.

Did You Know
Several Sages, native to the U.S., are growing throughout Illinois. Blue Sage (*S. azurea*), and Rocky Mountain Sage (*S. reflexa*) are naturalized here and may be incorporated into gardens. They seem to prefer rocky or sandy sites.

Shasta Daisy

Leucanthemum × superbum

When, Where, and How to Plant

Shasta Daisy is best planted in spring. Containerized plants can be planted at any time. Plant in full sun, though midday shade may be helpful in the southern part of the state. A fertile, moist, well-drained soil is best. Do not plant where water will stand in winter; if necessary, consider raised beds. Shasta Daisies can be naturalized in prairie plantings. Plants are available as divisions, or in pots and 1-, 2-, and 6-gallon cans, sometimes in bloom. Prepare the soil by tilling or spading to a 12-inch depth. Incorporate organic matter and sand to improve structure, and provide drainage if necessary. Dig the holes for containerized plants the same depth and twice as wide as the plant ball. Set divisions at the depth they were growing, spacing the plants 2 feet apart. Water to settle the soil around the roots.

Growing Tips

Shasta Daisies need to be watered in dry weather to continue flowering. Apply a complete fertilizer such as 20-20-20 liquid (Peters, Miracle-Gro, or similar) as growth begins in spring, and every month during the season.

Care and Maintenance

Shasta Daisies do not have many pest problems. Pinch taller cultivars as they grow to improve their branching. Cut the flowers or deadhead to stimulate continuing bloom. In fall, cut down the plants; in Zones 4b and 5, mulch with straw to prevent heaving and cold injury. Divide the clumps every two or three years. Discard the woody center of the clump and replant the perimeter pieces. If growing for cut flowers, do not pinch the stems as they grow; if they are too long to stand up, tie them to stakes. Keep them growing straight up for nice, straight stems. Disbud (remove all side buds) to develop large central flowers. Certain varieties are better suited for cut flowers.

Companion Planting and Design

Daisies are best at the back of the garden due to height.

Did You Know

Shasta Daisies are excellent cut flowers.

Shasta Daisy is what most people envision when they think of a Daisy: neat white petals (ray flowers) and a bright-yellow center. Daisies fit well in the garden. Daisies are excellent cut flowers. The cultivar 'Thomas Killen' is most popular for growing in gardens. Shasta Daisies are available as single or double flowers on plants from 1 foot to about 3 feet tall. They can fit almost anywhere. Not all cultivars of Shasta Daisies are fully hardy throughout Illinois. Some cultivars listed for Illinois conditions are 'Alaska' (with large single flowers) and 'Snowcap' for profuse blooming. 'Thomas Killen' has the long, thick stems which make it good for cutting. 'Esther Read' has fully double flowers, and 'Polaris' has flowers more than 6 inches across.

Bloom Period and Color

June to September blooms in white with yellow centers.

Mature Height × Spread

1 to 3 feet × 6 inches to 18 inches

Speedwell
Veronica sp.

Speedwells are some of the most hardy of garden perennials. They are semi-woody plants that produce spikes of blue flowers most of the summer. The foliage is rich green or, in the case of Woolly Speedwell, woolly-white. The plants are generally orderly and upright, though Hungarian Speedwell tends to fall over. Veronicas are easy to work into the garden because they flower almost all season, and the plants are attractive even when not in bloom. V. spicata, Spike Speedwell, has a good, upright habit and shiny green leaves. Some cultivars are 'Blue Spires', with glossy green leaves and blue flowers; 'Heidekind', 10 inches tall with rose-pink flowers; and 'Icicle', a true white. Woolly Speedwell, V. incana, has woolly leaves and lavender-blue blooms.

Other Name
Veronica

Bloom Period and Color
Summer blooms in white, rosy-pink.

Mature Height × Spread
1 to 3 feet × 1 to 3 feet

When, Where, and How to Plant
Speedwells can be planted in spring or fall. Full sun is best, but these plants will tolerate some light shade. Shaded plants may grow more loosely and tend to flop. Soils should be moderately fertile and well drained. Standing water in winter will kill the crowns. Plant in the front to middle of the border, in masses, in beds, or in the cutting garden. Speedwells are available in pots or 1- to 6-gallon cans, often in bloom. Divisions can be made in spring or fall. Prepare the soil by tilling or spading to a 6-inch depth. Incorporate organic matter for improved condition. If drainage is poor, consider tiles or raised beds. Set the plants at the same depth they were growing in their containers. Dig the holes for containerized plants the same depth and twice as wide as the plant balls.

Growing Tips
Speedwells need water and fertilizer for best flowering. Apply an inch of water per week. Apply a complete fertilizer such as 20-20-20 liquid (Peters, Miracle-Gro, or similar) as growth begins in spring, and every month during the season.

Care and Maintenance
Speedwells have very few pests. Leaf spot diseases may turn lower leaves brown in wet weather. Care consists of watering in dry weather, and deadheading the plants to keep them blooming. Cut the plants down after frost has killed the leaves in fall. Divide the plants in early spring or fall when they become crowded, which will be every three to four years.

Companion Planting and Design
Plant Speedwells anywhere in the garden. They are excellent for edging and among the other perennials. Trailing types can grow over walls on in the rock garden. Plant some in the cutting garden, too.

Did You Know
Taller Speedwells will need support. Newer varieties such as 'Sunny Border Blue', the 1993 Perennial Plant of the Year, are stronger and more compact. They stand up better.

When, Where, and How to Plant

Stonecrop may be planted in spring or fall. Cuttings can be taken and will root easily in summer. Containerized plants are available all season, often in bloom. Plant Stonecrop in full sun in a well-drained, well-prepared soil. They are suitable in borders, as edging, in masses, over rocks, or as groupings of three to five plants. These plants are available potted or in 1-gallon cans. Divisions are available in spring and fall. Prepare the soil by spading or tilling to a depth of 6 inches. Set the plants at the same depth they were growing in their containers. Dig the holes for the containerized plants the same depth and twice as wide as the plant ball.

Growing Tips

After planting, water the plants to settle the soil. Do not water again until the soil is dry. Remember, these plants can be killed by overwatering. Fertilize cautiously. Overfertilized plants will be floppy and subject to root rot.

Care and Maintenance

Once established, a Stonecrop requires almost no attention, and it has no serious insects or diseases. The plants will grow unattended, requiring no watering, fertilizing, pinching, or staking. If weeds invade before the Stonecrop has filled in, remove them. Before new growth begins in spring, remove the dead, overwintering plant tops.

Companion Planting and Design

Most Stonecrop plants are distinct enough to stand on their own. 'Autumn Joy' Sedum is a large plant and is used in borders and in beds. Its flowers blend well with bronze Hardy Mums or golden Coreopsis. Smaller kinds are best in borders or rock gardens where they can be interplanted with spring bulbs. Other low-growing flowers and shrubs such as Creeping Phlox, Sweet Woodruff, or Blue Rug Junipers can be worked into the planting. Some Sedums are excellent in hanging baskets.

Did You Know

The name Sedum is from Latin, "to sit." Stonecrop refers to their seeming ability to grow from stones.

Stonecrop plants are among the easiest garden plants to grow: plant them and forget them. There are many kinds of Stonecrop, all succulents with fleshy leaves. The flowers are tiny and star-shaped and usually grow in masses of showy heads. Many of the Stonecrops are rock garden plants, low-growing and perfectly satisfied with a hard, infertile soil. Some are invasive, but the upright-growing ones are not. They are just about indestructible; the only thing that kills them is too much water. Sedum kamtschaticum grows 9 inches tall, covered with yellow flowers. Two-row Stonecrop, Sedum spurium, has scalloped leaves and grows to about 6 inches tall. It is a ground cover type, used for edging. It has pink to deep red blooms. 'Dragon's Blood' is another popular cultivar.

Other Name
Sedum

Bloom Period and Color
Summer blooms in pink, yellow, red.

Mature Height × Spread
6 inches to 2 feet × 2 feet

Yarrow

Achillea millefolium, A. filipendulina

Yarrow is often overlooked for the perennial garden. It is a very useful plant, with larger kinds that are suited to the middle of the border, and shorter ones that can be used as edging. The flowers are excellent for cutting, lasting well and keeping their color after drying. Yarrow flourishes in poor soil as long as drainage is good. It does best in full sun, but it can be grown in light shade. Yarrow quickly becomes adapted in natural areas. Common Yarrow is a floppy plant, but the hybrids stand up well. The species is better as a naturalized plant, in poor, infertile soils. In fertile soils the plants spread very quickly. 'Appleblossom' has rosy-pink blooms and an open habit and it needs staking.

Other Name
Common Yarrow

Bloom Period and Color
June to September blooms in pink, yellow, lavender.

Mature Height × Spread
1 to 3 feet × 2 to 3 feet

When, Where, and How to Plant

Yarrow may be planted in spring or fall. Plant in full sun in a soil with good drainage. These plants can thrive in tough situations. Use them in the border, in naturalized masses, or in the cutting garden. Plants can be divided in spring or fall. Yarrow is available in pots or 1- and 6-gallon cans, often in bloom. Prepare the soil by tilling or spading to a 6-inch depth. Any decent garden soil is satisfactory. Dig the holes for containerized plants the same depth and twice the width of the plant ball. Set the plants or divisions at the same depth they were growing in their containers. Water thoroughly to firm the soil. Do not water again until the soil dries out.

Growing Tips

Yarrow does not tolerate soggy soils. Water only when the plants are dry. Keeping them too wet will result in weak floppy plants and may cause root rot. These plants do best in poor, infertile soils. Apply fertilizer only if the plants show deficiency symptoms.

Care and Maintenance

Yarrow does not require a lot of care. Taller cultivars or plants growing in partial shade may need to be staked and tied to keep them from falling over. Plants in fertile or moist soils will be larger and weaker. Remove spent blooms to keep the plants flowering. In fall, cut the plants to the ground.

Companion Planting and Design

Yarrow is suited for the border and the cutting garden. The plants tend to fall over and they may need to be supported. They blend well with the blues and lavenders of Salvia and Veronica as well as with the golds of Black-Eyed Susan or Goldenrod.

Did You Know

Yarrows make excellent cut flowers, and if cut before the pollen ripens, can be dried as well. The dried flowers can be used in dried arrangements and will retain their color for years.

Roses *for Illinois*

I received and planted a rosebush when I was still a teenager in Pasadena, California, working for Campbell's Seed Company. It was a 'Chrysler Imperial' and, I think, an AARS (All-America Rose Selection) that year. It was about 1952.

I had no intention of becoming a rosarian. (I had no intention of becoming a horticulturist then either.) I had the plant and had a place to plant it. When that plant began to bloom it piqued my interest, because the only flowers I had ever grown were things like Zinnias and Nasturtiums. This plant actually made a gorgeous, big red flower, and people came to smell and admire it. Eventually my gardening space expanded to include a dozen or so different Roses, including 'Peace'. Not long after that I headed off to college; not as an aspiring musician as I had once planned, but to learn as much as I could about the fascinating world of horticulture. Other factors were involved in this decision, but roses started it all. I still grow Roses and, for a good part of my career, grew them commercially.

Choosing Roses for the Garden

Roses are the most popular flower with gardeners across America, and we are no different in Illinois. We had Roses in our garden when I was a child, and there were Roses in Grandma's garden, too. Ours were not Hybrid Tea Roses, but Shrub Roses with deliciously fragrant double pink flowers that bloomed every June. They were Moss Roses, I suppose, because the stems were covered with moss-like thorns. I can still remember the aroma.

Since the end of World War II, Rose gardeners have embraced the Hybrid Teas as the ultimate Roses. In our part of the country the flowers are beautiful, but getting them through the winter is a hit-or-miss adventure. I have to admit that I made lots of misses. Caring for them requires spraying, fertilizing, watering, pruning, and worrying.

There had to be a better way. The Shrub Roses are an answer. The current popularity of things Victorian means a resurgence of interest in the old-fashioned Roses, including Shrub Roses. They are nearly maintenance free, and most will survive Illinois winters without protection. The newer landscape-type Bush Roses, many of which are from the House of Meilland, are smaller, hardy, and just about trouble free. Simply plant these Roses like any other shrub, get out of the way, and let them grow!

The Bush Roses flower in spring, and some flower throughout the summer. The flowers can be singles or doubles, sometimes cabbage-like. They have a singular beauty. Many are scrumptiously fragrant. I hope there are enough Rose lovers who would be perfectly happy each spring with a cluster of single Roses or Roses the size and shape of cabbages. Maybe Shrub Roses will become respectable, and everyone can grow at least one Rosebush.

For many Rose fanciers, the Bush Roses, in spite of their admirable qualities, just can't compete with the classical roses such as Hybrid Teas, Floribundas, and Grandifloras. Most Rose gardeners persist in growing these admittedly beautiful, but cantankerous, plants. So . . . how do you grow Roses in Illinois?

Planting

Hybrid Tea Roses—and the closely related Floribundas, Grandifloras, and Miniatures—must have full sun and a well-drained soil. Throughout this book we talk about the necessity of good drainage, but for no plant is it more important than for Roses. Without good drainage they simply will not survive the winter. If the soil does not drain, construct raised beds or install drain tiles.

If the soil is a good loam with plenty of organic matter (a good black soil), the Roses can be planted directly in it. If the soil is poor, prepare it by turning it over to at least one spade depth. If you are planning to plant just one or two Roses, spade just the couple of square feet where each plant will be set. Incorporate into the soil organic matter such as compost, peat moss, or whatever you can get your hands on. Shredded leaves, manure, shredded bark, or even corn cobs will work.

Hybrid Tea types are all grafted plants. The flowering part (the scion) is grafted to a root that is a different kind of Rose. The roots are vigorous plants that do not flower. When planting, the scion must be placed so that it is just at or below the soil's surface, so that the graft and part of the scion can be covered for winter. An unprotected scion exposed to the rigors of an Illinois winter will not survive, and the rootstock, ultimately more hardy, will grow instead. Roses of the Hybrid Tea type require continuous care throughout the season.

Watering and Mulching Roses

Water to provide a measured inch a week if nature does not cooperate. Keeping water off the leaves reduces diseases. Drip irrigation or leaky pipe systems will put the water on the ground instead of on the plants.

Mulching reduces the chances of rainstorms splashing water and soilborne diseases onto the leaves. Mulches keep the soil from compacting and reduce surface evaporation. Use leafmold, shredded bark, wood chips, or compost. When I started growing Roses, cracked corncobs were the only mulch, according to most rosarians. Nothing else would work. Of course, there are really many things that will work. Use whatever you can find that stays put and looks attractive. I wouldn't use any of the landscape stones.

Fertilizing Roses

Roses must be fertilized throughout the spring and early summer. Use a complete, balanced fertilizer (such as 10-10-10) three times per season . . . early spring, after the first flush of blooms, and about

mid-July. An alternative is a soluble fertilizer such as Peters or Miracle-Gro. Follow label directions. Do not fertilize after August 1, or the plants might not harden off for winter.

Controlling Rose Pests

Blackspot and mildew, the most serious diseases, can be quite troublesome in rainy weather. Spray with triforine (Funginex) every week as long as the weather is wet.

Insect pests include aphids and mites; insecticidal soap will control both of them. Orthene will control most other insects. Be sure to read and follow the directions on the label.

Pruning Roses

Roses are pruned in early spring, to remove weak and dead stems and to shape the plant. Select two or three strong canes. Cut them back to side buds facing away from the center of the plant, leaving the canes about a foot long. Remove all other canes.

When cutting flowers or deadheading, cut to a "five" (a leaf with five leaflets) near the middle of the stem. Try to leave two "fives" on the remaining stem. The cut should be made $1/4$ inch above the leaf. If you have had trouble with cane borers in your area, dab the cut with a little yellow shellac or white household glue to protect it.

Winter Protection for Roses

Rose plants will lose their leaves in fall when temperatures begin to go below freezing. Cut the canes back to 15 or 18 inches high. When the ground begins to freeze in late fall, cover the bases of the plants with foot-high piles of topsoil from elsewhere in your garden. After the soil freezes, cover the piles of topsoil with another foot of mulch.

A few of the many kinds of Roses are discussed in this chapter, and some cultivars are listed as well. These may have received AARS recognition, or they may have rated very high on the ARS evaluation scales. Since this chapter is only an introduction to the wonderful world of Roses, lots of good Roses are left out. For more information on roses, contact your local Rose Society chapter or the American Rose Society, P. O. Box 30000, Shreveport, LA 71130-0030.

Floribunda Rose
Rosa hybrids

Floribundas are small-flowered Roses that bear clusters of blooms at the ends of their stems. The flower forms are varied, but most are button like with twenty-five to forty petals and typical Rose form. There are some cultivars that have few petals and even a few singles. The plants produce a good display with all the flowers in the clusters blooming about the same time; a plant covered with these clusters is spectacular indeed. There are literally dozens of hybrid Floribundas. 'Iceberg' is a highly rated white and 'Europeana' is a top-rated velvet red. An excellent yellow is 'Sunsprite'. These have all performed well; the 'Europeana', however, does sunburn in the hottest weather, even though it is better than most reds.

Bloom Period and Color
Summer blooms in white, pink, red, orange, yellow, bicolors.

Mature Height × Spread
3 feet × 3 feet

When, Where, and How to Plant
Floribunda Roses are planted in the spring in Illinois—they are too susceptible to winter injury to risk losing them by planting them in fall. Blooming plants are available in containers all season long. Plant dormant bareroot Roses in March. The plants can stand a freeze even if they have started to grow. Any good garden soil will suffice, but it must be well drained. Roses are at their best in full sun. Spade soil to a 12-inch depth. Incorporate organic matter. Drainage is essential. If the garden does not drain, consider constructing raised beds. Dig the planting holes deep enough so that the plants may be set with the graft 1 inch below ground level. Trim off any damaged roots. Form a cone in the bottom of the hole, set the plants at the correct depth, and spread the roots out evenly. Be sure to properly set plants from containers; these plants are often potted too shallowly and will need to be set so that the grafts are at the correct depth. Fill the hole with soil, taking care to firm it around the roots. Water thoroughly to settle the soil.

Growing Tips
Floribunda Roses require a lot of care. Water them when the soil is dry—do not let them wilt. Water early in the day and keep water off the foliage. The major diseases of Roses are severe if the leaves are allowed to be wet overnight.

Care and Maintenance
Deadhead the plants to keep them blooming. To control blackspot disease in wet weather, use Funginex (triforine) according to label directions. Mites and aphids may be troublesome; control them with insecticidal soap.

Companion Planting and Design
Plant in the shrub border, in the perennial garden or in the Rose garden. These small-flowered plants provide an attractive display all season.

Did You Know
Florist corsage Roses are Floribundas. Most Floribundas are excellent cut flowers.

Grandiflora Rose

Rosa hybrids

When, Where, and How to Plant

Plant Grandiflora Roses in the spring. If planted in fall, you risk losing them to winter injury. Plant dormant bareroot Roses in March. The plants can stand a freeze if they have started to grow. Plant in a well-drained garden soil. Spade to a 12-inch depth, incorporating organic matter. Drainage is essential. If the garden does not drain, consider constructing raised beds. Dig the planting holes deep enough so that the plants may be set with the graft 1 inch below ground level. Trim off any damaged roots. Form a cone in the bottom of the hole, set the plants at the correct depth, and spread the roots out. Set plants properly; these plants are often potted too shallowly and need to be set so that the grafts are at the correct depth. Fill the hole with soil, taking care to firm it around the roots. Water thoroughly to settle the soil.

Growing Tips

Grandiflora Roses require a lot of care. Water them when the soil is dry-do not let them wilt. Water early in the day and keep water off the foliage.

Care and Maintenance

Deadhead the plants to keep them blooming. Each spring, prune out dead wood and small weak canes. Leave two or three good sturdy canes, and trim them to an outside bud so they will spread instead of growing to the center of the plants. The major diseases of Roses are severe if the leaves are allowed to be wet overnight. Control blackspot disease in wet weather. Dust or spray with Funginex (triforine) according to label directions. Mites and aphids may be troublesome; control them with insecticidal soap.

Companion Planting and Design

Grandifloras can be planted as specimens in the border or perennial garden, but they are usually best in a rose garden where they can be given the necessary care.

Did You Know

Grandifloras will need to be protected for the winter.

Grandiflora Roses include some of the best hybrids, and they have received many AARS awards. The flower size approaches that of many Hybrid Teas, but the flowers are borne in clusters that all open at about the same time. Grandifloras are better specimens than Floribundas, but they do not put on the mass floral display typical of beds of Floribundas. Grandifloras are the result of crossing Hybrid Tea Roses and Floribundas. The first Grandiflora was 'Queen Elizabeth' in 1955. It is a tall plant, growing very strongly upright with well-shaped pink blooms. It is a one-of-a-kind—there is nothing else quite like it. 'Gold Medal', a medium yellow, is the only other Grandiflora rated higher than 8.5 by the American Rose Society.

Bloom Period and Color
Summer blooms in all colors except blue.

Mature Height × Spread
3 feet × 2 feet

Ground Cover Rose
Rosa hybrids

Ground Cover Roses are hardy, low-growing ramblers. They cover the ground with a thicket of canes dense enough to keep weeds out. These plants can be described as procumbent (they have stems that trail along the ground without rooting). They are much wider than they are high, making them very useful in the landscape. Some older Ground Cover cultivars are 'Max Graf', a hybrid from 1919, and 'Raubritter', a low-mounded plant with pink single flowers in early summer (1936). More recent is 'Ferdy', a taller pink (3 feet tall), spreading at least 6 feet. The most exciting Ground Cover Rose is 'Flower Carpet' Pink. It blooms from spring to fall with pink-and-white flushed flowers in clusters. The plants are 2 feet tall and spread 6 feet or more.

Other Name
Carpet Rose

Bloom Period and Color
Summer blooms in pink, white, red, yellow.

Mature Height × Spread
1 or more feet × 1 to as much as 6 feet

When, Where, and How to Plant
Plant in spring so Ground Cover Roses become established before the onset of winter. Plant containerized plants until the ground freezes up. While these plants are hardy, there is still the risk of damage to plants that are not well rooted. Ground Cover Roses should be in full sun in a well-drained soil. Ground Cover Roses are grown in 5-gallon-sized containers. The hole for planting should be no deeper than the depth of the ball of the plant, and at least twice as wide. Remove the plants from their containers and slice any circling roots. Set the plant in the planting hole and replace half the soil. Fill the hole with water. Replace the remaining soil, and fill the hole with water again. Make a saucer around the plant with any remaining soil. Space the plants at 2 to 4 feet apart.

Growing Tips
Water to provide an inch per week. Fertilize monthly until August 1.

Care and Maintenance
Other than some pruning and watering, these plants require very little care. Don't shear them; head them back. Cut overly long branches to a side branch growing in the same direction, but shorter. Prune in spring before growth starts, or as needed during the season. Ground Cover Roses are low and twiggy and tend to collect trash that blows into them. Rake them out, or have a landscape contractor vacuum them out in spring. Until they are established, the shade produced by these somewhat open plants is not dense enough to keep out weeds. Pull or hoe the weeds. Preemergent herbicides and grass preventers are also helpful.

Companion Planting and Design
Ground Cover Roses are useful as ground covers in beds, in parking lot islands, in office sites, or on banks and slopes in the landscape where mowing is difficult.

Did You Know
These Roses are just becoming popular in this country, but they have been used in Europe for many years. Some European cultivars are being used here now.

Hybrid Tea Rose

Rosa hybrids

When, Where, and How to Plant

Plant in the spring. Plant potted plants all summer, but late planting may not allow them to become established before the onset of bad weather. Hybrid Teas are marginally hardy in Illinois. If winter is unusually severe or very changeable, alternating hot and cold, the plants may be killed. Plant in a well-drained soil. Spade to 12 inches, incorporating organic matter. Drainage is essential. If the garden does not drain well, consider raised beds. Set the plants with the graft 1 inch below ground level. Trim off any damaged roots. Form a cone in the bottom of the hole, set the plants at the correct depth, and spread the roots out. These plants are often potted too shallowly and need to be set so that the grafts are at the correct depth. Fill the hole with soil, taking care to firm it around the roots. Water thoroughly to settle the soil. Space the plants 3 to 4 feet apart.

Growing Tips

Do not let Hybrid Teas wilt, but do not keep the soil continuously soaked either. Water them early in the day, and keep water off the foliage. The major diseases of Roses are severe if the leaves are allowed to be wet overnight.

Care and Maintenance

To increase the numbers of blooms, pinch out the center bud when it is the size of a grain of rice. For large blooms, disbud (remove the side buds) as soon as the buds are big enough to handle. Deadhead the plants to keep them blooming. Dust or spray using Funginex (triforine) to control blackspot disease in wet weather. Control mites and aphids with insecticidal soap.

Companion Planting and Design

Hybrid Tea Roses can be used in the border, perennial garden, cutting garden, or in the Rose garden where they can be given the extra attention they demand.

Did You Know

All American Rose Selections include more Hybrid Teas than any other class.

Hybrid Tea Roses created a sensation when introduced in 1867 by Jean-Baptiste Guillot. 'La France' was produced by crossing a Tea Rose with a Hybrid Perpetual. These were the first large Roses that would bloom all summer on fairly long stems. Prior to that, most Roses bloomed in early summer and sporadically after that. The Hybrid Perpetuals did bloom all summer, but they had shorter stems and their blooming was erratic, not at all predictable. Hybrid Teas can be situated as specimens in a border or planted in a Rose garden. There are hundreds of Hybrid Tea Roses. 'Peace' is a blend, pale yellow petals touched with pink, and an AARS in 1946. 'Touch of Class' is orange-pink. 'Olympiad' and 'Mister Lincoln' are red. The 2002 AARS, 'Love and Peace', is golden yellow edged with pink.

Bloom Period and Color

Summer blooms in red, white, yellow, pink, orange, bicolors.

Mature Height × Spread

4 feet × 3 feet

Miniature Rose
Rosa hybrids

Miniature Roses are not new, but they are enjoying a resurgence in popularity. These little Roses were popular as pot plants in Europe in the early 1800s. Shortly after World War I, a Swiss army medical officer named Roulet spotted a plant growing in a pot on a windowsill in Geneva. He propagated it under the name of 'Rouletii'. The modern Miniatures are the result of the hybridizer Ralph Moore, of Sequoia Nurseries in Visalia, California. 'Peggy T' is a medium red. 'Pacesetter' and 'Snowbride' are white. 'Pink Meillandina' and the yellow 'Rise 'n' Shine' are excellent choices, but 'Jean Kenneally', an apricot blend, rates an ARS 9.7, one of the all-time highest scores. It has classic-form flowers and blooms from June until frost.

Bloom Period and Color
Summer blooms in red, white, yellow, pink, orange, bicolors.

Mature Height × Spread
1 to 2 feet × 1 to 1¹/₂ feet

When, Where, and How to Plant
Most Miniatures are potted for sale. They are best planted in spring when the worst of the cold weather is over. Plant these little Roses in full sun in a well-drained soil. Raised beds work well, allowing the plants to be a little higher and more visible. Miniature Roses can be planted in borders, as edging, as accents, in masses, or in planters or containers. Prepare the soil by tilling or spading. If the drainage is not good, consider constructing raised beds. Miniature Roses are sold as potted plants in bloom, in 4- or 6-inch pots. When planting in beds, set them about 1 to 1¹/₂ feet apart, and only as deep as they were growing in their containers. When planted in planters, flowerboxes, urns, or hanging baskets, they are usually spaced plant-to-plant.

Growing Tips
Water them as needed, early in the day so the foliage dries before nightfall.

Care and Maintenance
Miniatures are beset with the same problems as their larger counterparts. Dusting or spraying will be necessary to control blackspot disease in wet weather. Use Funginex (triforine) according to label directions. Mites and aphids may be troublesome; control them with insecticidal soap. Prune out dead twigs and remove spent blooms as the flowers fade.

Companion Planting and Design
Miniature Roses can be planted in the garden as their larger relatives are. But, they are often lost because of their small size. Plant them in containers around the patio or porch where they can be seen. Then move them indoors for the winter. With adequate light and moderate temperatures, they will bloom all winter. Try growing them under lights if there is no bright spot in your home.

Did You Know
Miniature Roses are often hardier than the larger-flowered types, but they are best protected for the winter. After the ground has begun to freeze, cover the plants with top soil from elsewhere in the garden. Once the soil is frozen, mulch heavily.

Shrub Rose
Rosa hybrids

When, Where, and How to Plant

Shrub Roses are planted in spring, or from containers anytime during the season. They are hardy, but they do need to be established before the onset of severe weather. Plant Shrub Roses as accents, as specimens, in masses, for screens, as hedges, or in the shrub border. These plants need full sun. They will grow in partial shade, but the flowering will suffer. The soil should be fertile, moist, and well drained. Shrub Roses are generally sold in containers; sometimes small plants are sold bareroot. The hole for planting should be shallower than the depth of the ball, and at least twice as wide. Soak bareroot plants for several hours before planting. Space plants of landscape cultivars 3 to 6 feet apart in masses. Larger plants should be spaced 10 to 15 feet apart or farther, and specimen plants should be at least the same distances from any structure. Set each plant in the hole, keeping it slightly higher than it grew in the nursery. Remove the burlap from balled-and-burlapped plants, stuffing it in the hole. Soak the plants thoroughly after planting to settle the soil around the roots.

Growing Tips

Shrub Roses benefit from fertilizer applied in spring, and from water. Apply a complete fertilizer such as 10-10-10, 1 pound per 100 square feet of bed, and an inch of water per week if nature does not cooperate.

Care and Maintenance

Pruning to keep the plants tidy and in bounds is the major maintenance chore with Bush Roses. Remove old or damaged canes in spring. Disease control should not be required; insects that may stumble into the planting can be dealt with if necessary.

Companion Planting and Design

Landscape Shrub Roses can be used the same manner as other landscape shrubs. Species Shrub Roses can be used in the shrub border, as specimens, and in the rose garden.

Did You Know

Fruits of Shrub Roses are edible.

The Shrub Roses are a catchall classification for plants that don't seem to fit anywhere else. They may be large bushes, or they may be tame and easily controlled as are Landscape Roses. Here we tend to classify them as winter-hardy plants that are for all practical purposes disease resistant as well. The Landscape Roses are hybrids that have been bred for use as hedges, borders, or accents. Species Roses and hybrid Shrub Roses are of many forms, and may be either spring-blooming or they may repeat bloom. Landscape Roses are short and well behaved. The first of these to receive wide notice was 'Bonica'. 'The Fairy' and the 'Meidiland' series that includes pink-, white-, and scarlet-flowering types are being planted enthusiastically by landscape contractors. The 2002 AARS 'Starry Night' is pure white—the first Landscape Rose to receive AARS honors.

Bloom Period and Color
Summer blooms in pink, red, white, yellow, orange, bicolor.

Mature Height × Spread
4 feet × 4 to 6 feet

Shrubs *for Illinois*

Shrubs create a transition from the lawn to the home. If the landscape is well designed, shrub plantings point the way to the house's entrance. They identify the boundaries of spaces, the public and the private areas of your property. They provide a windbreak in winter and direct cooling breezes in summer. They can hide undesirable views while accenting desirable ones.

Shrubs provide flowers, attractive summer foliage, and fall color, and some display colorful fruit. The structure and texture of leafless stems provide contrast and interest in the winter landscape. Shrubs attract wildlife. They are refuges for birds, providing secure nesting sites and shelter from storms.

Using Shrubs in the Garden

Shrubs are the most used (and misused) plants in the home landscape. There are many, many kinds of shrubs, but if you drive down a typical street you are likely to see the same ones used over and over again in the same way: a line of evergreens in front of the house and a Christmas tree at the corner. (At the turn of the 19th century the overused shrub arrangement was a line of Vanhouttei Spireas on either side of the entrance walk in front of a porch.)

In this chapter are descriptions of more than two dozen shrub species and many more cultivars. Each of these has a place in a landscape. Some are familiar to almost everyone, while others are less well known. This is just a partial selection of the shrubs that are available.

Planning the Garden

When designing your plantings, try to think of
new things to do with your plants. There's no need
to do the same things your neighbors are doing.
Similar adjacent landscapes may be pleasing, but
variety is more interesting. And it is not necessary
to use evergreens in front of your house. It is true
that evergreens stay green all year, but other plants
have interesting things to offer during all four
seasons. The bare stems of winter will give way to
emerging leaves in spring, flowers in summer, and
colors in fall . . . these changes can be a lot more
interesting than the same old green stuff!

Visit the botanical gardens or arboreta in
your area. Each university maintains plantings, often labeled with plant names. When you try something
new in your garden, the worst thing that can happen is that you will change your mind after you plant
it. If this happens, pull it out and start again. Gardening is not a goal; it is an adventure. The fun is in
the doing.

Considering Shrub Location

Before buying shrubs, draw a plan of your yard, showing the garden and the various areas that are for
public viewing, for privacy, or for utility. Mark the things needing to be hidden, such as a telephone pole,
the neighbor's compost heap, or a church's parking lot.

Plantings in the front of the house should emphasize the entrance. Draw a picture of the front of
your house, marking the main entrance. Then draw lines from the bottom of the entrance, angling to a
point 2/3 of the way up to the corners of the house, and extend these lines to the property lines. All the
plants in front of the house should fit under those lines, smallest at the entrance, largest at the ends. Be
sure your plants will not hide windows.

Decide the sizes of the plants needed in each location in your yard. Then select suitable proper-sized
plants that you would enjoy seeing in your yard. Mix textures, shapes, and colors. Have some fun making
selections. Do a little bit at a time so it doesn't become a chore.

The plants in this chapter are shrubs we have used and enjoyed. We hope this information will get
you started on a fascinating adventure with shrubs that will brighten your Illinois garden.

Alpine Currant
Ribes alpinum

Alpine Currant is a dense, twiggy shrub with light green foliage. Adapted to shaded areas, it makes good hedges and borders. It is useful for formal hedges, as it takes shearing exceptionally well. It thrives in shaded spots, as well as surviving the perils of high-traffic areas. Alpine Currant does well in full sun, too. In the sun, its foliage is more dense and leaf spot problems are lessened. Quite a bit of selection has been done for shorter and more dense plants. Illinois growers have been leaders in this endeavor. Ribes alpinum 'Pumilum' grows to 3 feet. It spreads twice as wide, and produces tiny scarlet berries in early summer. 'Green Mound' is a little smaller, with bright-green color. It is used extensively in the landscape industry.

Bloom Period and Color
April blooms in green, not showy.

Mature Height × Spread
3 to 6 feet × 3 to 6 feet

When, Where, and How to Plant
Balled-and-burlapped Alpine Currant can be planted in spring or fall. Containerized plants can be planted at any time. Plant in sun or in semi-shaded locations. It does well in any good garden soil; acidity does not seem to matter to this adaptable plant. Sometimes small plants are sold bareroot. The hole for planting should be shallower than the depth of the ball and at least twice as wide. Soak bareroot plants for several hours before planting. Remove plants from containers, and slice any circling roots. Space plants 1½ to 2 feet apart in hedges, 5 feet apart in masses. Set each plant in its hole, keeping it slightly higher than it grew in the nursery. Remove the burlap from balled-and-burlapped plants, stuffing it in the hole. Replace the soil and fill the hole with water.

Growing Tips
Currants will need regular watering their first year after planting.

Care and Maintenance
Alpine Currant can be sheared to fit nearly any location. Shear in spring after the first flush of new growth. Trim hedges wider at the bottom than at the top; vase-shaped hedges soon lose their lower leaves, ending up with leaves only at the tops of the plants. Leaf spot disease can be troublesome during wet weather. Control with maneb or mancozeb, applied as leaves emerge in spring. Almost all *Ribes* species are alternate hosts of white pine blister rust. This is a serious disease of White Pines, often killing them one branch at a time. If there are large plantings of White Pine in your county, check with the state forester to see if Alpine Currant is safe to plant.

Companion Planting and Design
Alpine Currants are especially adapted to shade gardens. Use them as a backdrops for other shade plants or use smaller cultivars as accents. They complement the brighter colors of Coleus, Caladiums, or Tuberous Begonias.

Did You Know
Clove Currant (*R. odoratum*) with yellow, clove-scented flowers is native to Illinois.

Arborvitae
Thuja occidentalis

When, Where, and How to Plant

Plant Arborvitae in spring or fall. Plant containers any time during the season. In heavy shade, a plant will lose its needles, and its crown will be quite thin and open. Soil should be deep, moist, and well-drained. In the wild, these plants can tolerate soils that are either too wet or too dry, but the quality of the plant suffers. Most of the dissatisfaction with Arborvitae comes from buying plants of unknown origin, only to discover that the cultivar is not hardy, or from buying plants grown in a soil different from that into which they are planted. Buy plants selected for local conditions and grown in local soils. Arborvitaes are grown as balled-and-burlapped plants and in containers. The hole for planting should be no greater than the depth of the ball of the plant, and at least twice as wide. Remove the burlap from a balled-and-burlapped plant, and stuff it down in the hole. Replace the soil, and fill the hole with water.

Growing Tips

It is essential that these plants receive adequate water. If they dry out, their needles will drop.

Care and Maintenance

Trim the plants after the first flush of new growth has hardened off in late spring. Pruning can be severe if necessary, but do not cut into the "dead" zone in the middle of the plant. Twigs with no needles will not grow again. Keep the plants wider at the bottom than at the top. Mites can be troublesome in hot weather. Treat with insecticidal soap. Bagworms can strip trees in a short time. Control them with *Bacillus thuringiensis kurstaki*, following the directions.

Companion Planting and Design

Use in shade or sun for excellent screening or mix clusters of Arborvitaes with deciduous shrubs for a more interesting planting. Use smaller kinds as foundation plantings, but give them room to grow.

Did You Know

Arborvitae literally means tree (Arbor) of life (vitae).

Arborvitae is a native woodland evergreen tree that grows among deciduous trees such as Ash and White Pine in Illinois, and among Oaks in Michigan. It grows as an understory tree in fairly dense shade, often in wet areas. In the landscape it can be grown as a specimen or accent, foundation plant, windbreak, living fence, or screen. Arborvitae is an excellent hedge plant, and will take shearing. These plants are used for screening; as they are evergreen, they work well during all seasons. Properly located, they are effective for many years, and with judicious trimming can be kept attractive and within bounds indefinitely. There are many cultivars of Arborvitae, with differing forms, sizes, and colors; they differ in winter hardiness as well.

Other Name
Arbor Vitae

Bloom Period and Color
Evergreen foliage.

Mature Height × Spread
20 feet × 6 feet wide

Barberry

Berberis sp.

Barberries comprise a large group of landscape plants that are all thorny and make good barriers. Barberries are tough plants. Growing best in full sun, they can stand drought better than most ornamental plants. They are not affected by the pollution and grime of the city. All take shearing without difficulty. Barberries will not tolerate wet sites. Barberries have attractive red berries that may persist well into the fall. Some cultivars have green foliage, but the red kinds seem to be the most popular. The most commonly grown selections are those of Japanese Barberry, Berberis thunbergii. Many are varieties of B. thunbergii 'Atropurpurea', the Red Barberry, and they come in all sizes. 'Crimson Pygmy' is one of the best, 2 feet tall and wide.

Bloom Period and Color
Spring blooms in yellow, not showy.

Mature Height × Spread
1^1/2 to 6 feet × 3 to 12 feet

When, Where, and How to Plant
Barberries are grown mostly in containers. Larger sizes are balled and burlapped. They can be planted any time the soil can be worked. Plant as specimens, in masses, in groupings, or as barriers or hedges. Any garden soil will suffice for Barberries. Dig the planting hole the same depth and twice as wide as the plant ball. Space the standard cultivars 4 feet apart, dwarf cultivars 1^1/2 feet apart. In hedges, set them plant to plant. Hedges can be planted by opening a trench, setting the plants at the right spacing, and backfilling all of them at the same time.

Growing Tips
Newly planted Barberries benefit from an inch of water per week the first year. After that they seldom need watering. Fertilize young shrubs in early spring before they begin growing. Large established plants do not need regular fertilizing unless they show obvious signs of malnutrition.

Care and Maintenance
Barberry does not require a lot of care. Shearing of hedges is best done after early growth has hardened off in late spring. Few insects or diseases affect it, though verticillium wilt, a soil-borne disease, can kill these plants. If the disease is introduced into the planting on soil or other plants, it will often kill one plant and then work its way down a hedge, for instance, killing a plant at a time on either side. There is no cure for this disease. Remove the plants, and replant the hedge with a resistant variety.

Companion Planting and Design
Barberries are most commonly used as hedges, and are sheared to shape. These plants can be used as specimens or in groupings or masses.

Did You Know
While Barberries are most often trimmed by shearing, the specimen plants look best if hand trimmed. Don't mind the thorns; they point up instead of down as on Roses, so they do not grab your clothing. Wear gloves and long sleeves. Remove dead twigs and overly long branches.

Boxwood

Buxus microphylla koreana × B. sempervirens

When, Where, and How to Plant

Plant Boxwood in spring or fall. In either case, some protection will be needed from sun and wind until the plants are established. Plant in a well-prepared soil. The plants are tolerant of soil type, but a cool, moist soil is best. Good drainage is important; they cannot stand in water. Boxwoods are nearly always sold as balled-and-burlapped plants. Prepare the soil by tilling or spading to a 6-inch depth, and incorporate organic matter. Dig the planting hole the same depth and twice as wide as the plant ball. If the soil in the ball is much different from that in the hole, mix some soil from the ball with that going back into the hole to avoid an interface problem. A couple of inches of mulch will help maintain soil moisture and coolness. It is best to buy plants grown on a soil as nearly like that in your yard as you can find. Locally grown plants are best. Soak the plants well after planting.

Growing Tips

During the first season, Boxwood needs to be watered during dry spells.

Care and Maintenance

Boxwood will need protection from midday sun and from drying winds in summer and especially in winter. During winter, a temporary burlap screen will work fine. Drive stakes around the south and west sides and tack the burlap to them. Several insects and diseases can damage Boxwood, though most of these are minor problems. Poorly drained soil will result in root rot and affected plants will die. If the plants are growing in a hedge, the plants nearest a downspout will be the first to turn yellow; redirect the downspout.

Companion Planting and Design

Use these adaptable evergreen plants for sheared hedges, but don't neglect their value as specimens or in clumps for accents.

Did You Know

Extensive plantings of 'Wintergreen' Boxwood at the Chicago Botanic Garden in Glencoe survived even the severe winters of 1995-96.

Boxwoods have been part of gardening in America since colonial times. Most are Common Box, which will reach a height of 20 feet. Boxwoods have evergreen foliage and a neat form. Even when allowed to grow without trimming, these plants maintain good form. They are usually severely trimmed into hedges in formal gardens, knot gardens, and foundation plantings. Common Box is not hardy in Illinois. The Korean Box, B. microphylla koreana, has been crossed with Common Box, and the result is a series of hardy evergreen Boxwoods that can stand the Northern winters. They are delightful little plants. They stay small without shearing, but they take shearing very well. The color is bright green, and some of them hold their color into winter.

Other Name
Korean Box

Bloom Period and Color
Evergreen foliage.

Mature Height × Spread
4 feet × 4 feet

Burning Bush

Euonymus alatus

Burning Bush is an adaptable plant attractive in all seasons. It is especially known for its brilliant red fall color. After the leaves drop, the corky winged stems provide interesting texture all winter. In winter, the "wings" hold snow that falls on them, but the stout branches are strong enough to avoid being broken down by the weight. Burning Bushes can be used as specimen plants, in groups, and as sheared hedges. They are excellent foundation plants due to their horizontal branching, clean crisp foliage and interesting stems. Burning Bushes are members of the diverse Euonymus family and are some of the best of the landscape plants available today. Fall color may be diminished in plantings that get too little light. They tolerate nearly any situation except soggy soils.

Other Name
Winged Euonymus

Bloom Period and Color
Green, in April or May. Flowers inconspicuous.

Mature Height × Spread
15 to 20 × 15 to 20 feet. Dwarf forms are half as large.

When, Where, and How to Plant
Tolerant of shade, these plants are at their best in full sun. They do well in almost any soil, heavy or light, acid or alkaline, but don't like wet feet. They do well in hot, dry situations as long as they are watered during extended dry periods. Use in shrub beds, foundation plantings, as screening, or as hedges. Burning Bush plants are grown in 5-gallon-sized containers, and as balled-and-burlapped plants. The hole for planting should be no deeper than the depth of the ball of the plant, and at least twice as wide. Remove the plants from containers, and slice any circling roots. Prepare the soil by spading or tilling to a 12-inch depth, incorporating organic matter if possible. Space the plants 5 to 6 feet apart in beds or screening, and 2 feet apart in sheared hedges.

Growing Tips
New plantings need watering in dry weather. These plants need little care once well established. Avoid overfertilization with nitrogen—it diminishes fall color, and may increase the incidence of winter injury.

Care and Maintenance
Prune to maintain the shape and size in spring before growth begins. Hedges should be trimmed to size before growth begins, and can be sheared during the season, leaving at least half of the new growth on the plant. While Burning Bushes are not attacked by Euonymous scale, they are susceptible to oystershell scale and scurfy scale, which are capable of killing stems or entire plants. Treat in May with summer grade insecticidal oil.

Companion Planting and Design
These plants are so distinctive that they do not blend well with other plants. Use them as specimens, in groupings, in borders, for screening, or as hedges. Set them where their spectacular fall color can be appreciated.

Did You Know
Dwarf Burning Bush, *Euonymus alatus* 'Compactus' grows half the size of the species. 'Nordine' is 6 to 8 feet tall and wide, more winter-hardy, and has attractive fruit.

Butterfly-Bush
Buddleia davidii

When, Where, and How to Plant

Best planted in spring before growth begins, containerized plants can be planted out in early summer, but leave sufficient time for them to become well established before winter. Plant in full sun in a well-drained soil. Dig the planting holes the same depth and twice as wide as the root ball. Remove plant from container and shake off as much of the potting soil as you can without damaging the roots. Mix with the soil from the hole. Set the plant at the same depth it grew in the container, fill the hole with the mixed soil, and water thoroughly.

Growing Tips

Do not be too quick to dig out plants that die to the ground in winter. Cut the stems back to about 6 inches from the ground. By June, the plants will sprout from the bases. Watering will be necessary the first year, especially if the plant was grown in an artificial soil. Keep the soil moist but not wet. Fertilize in spring after growth begins, using a complete garden fertilizer.

Care and Maintenance

As blooms begin to fade, clip them off to a lower side shoot. The plants will continue to produce smaller blooms until frost. Leave the old plants standing all winter. If the weather is mild, they may not be killed back. Butterfly-Bush is not long-lived in the garden, although I have seen plants that are fifteen years old in some surprising places. Expect them to live five or six years before they begin to get ragged. In spite of their special needs, they are such good additions to the garden that they are worth the extra effort.

Companion Planting and Design

Use in the shrub or perennial border, in the cutting garden, or in masses to attract butterflies. This is not a plant for foundation plantings.

Did You Know

There are many cultivars of these special plants. The 'Nanho' series, available in various colors, is more compact and more floriferous than the species.

Butterfly-Bush is aptly named as it is one of the best for attracting butterflies to your garden. The 6-to-8-inch long panicles of blooms are delightfully fragrant and last all summer if old blooms are clipped off. The plant is loosely arching with blue-green leaves, making a nice contrast to the normal greens of the shrub border. In milder climes the plant overwinters well, attaining its full size. In the colder zones it may be killed down to the snow line in winter. But do not dismay. You will be surprised how fast it grows back, growing vigorously, like a herbaceous perennial, and flowering prolifically by early summer.

Other Name

Summer Lilac

Bloom Period and Color

July until frost. Lilac, purple, white, pink.

Mature Height × Spread

6 to 8 feet × 6 to 8 feet

Cotoneaster

Cotoneaster sp.

Cotoneasters are among the more attractive shrubs, with their glossy foliage and red fruits. They are large plants and need plenty of room. Some types are upright and suited for hedging or screening. Cotoneasters tolerate pruning well. With judicious pruning, spreading types can be kept in bounds and present a nice appearance. Hedge Cotoneaster and Peking Cotoneaster, both high-quality hedges, can be sheared. Cotoneasters have vigorous fibrous root systems, transplant easily, and will grow in almost any kind of soil. Cotoneaster divaricatus, Spreading Cotoneaster, is an arching shrub reaching about 6 feet tall and wide. It has tiny leaves and its flowers are rose-colored in spring, partially hidden by the leaves. Bright-red fruit in fall persists until the leaves turn red and yellow before dropping.

Bloom Period and Color
Spring blooms in pink, white, rose.

Mature Height × Spread
6 to 12 feet × 6 to 12 feet

When, Where, and How to Plant
Cotoneasters are planted in either spring or fall. Tolerant of some shade, these plants are at their best in full sun. They do well in almost any soil, but they don't like wet feet. Use in shrub beds or foundation plantings, or as screening or hedges. Cotoneaster plants are grown in quart- to 5-gallon-sized containers or as balled-and-burlapped plants. The hole for planting should be no deeper than the depth of the ball of the plant, and at least twice as wide. Remove the plants from their containers and slice any circling roots. Prepare the soil by spading or tilling to a 12-inch depth, incorporating organic matter if possible. Space the plants 5 to 6 feet apart in beds or screening, 2 feet apart in hedges. If planted too close together, they will need excessive pruning.

Growing Tips
Cotoneaster plants do well in hot, dry situations as long as they are watered during extended dry periods.

Care and Maintenance
These plants require very little care. Don't shear the spreading types; head them back. Cut overly long branches to a side branch growing in the same direction, but shorter. Prune in spring before growth starts, or as needed. Shear hedge types after the new growth has hardened off in late spring. The shade produced by these somewhat-open plants is not dense enough to keep out weeds. Pull or hoe when necessary. Preemergent herbicides and grass preventers are helpful. Cotoneasters are susceptible to attack by leaf-roller caterpillars, webworms, mites, and fire blight disease. Control the insects with *Bacillus thuringensis*, control mites with insecticidal soap, and control fire blight with Phyton 27 copper sulfate. Follow label directions carefully.

Companion Planting and Design
The low-growing Cotoneasters are good replacements for the overused Junipers or Yews in foundation plantings.

Did You Know
The name Cotoneaster has nothing to do with the fabric or Resurrection Sunday. It comes from the Greek *ketonen*, "quince," and *aster* meaning "similar."

Dogwood
Cornus sp.

When, Where, and How to Plant

Plant Dogwoods in spring or fall. Plant containers at any time. Plant in full to filtered sun in the shrub border, for screening, as hedges, in foundation plantings, in naturalized areas, or in masses. Dogwoods are tolerant of many conditions. Soils should be well drained, but moist. Dogwoods are available balled and burlapped or in containers; sometimes small plants are sold bareroot. The hole for planting should be shallower than the depth of the ball, and at least twice as wide. Soak bareroot plants for several hours before planting. Space plants of the smaller cultivars 2 feet apart in hedges, 5 feet apart in masses. Space larger plants 10 to 15 feet apart. Set each plant slightly higher than it grew in the nursery. Remove the burlap from balled-and-burlapped plants, stuffing it in the hole. Plant hedges by opening a trench, setting the plants at a 2-foot spacing, and backfilling all at the same time.

Growing Tips

Dogwoods will need to be watered during dry spells their first season after planting.

Care and Maintenance

Shrubby types with colored stems should be renewed annually by cutting one-third of the stems to the ground; the new shoots will exhibit brighter color for the next two or three winters. If the plants become overgrown without proper pruning, cut them down completely. They will regrow in two seasons. The shrubby Dogwoods are susceptible to cankering, which kills a branch at a time from the bottom. Scale can be serious as well. Cankering affects only older branches and can be reduced by systematically renewing the plants annually. The removal of the branches eliminates scale at the same time.

Companion Planting and Design

Use shrubby-type Dogwoods as foundation plantings or informal hedges, larger types in shrub borders or masses, and treelike forms, such as Pagoda as specimens.

Did You Know

Flowering Dogwood is described in the tree section of this book.

Dogwoods are among our best woody ornamentals. They are four-season plants with something of interest to see at any time of the year. Their flowers are usually tiny but are often present in such numbers as to be highly effective. Cornelian Cherry is covered netlike with yellow flowers before the leaves appear in spring. Foliage in this genus is usually bright green, but some types have variegated foliage. Fruits are berrylike—red, white, or black. The fruit is readily eaten by birds, but pink fruit stalks of some species persist all winter. Fall color is brilliant red on most; twigs of some are bright yellow or red all winter. Red-twig and Yellow-twig Dogwoods are adapted to moist soils and will naturalize in wetland settings.

Bloom Period and Color
Spring blooms in white or yellow.

Mature Height × Spread
6 to 20 feet × 6 to 20 feet

Forsythia

Forsythia sp.

Forsythias are gracefully arching or upright plants covered with masses of bright-yellow blooms along their stems in early spring. This is the reason we grow these delightful plants. Forsythia blooms are our first reminder that spring is on the way after the long, dreary Illinois winter. Standard Forsythias are large plants. Dwarf types are shorter, but they do spread and need room. Some of Forsythia's popularity is due to the ease with which it can be grown. It tolerates almost any soil, and is unaffected by urban conditions. If properly selected for the conditions and placed where it has room enough to grow, it can be planted, and, with minimal care, forgotten, blooming happily year after year. Plant only cultivars with known flowerbud hardiness.

Bloom Period and Color
Spring blooms in yellow.

Mature Height × Spread
3 to 9 feet × 4 to 6 feet

When, Where, and How to Plant

Plant Forsythias in spring or fall. Plant containers anytime during the season. Plant in full sun for best blooming, allowing plenty of room for the plants to spread out. Many Forsythias are planted in such cramped quarters that they must be pruned yearly to fit, resulting in mutilated plants and poor flowering. Any well-drained garden soil will suffice. Forsythias are available balled-and-burlapped or in containers, and sometimes small plants are sold bareroot. In spring, garden centers are full of them in bloom. The hole for planting should be shallower than the depth of the ball and at least twice as wide. Soak bareroot plants for several hours before planting. Space plants of smaller cultivars 6 feet apart in masses, and larger plants such as Border Forsythia or Weeping Forsythia 10 to 15 feet apart. Set each plant slightly higher than it grew in the nursery. Soak the plants thoroughly after planting to settle the soil around the roots.

Growing Tips

New plants need about an inch of water per week. Fertilizer generally is not needed unless plants show obvious nutrient deficiencies.

Care and Maintenance

Forsythias are essentially pest-free, but yearly pruning to renew the plants is important. Flowers are produced on one-year-old stems; buds for the next year are set soon after flowering. If you prune after the buds are set, you will remove the flowers for the next spring. Immediately following flowering, remove $1/4$ to $1/3$ of the oldest branches all the way to the ground. This will stimulate new stems from the bases of the plants. If the plants get out of hand, they may be cut to 6 inches above the ground and will regrow in about three years. In either case, flowering will not be interrupted.

Companion Planting and Design

Plant these shrubs where they will not need trimming to keep them in bounds. Trimming can remove the flower buds, eliminating flowers the next spring.

Did You Know

For early indoor blooms, cut a few stems after midwinter to force.

Fragrant Sumac

Rhus aromatica

When, Where, and How to Plant

Fragrant Sumac can be planted either in spring or fall. Containerized plants can be planted at any time. Sumac is tolerant of soils and locations. Plant it in sun or shade; it is one of the few plants that will grow in full shade. Use it for masses, shrub borders, or screening. Fragrant Sumac plants are sold balled and burlapped or in containers, and sometimes small plants are sold bareroot. The hole for planting should be the same depth as the plant ball, and at least twice as wide. Soak bareroot plants for several hours before planting. Remove plants from containers and slice any circling roots. Space the plants 5 feet apart. Set each plant in its hole, keeping it at the same height it grew in the nursery. Remove the burlap from balled-and-burlapped plants, stuffing it in the hole. Replace the soil and fill the hole with water.

Growing Tips

Sumac may need watering during its first season. Apply a measured inch per week if rain does not fall. Fertilizer is generally unneeded unless plants show obvious nutrient deficiencies. Fertilized too vigorously, plants will be rank, with diminished fall color.

Care and Maintenance

Sumac is relatively trouble-free, though leaf spot diseases may be troublesome in wet seasons. Hot dry seasons may result in mite infestations. Generally these problems do not require treatment. Fragrant Sumac is a loosely branched plant and may become overgrown and straggly. If so, it can be cut down to the ground and will regrow.

Companion Planting and Design

Fragrant Sumac is well suited to massing and to naturalized landscapes. The plants require little care. Fall color can be quite nice, especially on plants in full sun.

Did You Know

At 2 to 3 feet, 'Gro-Low' is the lowest-growing of the Fragrant Sumac selections. 'Green Globe' is larger, 6 feet tall and wide. It can be sheared to any height, but since it is naturally tall, it will be a continuous chore to keep it in bounds.

Fragrant Sumac is an excellent plant for naturalized or wooded areas, shrub borders, screens, or roadsides. The tiny-but-lovely yellow flowers produced before the leaves emerge on many plants are certainly welcome after the dark, dreary Illinois winter. The foliage appears in mid-spring and turns crimson in fall. It grows best in dry, poor soils. This makes it well suited for use in the damaged soils common in new developments. It thrives in urban conditions with the grime and pollution, so it is useful in inner-city locations. Where the stems touch the ground, the branches take root, which makes it unusually good at stabilizing damaged banks and slopes. An aroma is emitted when leaves or stems are crushed.

Bloom Period and Color

Spring blooms in yellow.

Mature Height × Spread

6 feet × 6 to 10 feet

Holly
Ilex sp.

Hollies will grow in Illinois; they won't all look like Christmas Holly, but they usually have bright, red berries (drupes). Only female plants have drupes, so there must be a male pollen-plant in your planting and you must have at least two plants for the colorful berries. Male cultivars are listed separately from the female, drupe-producing cultivars. Red drupes develop in late summer while the leaves are still green. Ilex verticillata, or Winterberry, is a deciduous Holly that keeps its leaves well into the fall. Two male cultivars are 'Southern Gentleman' and 'Jim Dandy'. Among the female plants are 'Red Sprite', 'Harvest Red', and 'Winter Red'. American Holly, Ilex opaca, will grow throughout Illinois in protected spots, and if allowed, will grow into a large tree.

Bloom Period and Color
Late spring blooms in white.

Mature Height × Spread
9 to 18 feet × 4 to 9 feet

When, Where, and How to Plant
Plant in a protected, semi-shaded area that is safe from the wind. Evergreen American Holly in particular needs to be in a protected location for the winter. Soils for Hollies need to be moist and well drained. Hollies tolerate alkalinity, but they will be chlorotic (yellow) in soils that have a high pH. An organic soil is best; it holds moisture without excluding air. Winterberry will withstand wet soils, while American Holly will not. Transplant balled-and-burlapped or containerized plants in the spring. The soil should be a good garden loam and it must have adequate drainage. Dig the planting hole the same depth and twice as wide as the plant ball, and set the plant at the same depth it was grown at the nursery. If planting a container-grown plant, mix some of the soil in the container with the soil that goes back into the planting hole. This will create a gradual change from one soil to another, preventing a soil interface problem.

Growing Tips
It is most important to give Hollies winter protection and adequate water during dry periods.

Care and Maintenance
Hollies resent pruning until they have been established for several years; then they will stand some shearing. American Holly cannot stand winter wind. Plant the Holly in a sheltered location or install protection such as a burlap screen to stop the wind. Except for requiring this kind of care, Hollies thrive on neglect. Once it is established, American Holly can be cut or sheared to keep it adequately small. Prune in the fall to collect berry-laden stems. This will help keep the plants in shape and at a manageable size.

Companion Planting and Design
The spectacular red fruit of Winterberry is best set off in front of evergreens such as Spreading Yews.

Did You Know
American Holly is the Holly of winter holidays. Cut some foliage and berries for holiday decorations.

Honeysuckle

Lonicera sp.

When, Where, and How to Plant

Honeysuckle can be planted anytime plants are available: spring, summer, or fall. Plant in sun or partial shade in any soil that drains well. Use in shrub borders, masses, or screens. Dwarf types are suitable for hedging. Honeysuckle plants are available in containers, balled and burlapped, or bareroot. Dig the planting holes the same depth and twice as wide as the plant balls and set the plants the same depth they were growing in their containers. Soak bareroot plants for 12 hours before planting them. Hedges may be planted by digging a trench, setting the plants at the right spacing, and backfilling the trench. This is a great labor-saving system. Space large plants 10 feet apart. Dwarf plants can be set 3 to 4 feet apart, or 2 feet apart in hedges.

Growing Tips

New plants need about an inch of water per week. Established plants are drought-tolerant. Fertilizer is generally unneeded unless plants show obvious nutrient deficiencies. Fertilized too vigorously, plants will be rank and weak.

Care and Maintenance

Honeysuckles should be renewed after flowering to remove 1/4 to 1/3 of the branches to the ground. Head back overly long branches to a shorter side shoot growing the same direction. Hedges may be sheared after new growth hardens off in spring, about the end of June. Overgrown plants should be renovated by cutting them all the way to the ground in midwinter. They will regrow in two to three years, full to the ground.

Companion Planting and Design

Honeysuckles can be used as screening, in the shrub border, or as masses; use the dwarf forms for hedges, either formal or informal.

Did You Know

Honeysuckle aphid has reduced the value of Honeysuckles. It seems to have hopped off a plane at O'Hare Field and settled on the first Honeysuckle it found. Tartarian Honeysuckle, and the dwarf types 'Clavey's Dwarf', 'Hedge King', and 'Emerald Globe' are aphid-resistant.

Honeysuckles are the workhorses of the landscape industry. The main advantages are that they have fragrant flowers in early summer, and they can take mistreatment and keep right on growing. Honeysuckle never looks really good. It is stemmy, and its foliage is dull. Its flowers last only a short time. But these plants can be stuck in the ground and forgotten. They never look great, but they don't die. They can be sheared to death, but they always come back with new shoots. When they get overgrown and straggly, cut them to the ground. They'll come back better than ever. Honeysuckles are still extremely popular and useful plants, especially in newly developed sites and other tough situations. They fulfill an important function in the landscape.

Bloom Period and Color
Spring blooms in white, pink, yellow.

Mature Height × Spread
3 to 10 feet × 3 to 10 feet

Hydrangea
Hydrangea sp.

Hydrangeas are grown for their massive clusters of flowers produced in summer when few other shrubs are in bloom. *Smooth Hydrangea,* H. arborescens, *is the Snowball Bush of early summer. It grows to a height of about 5 feet, spreads, and will sucker if allowed to do so. These are specialty plants. Often they are killed to the ground by winter cold, but their flowers are borne on current-season wood. Panicle Hydrangea,* H. paniculata, *is a large plant. It produces pyramids of white blooms that change to pink, rose, and brown and persist all winter. The flowers make this plant worthwhile, but it must be planted where it has room, and it must be kept under control. Hydrangea arborescens, 'Annabelle', has extra-large heads, sometimes a foot in diameter.*

Other Name
Snowball Bush

Bloom Period and Color
Summer into fall blooms in white.

Mature Height × Spread
6 to 15 feet × 6 to 15 feet

When, Where, and How to Plant
Hydrangeas may be planted in spring or fall. Spring planting will allow a full season of growth before freeze-up, and may be advantageous where the plants are killed to the ground in winter. These plants prefer a well-drained, loamy, moist soil and are partial to full sun. Hydrangeas are available balled and burlapped or in containers. Dig the hole for planting the same depth and twice as wide as the plant ball. Roots are fibrous and transplant well. If the soil in the container is one of the soilless mixes or is much different from the soil from the planting hole, shave some from the ball and mix it with the soil going back into the hole. This will prevent any interface problems. (See the section on soils in the introductory chapter for futher explanation.)

Growing Tips
The plants will need watering during dry spells the first season after planting. For best flower production, plan to water the plants thoroughly any summer when the weather is dry.

Care and Maintenance
Hydrangeas are messy plants—remove the spent blooms when they have faded. The plants need severe pruning in winter or early spring. If not winter-killed, these plants are best cut to the ground in spring. This will keep them tidy and symmetrical, and flowering is enhanced if all of the stems are fresh each spring. Cut Smooth Hydrangea to the ground; Panicle Hydrangea should be pruned hard to remove weak stems and reduce the number to about a dozen or so main stems. These stems will produce uniformly large clusters of blooms. Remove the blooms before they turn brown and ugly.

Companion Planting and Design
Hydrangeas are planted as specimens, in masses, or incorporated into the shrub border. They are excellent for cutting.

Did You Know
The pink and blue Hydrangeas such as 'Nikko Blue' will grow throughout Illinois, but are killed to the ground most winters, eliminating the flower buds which are produced the previous year.

Juneberry
Amelanchier sp.

When, Where, and How to Plant

Juneberries may be planted in spring or fall. Containerized plants may be planted at any time. They can be planted in slight shade or full sun. They prefer a rich, woodland soil, but any good garden soil with adequate drainage and organic matter will suffice. Use in naturalized plantings, shrub borders, foundation plantings, or near water features. Transplant plants that are balled and burlapped or from containers in spring. Try to buy plants grown in a soil as much like that in your garden as you can find. The soil should be a good forest soil or garden loam, and it must have adequate drainage. Dig the planting hole the same depth and twice as wide as the plant ball. Set the plant at the same depth it was grown at the nursery. If planting a container-grown plant, mix some of the soil in the container with the soil that will back into the planting hole. This will create a gradual change from one soil to another and will prevent an interface problem. (See the soils section in the introductory chapter for further explanation.)

Growing Tips

Provide an inch of water per week during extended dry weather. Fertilizer is generally unneeded unless plants show obvious nutrient deficiencies. Fertilized too vigorously, plants will be rank and weak.

Care and Maintenance

Juneberries are nearly maintenance-free. They don't need pruning if allowed to assume their normal branched shape. Once established, these plants need very little care. These are relatively clean plants. Some diseases will occur in unusually wet weather. The plants are related to Crabapples. Insects are seldom troublesome.

Companion Planting and Design

Juneberries are woodland plants and do well in naturalized settings. Use them where their flowers can be enjoyed.

Did You Know

Few gardeners know about the delicious purple, berry-like Juneberry fruit. They make excellent pies. Birds feast on them. In fact, if you are late in getting to them, the birds will harvest them for you.

Juneberries are native woodland plants. The plant is delicate in spring, has pleasant gray-green foliage, orange to rusty-red fall color, and smooth red-gray bark in winter. Juneberry is an attractive plant at all seasons. It can be trimmed into tree form, but it is generally grown as a multi-stemmed shrub, as it is much more interesting and easier to handle in that form. Many selections and crosses of Amelanchier have been made for improved flowering and winter hardiness. The taxonomy of these plants is confused. Usually the cultivar names are correct, but the species may not actually be as labeled. Many of the Amelanchier cultivars sold in Illinois are actually A. × grandiflora selections. 'Autumn Brilliance', 'Cole's Select', and 'Forest Prince' are three cultivars worth trying.

Other Name
Serviceberry

Bloom Period and Color
Spring blooms in white.

Mature Height × Spread
15 to 20 feet × 6 to 10 feet

Juniper

Juniperus sp.

Junipers are members of a large family of evergreens that come in all growth types: trees, ground covers, and shrubs. The low-growing Junipers are discussed in the chapter on ground covers. The shrub types are widely planted as foundation plantings and in shrub borders. These are some of the toughest evergreen landscape plants, as long as they are growing in enough light. In shade they become thin and decline to a point at which they are no longer attractive. Shrub-type Junipers vary in size and texture. They tolerate almost any well-drained soil; some will grow in sand and endure droughty soils. They seem unaffected by soil pH. We have seen them growing nicely where the soil pH is near 8.0. Some will stand salt from snow removal.

Bloom Period and Color
Evergreen foliage.

Mature Height × Spread
5 to 20 feet × spreading 5 to 10 feet or more

When, Where, and How to Plant

Junipers can be planted at any time from containers. Balled-and-burlapped plants are available in spring and fall. Plant Junipers in full sun on a well-drained site. Junipers are grown in 1- to 5-gallon-sized containers, and as balled-and-burlapped plants. The hole for planting should be no deeper than the depth of the ball of the plant, and at least twice as wide. Remove the plants from their containers, and slice any circling roots. Set the plant in the planting hole and replace half the soil. Fill the hole with water. Be sure to remove the burlap from a balled-and-burlapped plant, and stuff it down in the hole. Replace the remaining soil and fill the hole with water again. Make a saucer around the plant with any more remaining soil. Space the plants 5 feet or more apart, depending on the variety.

Growing Tips

Make sure plants are well watered in fall to avoid winter desiccation.

Care and Maintenance

Junipers require pruning. Winter-killed branches need to be cut out in spring and overly long branches encroaching on walks or other plantings need to be headed back. Cut out entire branches to a vigorous side shoot growing in the same direction. If the cut is made beneath an overhanging branch, it will not be exposed. When cutting back severely, be sure to leave at least some green growth on the remaining branch or it will cease growing. Do not cut into the dead area in the center of the plant. Junipers are susceptible to mites, which can be controlled by insecticidal soap. Tip blight (Phomopsis) can be severe in wet weather. Spray affected plants with benomyl or triforine, following label directions.

Companion Planting and Design

Use these tough plants for hedges, foundation plants, screens, masses, or specimens.

Did You Know

There are hundreds of Juniper cultivars of all sizes and shapes. Save yourself a lot of trimming by selecting one that fits your space.

When, Where, and How to Plant

Plant Lilacs in spring or fall. Plant containerized plants any time during the season. Plant in full sun for best blooming and allow plenty of room for the plants to spread. Any well-drained garden soil will suffice. Lilacs are available balled and burlapped or in containers, and sometimes small plants are sold bareroot. The hole for planting should be shallower than the depth of the ball, and at least twice as wide. Space smaller varieties 6 feet apart in masses. Larger plants should be spaced 10 to 15 feet apart. Set each plant slightly higher than it grew in the nursery. Remove the burlap from balled-and-burlapped plants, stuffing it in the hole. Soak the plants thoroughly after planting.

Growing Tips

Fertilizer is generally unneeded unless plants show obvious nutrient deficiencies. Fertilized too vigorously, plants will fail to flower.

Care and Maintenance

Prune Lilacs to keep them blooming and in bounds. Remove blooms when they have faded, and renew the plants by cutting out 1/4 to 1/3 of the oldest stems all the way to the ground. Head back overly long stems to shorter side shoots growing in the same direction. Complete all pruning as soon as possible after blooms fade to allow the plants to develop flower buds for the next season. Control scales with summer oil or acephate, borers with lindane in June. Mildew will damage leaves in August, but while it is unsightly, it does no harm. Applying triforine will help. Be sure to read and follow the instructions on the labels. Sometimes Lilacs refuse to bloom. This may happen after transplanting, and it can happen to plants growing in the shade. The transplant problem will solve itself with time; correct the shade problem or the plants will never bloom.

Companion Planting and Design

Plant with enough room to develop to their full size, as specimens, in shrub borders, or in masses.

Did You Know

There are many species and hundreds of varieties of Lilacs.

Who doesn't like Lilacs? The blooms in spring aren't just beautiful, the fragrance (as Jane, my wife and best friend says) is "Heavenly!" For a short time in May, these wonderful plants burst forth with their wonderful blossoms, becoming the center of attention in the shrub border. The flowers are good for cutting. Lilac plants are untidy and difficult to fit into the landscape. The larger types are upright and woody, best used in the shrub border or in masses. Often they are planted next to the house where they either demand severe pruning to stay in bounds, or simply overwhelm everything else. Dwarf cultivars are easier to use; they stay smaller and they fit into foundation plantings. Their flowers, however, are not as spectacular.

Bloom Period and Color

May blooms in white, pink, lilac, violet.

Mature Height × Spread

4 to 10 feet × 4 to 10 feet

Mock Orange

Philadelphus coronarius

Mock Oranges are grown for their fragrant white blooms in June. These plants are no bother to grow, they flower easily, are completely hardy, have no serious pests, can be pruned and shaped without flinching, and make a beautiful, fragrant, display every year—just about the time we begin to spend a lot of time outdoors. Philadelphus × lemoinei has a mounded habit to 6 feet. Some cultivars are smaller. 'Avalanche' grows to 3 or 4 feet and has arching branches and flowers more than 2 inches across. The upright Philadelphus × virginalis 'Minnesota Snowflake' grows to 8 feet tall and half as wide with double flowers 2 inches in diameter. 'Frosty Morn' grows to 5 feet, and 'Miniature Snowflake' is compact growing to 3 feet.

Other Name
Sweet Mock Orange

Bloom Period and Color
June blooms in white.

Mature Height × Spread
3 to 10 feet × 3 to 10 feet

When, Where, and How to Plant

Mock Orange can be planted balled and burlapped in spring or fall, or from containers any time during the season. Plant in full sun or light shade. Any fertile garden soil is satisfactory as long as it is well drained. The taller kinds are suited to shrub borders or mass plantings. Lower-growing cultivars are suitable in borders, or they may be worked into foundation plantings. A single specimen in the middle of a front yard will be beautiful when in bloom but unattractive the other fifty weeks of the year. The hole for planting should be shallower than the depth of the ball and at least twice as wide. Space plants of smaller varieties 6 feet apart in masses, larger plants 10 to 15 feet apart. Set each plant in its hole, keeping it slightly higher than it grew in the nursery. Remove the burlap from balled-and-burlapped plants, stuffing it in the hole. Soak the plants thoroughly after planting to settle the soil around the roots.

Growing Tips

Provide new plants an inch of water per week. Fertilizer is generally not needed; fertilized too vigorously, plants will fail to flower.

Care and Maintenance

Mock Oranges are essentially pest-free, but yearly pruning to renew the plants is important. Immediately following flowering, remove $1/4$ to $1/3$ of the oldest branches all the way to the ground. This will stimulate new stems from the bases of the plants. If the plants get out of hand, they may be cut to 6 inches above the ground; they will regrow in about three years. In either case, flowering will not be interrupted.

Companion Planting and Design

Some forms of Mock Oranges fit into the landscape. Relegate the more difficult ones to the shrub border, or to mass plantings to be enjoyed when blooming, but ignored the rest of the season.

Did You Know

These plants are sometimes called Syringas, which is unfortunate because that is the botanical name for the Lilacs.

Mugo Pine

Pinus mugo

When, Where, and How to Plant

Mugo Pines can be planted either in spring or fall. Containerized small plants may be planted any time during the season. Shrub Pines are suitable for massing, and for foundation plantings. Plant in a well-drained soil in full sun or light shade. Mugo Pines are grown as balled-and-burlapped plants, and in 1-gallon to 5-gallon-sized containers. The hole for planting should be no deeper than the depth of the ball of the plant, and at least twice as wide. Set the plant in the planting hole, and replace half the soil. Fill the hole with water. Be sure to remove the burlap from a balled-and-burlapped plant, and stuff it down in the hole. Replace the remaining soil and fill the hole with water again. Make a saucer around the plant with any remaining soil. Dwarf selections are preferred for most landscape plantings. Space the plants 5 to 10 or more feet apart, depending on the cultivar.

Growing Tips

Newly set Pines need to be watered freely the first year. Fertilize cautiously. Excess fertilizer will result in faster growth and larger plants.

Care and Maintenance

Mugo Pines are subject to attack by pine sawflies; their larvae appear magically in mid-spring as masses on individual branches. When disturbed, they all jump at once, startling predators (or unsuspecting people). You can solve the problem by wiping them off by hand or spraying with malathion. Follow directions on the label carefully. These Pines can be kept within bounds indefinitely by shearing or by removing half the new growth every summer. Christmas-tree growers use machetes to shear pines. Hedge trimmers work as well. Be sure to leave some green needles on each branch or it will cease growing.

Companion Planting and Design

Mugo Pines are suitable for use where small evergreens can add to the interest of the planting. They are a bit more coarse than Yews or Junipers, providing different texture.

Did You Know

While not often considered for such use, Mugos are quite attractive around water features.

Mugo Pine is a confusing plant. It is a bush Pine, but how big the bush will become is anyone's guess. This plant is an excellent one for use in small and large landscapes. The truly dwarf Mugo is an excellent plant for foundation plantings, masses, and specimens. But, since most Mugos are seed-produced, it is difficult to predict just how they will develop. If cultivars available from local nurseries have been grown by a reliable grower, the chances are better that you will get what you expect. 'Compacta' is very dense and round, reaching a height of 4 feet and a width of 8 feet. The variety 'Pumilo' grows a couple of feet tall and spreads 10 feet. 'Mops' is 3 feet high and wide.

Other Name

Swiss Mountain Pine

Bloom Period and Color

Evergreen foliage.

Mature Height × Spread

4 to 10 feet × 8 to 20 feet

Potentilla

Potentilla fruticosa

These little plants are welcome in the landscape because of their profusion of bright-yellow flowers that last all summer. They are neat plants if properly maintained; they have dark bluish green or gray-green foliage and few pest problems. These are stemmy shrubs that form low mounds. They are low enough to use as facer plants, in the foundation planting, as low hedges, in the perennial border, and in masses. If used in masses, it is important to renew them regularly or they will deteriorate into a twiggy mess. Use them in raised beds and planters, or they may be potted as specimens. 'Gold Drop' has small-ish blooms on a 2-foot plant, but this seems to have become a common name for many different yellow-flowered Potentillas.

Bloom Period and Color
June to frost blooms in yellow, white, red.

Mature Height × Spread
1 to 4 feet × 4 feet

When, Where, and How to Plant

Plant bareroot Potentillas in either spring or fall. Plant container-grown plants at any time during the season. Plant in any moist, well-drained, fertile soil. These plants will tolerate some light shade and will withstand dry soils. Potentillas will deteriorate in wet soils. Potentillas are sold as balled-and-burlapped plants, or in 2- or 5-gallon containers. Prepare the area to be planted by tilling a 6-inch depth. Incorporate organic matter and set the plants at the depth they were growing. Dig the holes the depth of the plant ball and twice as wide. Space the plants $2^1/2$ feet apart. For hedges, set them $1^1/2$ feet apart or plant-to-plant. Plant hedges by opening a trench, spacing the plants, and backfilling them all at the same time. Water thoroughly after planting to settle the soil around the plant roots. If the soil on the roots of the plant is much different from that in the hole, mix some with that going back into the hole to avoid a soil interface problem.

Growing Tips

Potentillas need watering in dry weather. If they are allowed to wilt, flowering is disrupted.

Care and Maintenance

Potentillas are completely hardy throughout Illinois. Winter damage may occur to plants standing in water or those exposed to wind and sun in extremely cold weather. These plants can be cut back and will recover when growth starts in spring. In late winter or early spring, cut out any dead or overly long branches. Reduce the overall height of the plants by $1/2$, and remove a few of the remaining branches to the ground. Pruning must be done before the start of growth in spring.

Companion Planting and Design

Potentillas mix well with annuals and perennials. Use them in the flower border, as small hedges, or in masses.

Did You Know

These little plants are native throughout the northern hemisphere, including Illinois.

Privet

Ligustrum sp.

When, Where, and How to Plant

Privets can be planted in spring or fall from balled-and-burlapped or bareroot plants. Bundles of two-year-old seedlings are sold in spring as economical starts for hedges. Containerized plants can be planted at any time during the season. Privets are useful only as hedges. They have no features that would foster them for any other purpose. (The exception is Golden Privet, which is sometimes used as a specimen.) Any garden soil will suffice for Privet. Dig the planting holes the same depth and twice as wide as the plant balls. Space the standard cultivars 3 feet apart, dwarf cultivars 1¹/₂ feet apart. Soak bareroot plants for twelve hours before planting them. Hedges may also be planted by digging a trench, setting the plants 1¹/₂ to 3 feet apart, and backfilling the trench. This is a great labor-saving system.

Growing Tips

Provide young plantings an inch of water a week. Fertilizer is generally unneeded unless plants show obvious nutrient deficiencies.

Care and Maintenance

Privets require little care—only shearing to maintain the hedge. Try not to keep these plants at the same size all season. Every time you shear, cut a little farther out to leave at least some new leaves. In late winter, cut the plants below the desired size, and let them grow out again. Keep the bottom of the hedge wider than the top so that all branches will receive some light and the plants won't become bare at the bottom.

Companion Planting and Design

'European', the most common Privet planted in our state, is a large, rank plant unless sheared. 'Densiflorum' keeps its form and good foliage cover even if untrimmed. 'Lodense' stays compact, under 5 feet indefinitely. Amur Privet has better resistance to a canker disease that is fatal to European types.

Did You Know

Amur Privet produces abundant clusters of blooms each year if trimmed just after flowers drop. If untrimmed, it will produce purple fruits readily sought by birds.

In Illinois, there are more Privet hedges than any other hedge, and it is unusual to see a Privet in any planting other than a hedge. There are only three or four kinds to discuss. They differ in size, color, and disease resistance. If left unsheared, Privets are dense, upright, stemmy plants. The flowers are slightly fragrant, and people either like or dislike the smell. Privets will tolerate severe conditions and mistreatment as well as any plant we know, even growing in poor, dry, high-pH soils. If Privets will not grow in a particular soil, then it is useless to try any other woody plant in that spot. They can stand the pollution and grime of the city, and they withstand pruning like no other plant.

Bloom Period and Color
May, June blooms in white.

Mature Height × Spread
5 to 15 feet × 15 feet

Rhododendron
Rhododendron sp.

Rhododendrons are plants that we Illinois gardeners wish we could grow as well as gardeners in other parts of the country. But while the list of kinds that will grow in our state is short, we can and do grow them. Rhododendrons may be either evergreen or deciduous. Their flowers are typically bell- or funnel-shaped and are borne in clusters at the tips of the stems in early to mid-spring. These are some Rhododendrons that can be grown in Illinois: 'Molle' hybrids are R. × kosterianum—Zone 5a; Korean Rhododendrons are R. mucronulatum—Zone 4b; Royal Azalea, R. schlippenbachii—Zone 5b; 'Exbury' and 'Knap Hill' Hybrids—Zone 5b; 'Ghent' hybrids, to 10 feet tall—Zone 5b; and 'Northern Lights' Azaleas are hardy to -40°F—Zone 2.

Bloom Period and Color
Spring blooms in lavender, pink, white, yellow, orange, red.

Mature Height × Spread
3 to 6 feet × 6 feet

When, Where, and How to Plant
Plant Rhododendrons in spring. Plant containerized plants until midsummer or later. The soil must be deep and well drained; hard and wet soils are not tolerated. Soil pH should be neutral or lower, though some grow in soils with a higher pH. They need protection from the midday sun in summer and winter. Winter sun and wind are especially damaging. Spade the soil to a 24-inch depth and incorporate organic matter, preferably generous volumes of acidic peat moss. If drainage is not adequate, install tiles or construct raised beds at least 5 feet wide. Rhododendrons are available balled and burlapped, or in containers. The hole for planting should be shallower than the depth of the ball, and at least twice as wide. Space the plants to allow for their mature size. Set the plant in the hole, keeping it higher than it grew in the nursery. Remove the burlap from balled-and-burlapped plants, stuffing it in the hole. Backfill the hole, adding 25 percent peat to the soil. Soak thoroughly. Mulch the plants with 2 to 3 inches of shredded bark or compost. Reapply mulch in spring and fall and provide winter protection if necessary.

Growing Tips
Watering will be needed in dry weather, as the beds of modified soil will not re-wet from the still-moist soil beneath the planting.

Care and Maintenance
Rhodies do not take kindly to pruning. Root and crown rot, *Phytophthora cinnamomi,* a devastating water mold disease of Rhodies, occurs where soils are too wet or poorly drained. If the wetness is due to something other than poor soil conditions or unusually wet weather, try drenching the planting with Banrot, Truban, or Banol fungicide.

Companion Planting and Design
The *Rhododendron* P. J. M. hybrids are large-flowered pinks and lavenders, the "top of the line" Rhodies for Illinois Gardens. They are hardy to Zone 5.

Did You Know
Azaleas and Rhododendrons are the same genus. That settles the confusion about whether particular plants are Azaleas or Rhododendrons. Now they all are classified as *Rhododendron.*

Rose of Sharon
Hibiscus syriacus

When, Where, and How to Plant
Plant Rose of Sharon in spring or fall. Containerized plants can be planted any time during the season. Plant in full sun or light shade. Any decent garden soil should suffice, but a well-drained soil with added organic matter is better. Rose of Sharon is available balled and burlapped or in containers. Dig the hole for planting the same depth and twice as wide as the plant ball. Roots are fibrous and transplant well. If the soil in the container is one of the soilless mixes or much different from the soil from that of the planting hole, shave some from the ball and mix it with the soil going back into the hole. This will prevent interface problems (see the section on soils in the introductory chapter).

Growing Tips
Rose of Sharon is thought by many to be drought-tolerant, but it does better when given adequate water during dry spells. The plants need watering during dry spells their first season after planting.

Care and Maintenance
Pruning is the most important maintenance practice for Rose of Sharon plantings. If they are allowed to grow wild, they will become upright, stemmy, and thinly branched, with all of their flowers at the top. Prune severely in spring. It tolerates shearing, but flowering will be sacrificed unless the shearing is done in early spring. Flower size can be increased by cutting back the previous year's growth to half a dozen buds on each shoot. This looks terrible until the plants start growing, but the flowers will be larger (if fewer in number).

Companion Planting and Design
In spite of the criticisms, these plants do serve a purpose. They are tough and will grow almost anywhere. This makes them very useful in disturbed sites, where they can be used in shrub borders or as specimens.

Did You Know
Rose of Sharon has been grown in this country since colonial days, having been brought from Europe to brighten American gardens.

In my opinion, Rose of Sharon has only one thing going for it, as far as beauty goes: it has beautiful flowers late in the season when there isn't much else going on. Let me temper my harsh criticism by agreeing that these plants are hardy, stand the dirt and grime of the city, will grow in almost any soil with drainage and some water, and flower faithfully year after year. They are indeed tolerant of difficult sites. They are planted in front yards where kids can run around them and along driveways where they get little water. I have seen Rose of Sharon in these situations, growing, not looking too good, but blooming with abandon. That is sufficient reason to include them in this listing.

Other Name
Shrubby Althea

Bloom Period and Color
July through September blooms in purple, pink, red, white.

Mature Height × Spread
10 feet × 10 feet

Saint John's-Wort
Hypericum prolificum

Saint John's-Wort is a low woody shrub forming a dense, twiggy mound that is covered with bright yellow flowers for much of the summer. Its attractive foliage is blue-green and has a medium-fine texture. This small plant is tidy enough to be used in the perennial border, as a facer plant, in the foundation planting, or in masses. The bright-yellow flowers are borne at a time when few other shrubs are flowering. Saint John's-Wort does very well in dry, rocky, or limey soils. The Kalm's Saint John's-Wort, H. kalmianum, is a plant native to cliffs and lakeshores in Illinois, Michigan, Quebec, and Ontario. Its form is more rank than that of Shrubby Saint John's-Wort, but its bright-yellow flowers are larger.

Other Name
Shrubby Saint John's-Wort

Bloom Period and Color
Late July blooms in yellow.

Mature Height × Spread
1 to 4 feet × 4 feet

When, Where, and How to Plant
Saint John's-Wort is best planted in light shade, but it will grow in full sun. Although these plants will grow in poor soils, they do as well or better in a moist soil that has good drainage. Sandy soils are ideal. These plants should be planted from containers. If the soil is quite heavy, prepare it by adding organic matter and sand. Dig the planting holes the same depth and twice as wide as the containers. Set the plants at the depth they grew in their containers. Soak the soil to settle it around the roots. Space the plants 1¹/2 to 2 feet apart.

Growing Tips
These plants will tolerate tough situations. They need little care, and if treated too well, become rank and readily die out. With minimal care, they do quite well. Fertilizer is generally unneeded unless plants show obvious nutrient deficiencies.

Care and Maintenance
Saint John's-Wort must be pruned to keep it tidy and blooming well. Prune it in very early spring to stimulate new growth. It flowers on current-season's wood. Faded flowers are messy; deadhead the plants by cutting off the old flowers.

Companion Planting and Design
Saint John's-Wort in bloom is so noticeable that people often ask what it is. Most have never heard the name and are surprised at the colorful plant, often found growing in a tough, dry place. It is not unusual to find one tucked into the corner of a parking lot or island planting where it seems unlikely such a bright little plant would thrive. Sometimes these are the sole survivors of a planting long since forgotten.

Did You Know
Spotted Saint John's-Wort, *H. punctatum,* is the Hypericum of the herbalists, once considered the most magical of all herbs for warding off "evil spirits and sickness." Currently, it is among the common herbals on pharmacy shelves, suggested for treating depression. Saint John's-Wort has been used in landscapes since the middle 1700s.

Smoketree

Cotinus coggygria

When, Where, and How to Plant

Smoketrees transplant easily, and they prefer any well-drained garden soil. They tolerate high pHs and will grow in dry, rocky soils. Plant Smoketrees in spring or fall. Container-grown plants can be planted any time during the season. Plant in full sun, in masses, or in the shrub border. Smoketrees are available balled and burlapped, or in containers. The hole for planting should be shallower than the depth of the ball and at least twice as wide. Space plants 10 to 15 feet apart. Set each plant in its hole, keeping it slightly higher than it grew in the nursery. Remove the burlap from balled-and-burlapped plants, and stuff it in the hole. Soak the plants thoroughly after planting to settle the soil around the roots.

Growing Tips

Newly set plants will benefit from an inch of water per week. Fertilizer is generally unneeded unless plants show obvious nutrient deficiencies.

Care and Maintenance

Smoketrees can be pruned to stimulate better flowering. The plants can be cut to the ground in late winter to stimulate vigorous shoot growth, larger leaves, and fewer but larger flower clusters. Scale insects, rodents, and verticillium wilt are the main pest problems encountered by Smoketrees. Severe pruning will eliminate the scales, or use dormant oil in late winter. Keep debris or weeds from accumulating around the trunks of the plants so that mice don't take up residence there before winter. If mice spend the winter there, they will girdle the plants. Verticillium is a soil-borne disease. Make every effort to avoid bringing this disease into the planting in soil or on other plants.

Companion Planting and Design

These plants are usually grown as specimens to exhibit their unusual, showy inflorescences. They are well adapted to the shrub border or planting in masses.

Did You Know

The cultivar 'Purpureus' has purple leaves and flowers. Several selections of this cultivar are available, but 'Nordine', a selection made at Morton Arboretum, Lisle, Illinois, is the hardiest of the group.

Smoketree is grown for the airy inflorescences, or clusters of fruits, that develop after its flowers drop. This display is produced by the pubescence (hairs) on the fruit stalks that persist in the cluster. These "hairs" turn smoky-pink and last through summer into fall. The effect is a haze of color surrounding the plant . . . like smoke. This is a large plant and is best used in masses or in the shrub border, though it is used most often as a specimen, typically in the middle of the front yard. I do not recommend planting this way, but people who dedicate their front yards to these plants so the rest of us can enjoy them are to be thanked, not disparaged.

Other Name

Common Smoketree

Bloom Period and Color

June blooms in yellow.

Mature Height × Spread

15 feet × 15 feet

Snowberry
Symphoricarpos albus

Snowberry is grown not for its flowers, but for its pure white berries (drupes) that appear in late summer and into winter. The plants are bushy and twiggy with a broad rounded form. The stems are ascending until loaded with berries; then they are pulled down by the berries, arching over and exposing the silvery undersides of the leaves. They are rather difficult to use in the landscape, but add another dimension: that of white fruit. Snowberry is very tolerant of soil conditions, and it will grow in places that generally provide difficulty for establishing plants, such as slopes, berms for sight and sound barriers, and banks for detention and retention ponds. Some improved selections develop more and larger fruit, and are more vigorous growers.

Bloom Period and Color
June blooms in pink.

Mature Height × Spread
3 to 6 feet × 6 feet

When, Where, and How to Plant
Snowberry can be planted at any time during the season. Plants are available balled and burlapped, and in 2- and 5-gallon cans. Plant in full sun to partial shade. These plants are probably more useful in shade, where other plants grow with difficulty. Any garden soil is satisfactory, but good drainage is important. The plants will deteriorate in soggy soils. The hole for planting should be the same depth as the plant ball and at least twice as wide. Remove plants from their containers, and slice any circling roots. Space the plants 3 to 4 feet apart. Set each plant in its hole, keeping it at the same height it grew in the nursery. Remove the burlap from balled-and-burlapped plants, stuffing it in the hole. Replace the soil and fill the hole with water. Snowberry may need watering during the first season.

Growing Tips
New plants need about an inch of water per week. Established plants are drought-tolerant. Fertilizer is generally unneeded unless plants show obvious nutrient deficiencies. Fertilized too vigorously, plants will be rank and weak.

Care and Maintenance
Once established, Snowberry needs little attention. Pruning early in the season will increase its flowering and fruiting. The plants flower on current season's wood. If suckering and spreading are to be controlled, hoe out the sprouts or kill them with glufosinate-ammonium (Finale) herbicide. Follow directions carefully and keep the material off desirable green plants.

Companion Planting and Design
Use in places where it is difficult to get other plants to grow. These plants tolerate tough situations and faithfully develop their attractive drupes.

Did You Know
Of selected varieties, *S. albus laevigatus* is one of the better ones. Some related species produce pink fruit. Coralberry, *S. orbiculatus,* grows about 4 feet high and wide with coral-colored drupes. *Symphoricarpos* × *chenaultii* is a 3-foot, arching shrub with showy pink flowers and pink drupes in the sun, or white or pink-tinged drupes in shade.

Spicebush

Lindera benzoin

When, Where, and How to Plant

Spicebush may be planted in spring or fall. Large plants do not transplant easily; the coarse, fibrous root system is slow to redevelop. Plant in light to full shade in a well-drained soil. Spicebush can be used in the shrub border, in some foundation plantings (especially in the shade), in masses, and in naturalized areas around water features or stream banks. It is a woodland plant and can be planted at the edge of wooded areas where its color can be appreciated and the birds it attracts can be seen. I have seen Spicebushes in naturalized areas on the North Shore, especially along the ravines leading to Lake Michigan. Large, overhead trees create almost continuous shade in summer. In the filtered sunlight of spring, the flowers of these plants are welcome after the dreary winter. Spicebushes are available balled and burlapped, sometimes in containers. Make sure the soil has adequate drainage. These plants do better in dry soil than in wet situations. Dig the planting hole the same depth and twice as wide as the plant ball. Set the plant at the same depth it was grown in the nursery. If planting a container-grown plant, mix some of the soil in the container with the soil that will go back into the planting hole. This will create a gradual change from one soil to another and will prevent an interface problem.

Growing Tips

Water Spicebushes their first season during extended dry weather.

Care and Maintenance

There is little that needs to be done to care for Spicebushes once they are established. No insect or diseases affect these plants.

Companion Planting and Design

These plants are natives of the moist woodlands. Use them where they have room to develop their natural shape.

Did You Know

Lindera, native to the eastern half of the U. S., is named for the 18th century Swedish botanist, Johann Linder.

Spicebush is a native shrub that will grow in deep shade to full sun, in any kind of soil at just about any pH. It is so adaptable that it can be grown in just about any situation. The plant is a rounded shrub, quite open and loose when grown in a shaded site. In the open in full sun, it will be dense and compact. Spicebush blooms in early spring with tiny yellow flowers in clusters along the stems. The flowers are fragrant, as are the stems and leaves when broken. The leaves turn clear yellow in fall. As they drop, the bright red berries (drupes) on female plants are gradually revealed, and the combination of yellow leaves and red fruit is quite attractive.

Bloom Period and Color
April blooms in yellow.

Mature Height × Spread
6 to 10 feet × 10 feet

Spirea
Spiraea sp.

Spireas are diverse and useful plants. They range in size from the small, upright Bumalda types with pink flowers, to the arching 7-foot S. × vanhouttei with white flowers. These plants are grown for their flowers, which are small and borne in flat clusters. The Vanhoutte Spirea used to be a fixture in landscapes, having found its niche as a foundation plant in front of the high front porches of early 1900, turn-of-the-century homes. The lower types are now fixtures in landscapes. They are colorful in bloom, and their flowers are produced all summer rather than just in spring. Another attractive feature of Spireas is their ability to grow almost anywhere. They tolerate almost any soil and will grow in sun or shade. They flower better in full sun.

Bloom Period and Color
Spring, summer blooms in white, pink.

Mature Height × Spread
2 to 10 feet × 2 to 10 feet

When, Where, and How to Plant
Spireas can be planted in spring or fall. Container-grown plants can be planted all season. Spireas are suited to shrub borders, mass plantings, and foundation plantings, or may be used as hedges or screens. They are sometimes planted as specimens, one plant in the middle of the front yard, but this is not the best use. Plant in full sun or partial shade. A moist, well-drained soil is best. Spireas are available in containers or balled and burlapped. Set the plants at the same depth they were growing in their containers. Hedges may be planted by digging a trench, setting the plants at the right spacing, and backfilling the trench. This is a great labor-saving system. Space large plants at least 10 feet apart and 10 feet from walls, fences, or other structures. Dwarf plants can be set 3 to 4 feet apart, or 2 feet apart in hedges.

Growing Tips
New plants need about an inch of water per week. Established plants are relatively drought-tolerant. Fertilizer is generally unneeded unless plants show obvious nutrient deficiencies. Fertilized too vigorously, plants will be rank and weak.

Care and Maintenance
Intelligent pruning is the key to success with Spireas. They should be allowed to develop their natural form, not sheared into artificial shapes. Renewal pruning to remove $1/4$ to $1/3$ of the stems to the ground each year will keep the plants in good shape. Sometimes it is a good idea to rejuvenate the plants by cutting them to the ground and allowing them to regrow.

Companion Planting and Design
Use the taller plants in the shrub border or as screens. Allow enough room to develop their natural, vase-shaped form. Use lower-growing types in beds and foundation plantings. Work into the perennial garden for a touch of color when other things aren't blooming.

Did You Know
Cut back spring-blooming Spireas as soon as flowers drop, and summer-flowering kinds in mid-winter or early spring.

Viburnum

Viburnum sp.

When, Where, and How to Plant

Viburnums transplant easily; move them in spring or fall. Containerized plants can be planted all season long. Plant in full sun or light filtered shade. A well-drained soil is important. Viburnums are available balled and burlapped and in containers. The hole for planting should be shallower than the depth of the ball and at least twice as wide. Space smaller cultivars 6 feet apart in masses. Larger plants should be spaced 10 to 15 feet apart. Set each plant slightly higher than it grew in the nursery. Remove the burlap from balled-and-burlapped plants, stuffing it in the hole. Soak the plants thoroughly after planting to settle the soil around the roots.

Growing Tips

Provide an inch of water per week. Fertilizer is generally unneeded unless plants show obvious nutrient deficiencies. Fertilized too vigorously, plants will be rank and weak.

Care and Maintenance

Viburnums must be pruned to keep them blooming and in bounds. Remove blooms when they have faded. Renew the plants yearly by cutting out 1/4 to 1/3 of the oldest stems all the way to the ground. Head back overly long stems to a shorter side-shoot growing in the same direction. All pruning should be completed as soon as possible after blooms fade to allow the plants to develop flower buds for the next season. Viburnums are subject to insect troubles: scales are controlled with summer oil or acephate, borers with permethrin in June. Leaf spot may damage leaves in August; spray with triforine. Be sure to read and follow the instructions on the labels. Crown borers can be serious on plants under stress. European Cranberrybush is one of the most susceptible; American Cranberrybush seems less so.

Companion Planting and Design

Use as backdrops for flower gardens. Plant Koreanspice Viburnum where the wonderful fragrance can be appreciated.

Did You Know

'Mohican' Viburnum has fruit that persists until November and attracts birds. American Cranberrybush Viburnum has bright fruit lasting all winter, if not gathered by birds. The edible fruit makes interesting jam.

The Viburnums are valued for their flowers, some of which are wonderfully fragrant; for their luxurious foliage; and for their various forms. They grow in most garden soils, tolerating alkalinity fairly well. They need decent drainage, and some will grow in relatively dry soils. Viburnums come in many forms and textures. The taller kinds are suitable for massing, screens, and shrub borders. Some are narrow and upright, good for narrow screens. Lower types are excellent for foundation plantings, massing, or borders. The smallest kinds are used for low masses in public areas, island planters, or low hedges. The flowers are borne in clusters, either flat, mounded, or snowball-like. One of the most fragrant is the Koreanspice Viburnum, outstanding for a couple of weeks in May. When it is in bloom, the fragrance fills the air, especially in the evening. Open the windows and let it in! Isn't there some way to bottle it?

Bloom Period and Color
Spring, summer blooms in white, pink.

Mature Height × Spread
3 to 10 feet × 3 to 10 feet

Witchhazel

Hamamelis sp.

There are two Witchhazels used in landscape plantings: Vernal Witchhazel blooms in January and February and Common Witchhazel blooms from October to December. These plants are quite unusual because they will bloom in winter-like weather, often when temperatures are below freezing. The flowers are fragrant, opening on sunny days and closing when temperatures drop. They bloom for several weeks. These plants are well adapted to Illinois conditions. They seem to grow equally well in heavy or light soils, as long as the soils are moist but well drained. Allow Witchhazels to grow to their full size. Use them in masses, shrub borders, screens, groupings, naturalized areas, or as specimen plants. Common Witchhazels, H. virginiana, are large plants growing up to 15 feet tall.

Bloom Period and Color
Spring, fall blooms in yellow.

Mature Height × Spread
15 feet × 15 feet

When, Where, and How to Plant
Witchhazels do not like to be moved. They are best transplanted in spring. Plant in full sun or partial shade. Soils should be well drained. Provide enough room so that they can grow without needing to be trimmed to fit the space. Plants are available balled and burlapped from local nurseries and garden centers. Dig the planting hole the same depth and twice the diameter of the plant ball. Make sure the hole drains—if there is doubt, check by filling the hole with water and allowing it to drain. Set the plant slightly higher than it grew in the nursery. If the soil on the plant is different from that of the planting hole, shave some from the ball and mix the two together for backfilling the hole. Water thoroughly to settle the soil around the roots.

Growing Tips
Provide an inch of water per week. Fertilizer is generally unneeded unless plants show obvious nutrient deficiencies. Fertilized too vigorously, plants will be rank and weak. Apply aluminum sulfate to lower the soil pH if plants become chlorotic (yellow).

Care and Maintenance
Witchhazels require very little care once they are established. Remove any dead stems in spring and head back overly long branches to a shorter side shoot growing in the same direction. In winter, protect plants from rabbits by encircling them with chicken wire fencing.

Companion Planting and Design
These plants flower when nothing else is in bloom. They are unique conversation pieces. Plant them where they can be seen, and where the fragrance can be appreciated. They are woodland plants and do best in that cool, moist kind of setting.

Did You Know
Extract of the bark of Witchhazel is a strong astringent and is used for many medical treatments for things such as wrinkles, bruises, sunburn, and other skin problems, and as an aftershave. The most effective divining rods are reported to be made from Witchhazel.

Yew

Taxus sp.

When, Where, and How to Plant

Yews transplant easily. If balled and burlapped, they may be moved in spring or fall. Plant containerized plants whenever the soil is workable. Protect from winter sun and wind. Use them for foundation plantings, masses, groupings, and as facer plants and hedges. Dig the planting hole slightly less deep and twice as wide as the plant ball. If the soil in the ball is much different from that in the hole, mix some soil from the ball with that going back into the hole to avoid an interface problem. Locally grown plants are definitely best. The importance of good drainage cannot be overemphasized. Poor drainage will result in loss of the plants. If the soil is not well drained, set the plants with the balls half out of the ground and hill soil up to them; or construct raised beds. Hedges may be planted by digging a trench, setting the plants at the right spacing, and backfilling the trench. Set the plants high. Space large plants 5 to 10 feet apart. Spreading Yews should be no closer than 10 feet from a structure. Space dwarf plants at their advertised spread. 'Hicks' Yew in hedges should be spaced 2 to 4 feet apart. Soak the plants well after planting.

Growing Tips

During their first season, Yews will need to be watered during dry spells. A couple of inches of mulch will help maintain soil moisture and coolness.

Care and Maintenance

In winter they will need protection from the mid-day sun and from drying winds. A temporary burlap screen will work fine; drive stakes around the south and west sides and tack the burlap to them.

Companion Planting and Design

The fresh green color and soft texture of Yews make them the first choice for evergreen landscape plants.

Did You Know

Yews are poisonous to many animals, but deer relish them. Protect them with wire cages.

Yews are the top-of-the-line evergreens for landscape use. They are attractive, bright-green, soft-needled plants that come in a wide variety of sizes and growth forms. They tolerate the soils of Illinois and will grow in either full sun or shade. They are the best shade-tolerant evergreens. Yews can be pruned severely, and they will keep growing. They can be systematically reduced in size so they can be used in places that might seem far too small. Yews produce colorful fruit, but the sexes are on separate plants. The red "berries" are not really fruits at all but fleshy arils, each surrounding a naked seed. For them to develop, you must have female plants, but there must be at least one male plant as well.

Bloom Period and Color
Evergreen foliage.

Mature Height × Spread
4 to 20 feet × 20 feet

Trees *for Illinois*

One of the most striking differences between the new communities emerging on the prairie lands of Illinois and the older, established neighborhoods is the presence of beautiful big trees. They provide a charm, a coziness, that cannot be created by anything else.

Growing up in an older community, I took trees for granted. They provided a link with the past. Some of those trees were very old. Some may have been there before our country was founded. As far as I knew, they had always been there and always would be. They provided shade in summer. They blocked the wind in winter. It was not unusual for children on the way home from school to take momentary respite from wintry blasts behind the trunk of a big friendly Elm. Birds nested in them in summer, and they provided a platform from which to view the neighborhood from an elevated perspective.

Something about trees provided a sense of security, something missing in that part of town where the new, postwar bungalows were being built.

The advent of Dutch elm disease changed all that. Entire communities were suddenly denuded of their trees, and the true value of the trees became apparent. Even today, mature Oaks are in jeopardy and wilt threatens Pines.

Using Trees in the Garden

Trees also tie the house to the land. They frame it and shelter it, making it more homey. And they provide interest throughout the year. The only rivals of the fresh, new, bright-green leaves of spring are the spectacular fall colors. Each fall, the dying leaves put on one of nature's most dramatic displays. Then in a few days, they tumble to the ground and the season is over. After the leaves drop, the

fascinating structure of the trunks and branches is revealed. Many trees have interesting bark that is often hidden by the foliage. In the midst of winter, it sometimes is hard to imagine that in a few short months the grayness of winter will be replaced by the green of spring.

Yet, trees aren't just aesthetically important. They are natural air conditioners. Just drive from an open highway into a forest preserve on a hot day and notice the difference. They block the wind in winter, which saves on the heating bills. They screen out sights and sounds, and they filter the dirt and grime from the air.

Trees provide shelter for birds and other wildlife. Some trees provide seeds and fruits to sustain the birds and small animals after the insects have disappeared for the winter.

Wooded building lots are premium properties. In our community, they are knocking down and replacing smaller, older houses that have trees on their lots with huge houses. Complete

with the full size trees, these homes have a real advantage over those being constructed on land that grew corn last year. Homes with big trees properly located are worth more. Real estate prices always reflect that.

Tree for Special Purposes

Trees with Good Fall Color:

Red

Black Tupelo	Oak, Red
Callery Pear	Oak, Scarlet
Flowering Dogwood	Sweet Gum
Maple, Red	

Yellow

Ash, Green	Katsuratree (apricot)
Beech (golden-bronze)	Larch
Birch, Paper	Magnolia
Birch, White	Maple, Norway
Ginkgo	Maple, Sugar (yellow, orange, red)
Hawthorn	Redbud
Hornbeam (yellow-orange)	

Purple-Bronze

| Ash, White ('Autumn Purple' selection) | Oak |

Trees with Attractive Flowers:

Callery Pear	Japanese Tree Lilac
Catalpa	Linden (fragrance)
Crabapple	Magnolia
Flowering Dogwood	Maple, Red
Hawthorn	Redbud
Horse Chestnut	Tuliptree

Trees with Interesting Bark:

Beech, American (silver, muscular)	Maple, Paperbark (cinnamon, pealing)
Birch, Paper (white)	Maple, Red (silver, smooth)
Birch, River (pink, cinnamon)	Pine, Scotch (cinnamon, pealing)
Hornbeam (smooth muscular gray)	
Japanese Tree Lilac (shiny brown, white lenticels)	

Small Trees for Use Under Power Lines:

Callery Pear	Japanese Tree Lilac
Crabapple	Maple, Amur
Flowering Dogwood	Redbud
Hawthorn	

Fast-Growing Trees:

Alder	Elm, Hybrid
Ash, Green	Hackberry
Ash, White	Honeylocust
Birch	Maple, Silver
Callery Pear	

Deer-Resistant Trees:

Ash	Japanese Tree Lilac
Beech	Redbud
Catalpa	Sycamore
Gingko	Tuliptree
Honeylocust	

Alder

Alnus glutinosa

Sometimes conditions are too poor for the more common ornamental trees, but something is needed to fill the void. Alders are well suited for that use. They are attractive in their own way, and are often better than some other choices such as Willows or Poplars. These trees are uniquely adapted to poor soils as they are able to fix atmospheric nitrogen for their own use. Thus, they are used in newly developed or reclaimed places where anything less tolerant would never grow. Often these can be used as temporary plantings to help improve the soil until more attractive trees can survive. These trees are more common in Europe where they are used in wet sites, often with the roots completely submerged; they are excellent for use around ponds.

Other Name
Black Alder

Bloom Period and Color
March. Purplish catkins, inconspicuous.

Mature Height × Spread
40 feet × 20 to 25 feet

When, Where, and How to Plant
Transplant in spring or fall balled and burlapped, or anytime from containers. Alder transplants easily. It prefers moist soil, for which it is especially well adapted, but I have seen it do well in dry parking lot islands. Dig the planting hole as deep and twice as wide as the root ball. Set the same depth or slightly shallower than it grew in the container or nursery. Remove the burlap and twine, and shove it down in the hole. Backfill, and water to settle the soil.

Growing Tips
Water as needed the first season. These are lowland trees and prefer moist soil. In most years rainfall will be sufficient to provide for these trees. However, in unusually dry years, water about an inch per week.

Care and Maintenance
Alders take little care once established. They may need trimming to remove the always-present dead twigs. Many insects will attack these trees, but most do little more than aesthetic damage. Tent caterpillars spin big webs that are easily clipped out. Wooly aphids exude sticky honeydew that drips on items below. Spray with malathion or insecticidal soap. The trees are tough and will tolerate a lot of damage without permanent harm. Alders are short-lived. Eventually, they begin to succumb to cankers that kill branches one at a time until the trees are unsightly and candidates for removal.

Companion Planting and Design
Use Alders where other more attractive trees will have a hard time growing, such as wet places, large open areas, parking lots, or next to ponds where they are immersed periodically. These trees will stand tough sites. Once established, the trees will often reseed themselves, resulting in a permanent, pure stand of Alders. Alders are much cleaner than Willows and are shallowly rooted so they do not invade underground sewer systems.

Did You Know
Alders have tough rot-resistant wood used to make products that receive a lot of wear such as sluice gates, bridges, and even wooden shoes in Holland.

Ash
Fraxinus sp.

When, Where, and How to Plant

Ash trees are best planted while dormant, in spring or in fall after leaves have fallen. With the advent of anti-desiccants, tree spades, and other innovations, they can be moved whenever the ground is workable. Tolerant of most soils, these trees can be planted almost anywhere there is sufficient room. An Ash will grow in sun or shade. They are grown as balled-and-burlapped plants and in containers. The hole for planting should be no deeper than the depth of the ball of the plant, and at least twice as wide. Remove the plants from their containers, and slice any circling roots. Set the plant in the planting hole. Remove the burlap from a balled-and-burlapped plant, and place it in the hole. Replace the soil and fill the hole with water. Make a saucer around the plant with any remaining soil.

Growing Tips

Trees suffer during droughty seasons. If no rains fall for three weeks, set a sprinkler and apply 2 inches of water under the branch spread of the tree. Measure it in a coffee can set beneath the sprinkler.

Care and Maintenance

Ashes are messy trees. They are often damaged by storms, and repairs are usually too difficult for the average homeowner. Obtain a certified arborist to evaluate and correct any problems. Borers, scales, mites, ash plant bugs, anthracnose, cankers, and verticillium wilt are among the difficulties these trees may encounter. If the trees are otherwise healthy, they will be able to withstand these problems and continue to prosper. Young trees struggling to overcome transplanting shock may require treatment.

Companion Planting and Design

They are suited to street tree plantings and to large yards for shade. Roots tend to be shallow in heavy soils and may pop up in the lawn and interfere with mowing.

Did You Know

Ash trees tolerate terrible soil conditions that might prevent using other trees. They may be short-lived, however.

White Ash and Green Ash are native American trees. White Ash is a huge plant, reaching as much as 60 to 80 feet in height and spreading at the same rate. It is a lowland tree, tolerant of wet and alkaline soils. Green Ash is smaller, growing 50 feet and spreading about 40 feet. It, too, is a lowland tree found along rivers and streams. Both trees are well adapted to all parts of Illinois. They tolerate wet soils, but also grow well in drier locations. They have been selected for type, size, and lack of seeds. Ash trees grow at a moderate rate, adding about 2 feet a year. Sometimes an Ash is planted as a temporary tree until conditions improve and another specimen is planted.

Bloom Period and Color

Spring blooms (insignificant) in green to purple.

Mature Height × Spread

50 to 60 feet × 60 feet

Bald Cypress
Taxodium distichum

Bald Cypress is one of three deciduous conifers grown throughout Illinois. It is the best of the three, with a fine texture, good form, and site tolerance. A stately, deciduous conifer, this is the Cypress of the Florida swamps, and hardy as far north as Wisconsin—quite a feat for any plant! It prefers moist soils but will stand upland sites. Bald Cypress is a fast-growing, durable tree that does well unless the soil pH is above 7.5. These trees are best suited for the southern parts of Illinois where soils are more likely to be acidic, although some are doing fairly well in northern municipalities. Older specimens develop the characteristic spreading, flat top. They are beautiful in full leaf, with a dramatic character in winter.

Bloom Period and Color
March, April blooms (insignificant) in yellow.

Mature Height × Spread
50 to 70 feet × 25 feet

When, Where, and How to Plant
Small container-grown specimens may be planted at any time, but spring is preferred. Full sun and moist, well-drained, acid to neutral soil are ideal conditions. These trees do not grow well in the shade. This is a narrow tree, requiring less room than most large trees. Bald Cypresses are grown as balled-and-burlapped plants and in containers. The hole for planting should be no greater than the depth of the ball of the plant and at least twice as wide. Remove the plants from their containers, and slice any circling roots. Set the plant in the planting hole. Remove the burlap from a balled-and-burlapped plant and place it in the hole. Replace the soil and fill the hole with water. Make a saucer around the plant with any remaining soil.

Growing Tips
When planted, Bald Cypresses need watering the first year. Later, they require little care.

Care and Maintenance
Acid soil is necessary for best results. Test the soil pH before deciding to plant a Bald Cypress. Maintaining soil acidity is an unnecessary maintenance chore. Instead of fighting high pH, plant something else. They are intolerant of pruning, so let them grow. Bald Cypresses are essentially free of pests.

Companion Planting and Design
These are large trees, achieving a height of 75 feet in landscape plantings. Their narrow crown makes them especially useful as street trees. They are excellent as background plants or specimens. The trees tolerate adverse conditions if the soil pH is low enough. A large 60-foot-tall specimen was located on the University of Illinois campus, pinched between a building and sidewalk. It received foot traffic, salt, and little care. It survived everything except the chain saw—when it succumbed to the need for more buildings.

Did You Know
Cypress wood is very durable and rot-resistant. In the past when the wood was plentiful, timbers were used for greenhouse benches, and the shredded bark for mulch.

Beech
Fagus sp.

When, Where, and How to Plant

Plant Beeches in spring only. Before investing in a Beech, I recommend seeing the specimens at the Missouri Botanical Garden, Chicago Botanic Garden, Morton Arboretum, or in a local planting. Give these large trees plenty of room. Plant in a sunny, well-drained site. They develop shallow root systems and dense shade where grass rarely grows. Beech trees are grown as balled-and-burlapped plants. Since these trees have shallow roots, they need well-aerated soil. Dig the hole for planting a little less deep than the plant grew in the nursery, and at least twice as wide as the ball. Set the plant in the planting hole; remove the burlap and place it in the hole. Replace the soil and fill the hole with water. Make a saucer around the plant with any remaining soil.

Growing Tips

In dry weather, thoroughly soak the soil under the branch spread of the tree once a month.

Care and Maintenance

Once established, these trees require little care. Beeches are susceptible to some diseases and several insects, including the two-lined chestnut borer. Healthy trees, however, are perfectly able to withstand these attacks without trouble. European Beech takes shearing very well and can be kept as a hedge.

Companion Planting and Design

Beech trees are big. They are beautiful specimens where there is room. Use them as accents where the scale of the landscape is grand enough.

Did You Know

Beeches are so spectacular that certain specimens remain in your memory. A tremendous row of American Beeches stood as sentinels along the shore of Lake Michigan south of Ludington, Michigan— their silver bark glistening at sunset. These trees, some with 4-foot diameter trunks, were removed to make way for the pumped storage reservoir. I'll never forget them. Three Copper Beeches in front of a modern high-rise along Chicago's Lake Shore Drive are worth an early-morning trip to see them as the rising sun illuminates them. Tricolor European Beeches have purple leaves with cream and pink edges . . . outstanding!

Among the deciduous trees of Illinois, there is nothing quite as magnificent as a Beech. These are large trees, slow growing and durable; but where there is room, there is no other tree that can compare with them. They are splendid in any season of the year with crisp dense foliage in summer, and sturdy with strong branches in winter. Beeches aren't particularly fond of pollution, so they are better off away from the inner city. They do tolerate our limey soils, however, if they are kept moist and well drained. The American Beech, Fagus grandifolia, has smooth silver-gray bark, dark-green summer foliage, and golden fall color. Even in a forest planting it stands out. American Beech is fully hardy throughout the state.

Bloom Period and Color
Unimportant.

Mature Height × Spread
40 to 90 feet × 40 feet or more

Birch

Betula sp.

White Birches are familiar, even to young children. The white, peeling bark creates interest at any time of the year. Stories explaining the use of the bark for canoes, shoes, and other items fill children's books. Visits to the north woods often include stops at souvenir shops where Birch-bark items are displayed. Birches are popular in landscapes because of their graceful form and striking bark. Birches are fast-growing, short-lived trees, grown for their graceful form and ornamental white, cinnamon, or yellow bark. River Birch or Red Birch, Betula nigra, are reported to be resistant to bronze birch borer. Red Birch has attractive cinnamon-colored bark that, when peeled, reveals a lighter-colored inner bark. 'Heritage' River Birch has bark that peels open white to salmon-white.

Bloom Period and Color
Unimportant.

Mature Height × Spread
40 to 50 feet × 20 to 25 feet

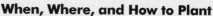

When, Where, and How to Plant
Some Birches do not transplant well. Plant them in the spring only. These are plants of the lowlands and ravines. They prefer moist, well-drained soils. Birch trees are grown as balled-and-burlapped plants and in containers. The hole for planting should be no deeper than the depth of the ball of the plant and at least twice as wide. Remove the plants from their containers and slice any circling roots. Set the plant in the planting hole. Remove the burlap from a balled-and-burlapped plant, and place it in the hole. Replace the soil and fill the hole with water. Make a saucer around the plant with any remaining soil.

Growing Tips
Birches require regular watering the first year after planting. All Birches should be watered in droughty periods.

Care and Maintenance
There is some indication that resistance to the bronze birch borer is improved if the plants are vigorous. River Birch will be less likely to become chlorotic if kept well watered. Chlorotic River Birch can be treated with chelated iron injected into the soil to improve the color. To protect White Birches from borers, spray the trees or apply a band of dimethoate concentrate to the trunks in early June. All pruning should be done in the fall to reduce bleeding.

Companion Planting and Design
Clump Birches are so distinctive that they are best used as accents in the landscape. They can be planted in front of evergreens or mixed with evergreens to simulate their natural setting in the North Woods. These plants are suited for use around water features where they appreciate the moist soil.

Did You Know
Bronze birch borers are deadly for Birches, and resistant cultivars are hard to locate. The only reliable resistant cultivar for Illinois is *B. platyphylla* 'Whitespire', developed at the University of Wisconsin. Unfortunately only plants grown from cuttings taken from the original plant have this characteristic, not those grown from its seeds.

Black Tupelo
Nyssa sylvatica

When, Where, and How to Plant

Black Tupelo reportedly transplants with difficulty. Plants in containers and smaller-sized plants, however, seem to move and become established quite easily. Plant in spring only. Deep, well-drained, acidic soil in full sun or a semi-shaded location is ideal. This plant makes a good street tree or an excellent specimen. It is not overly large and will fit into most residential yards. Black Tupelos are grown as balled-and-burlapped plants. They are hard to transplant because they develop deep taproots. The hole for planting should be no deeper than the depth of the ball of the plant and at least twice as wide. Set the plant in the planting hole. Remove the burlap from the ball and place it in the hole. Replace the soil and fill the hole with water. Make a saucer around the plant with any remaining soil.

Growing Tips

Tupelos require regular watering during the first year after planting. These trees prefer swampy soil, so water them thoroughly once a month, providing at least an inch of water during droughty periods.

Care and Maintenance

Black Tupelo is a trouble-free plant.

Companion Planting and Design

Black Tupelo is an excellent specimen and a good street tree, but since it is not tolerant of air pollution, it is not suitable for the inner city. The form is strongly pyramidal when the tree is young, with upper branches ascending, and descending lower branches.

Did You Know

This is a tree for the southern half of the state. It is hardy in Northern Illinois, but resents the alkaline soils. Local native populations in that part of the state are found on acid soils in Cook, DuPage, Will, and Kankakee Counties. Tupelo has outstanding summer and fall color. The leaves are deep lustrous green in summer turning flourescent yellow, to orange, scarlet, or purple in fall. This tree can be relied on to provide a wonderful fall display every year.

The Black Tupelo is a beautiful native tree with a distinctive pyramidal form, good branching, and excellent fall color. It is one of the most consistent of our native trees for its fall display of brilliant scarlet leaves. This tree prefers swampy places, but may be found in upland sites, woodlots, and abandoned farmlands. It does not tolerate alkaline soils or highly urbanized areas. This is an especially good tree to consider in the southern part of the state, where old soils tend to be acidic. This tree is seldom seen in the Chicago area, although there are a few in Cook County. It is common in the Indiana Dunes. The fruits are dark blue, about the size of cherries, and are attractive to birds.

Other Name
Black Gum

Bloom Period and Color
Insignificant.

Mature Height × Spread
50 feet × 30 feet

Zones
5b to 6

Callery Pear
Pyrus calleryana

Callery Pear was introduced from China in an attempt to introduce fire blight resistance into commercial Pear production. The experiment was unsuccessful, but the result is an interesting landscape plant. In spring these little trees are covered with small white single flowers. Fall color can be spectacular, but it will fail to develop fully if there is an early frost. 'Bradford' Callery Pear is the most common, most disease resistant, and has the best flowering; but is also the most likely to split open. It has a rounded form, as wide as tall. 'Chanticleer' is more upright and considered less likely to disintegrate. 'Aristocrat' has better form with a central leader and good vigor. Fire blight has been serious on this cultivar in the South.

Bloom Period and Color
Spring blooms in white.

Mature Height × Spread
30 feet × 30 feet

When, Where, and How to Plant
This plant is easily moved in either spring or fall if fully dormant. Do not move balled-and-burlapped specimens in leaf. Plant small containerized plants at any time. The Callery Pear is a small, short-lived tree suited for planting in restricted places. It grows well under power lines, is tolerant of many soil types and urban pollution, and makes an attractive street tree. Although Callery Pears are site tolerant, they require full sun. Callery Pears are grown as balled-and-burlapped plants and in containers. The hole for planting should be no deeper than the depth of the ball of the plant and at least twice as wide. Remove the plants from containers and slice any circling roots. Set the plant in the planting hole. Remove the burlap from a balled-and-burlapped plant and place it in the hole. Replace the soil and fill the hole with water. Make a saucer around the plant with any remaining soil.

Growing Tips
Although Callery Pears are drought tolerant, the trees will benefit from watering during extended dry periods. Pears require regular watering the first year after planting.

Care and Maintenance
These plants are somewhat messy. Prune in winter or early spring to remove damaged, diseased, and crossing branches. Later pruning may result in fire blight infection. Callery Pears are extremely brittle as they age. They have a multitude of small branches with narrow crotches that tend to split the tree open as it reaches maturity. Plan to replace these trees every twenty years.

Companion Planting and Design
Callery Pears are small trees and are well suited for planting in parkways with overhead obstructions such as power lines. They are also suited for planting near patios and in small city yards. These trees are commonly used in sidewalk cutouts in the inner city.

Did You Know
Callery Pears are relatively new additions to the inventory of landscape trees. Bradford Pear was the first, selected and named in 1963.

Catalpa
Catalpa speciosa

When, Where, and How to Plant
Catalpas transplant most easily in spring. Plants growing in containers can be planted anytime. While Catalpas probably do best in a well-drained, moist soil, they seem to tolerate wet, dry, or compact alkaline soils without difficulty. Allow growing room and plant in full sun. These trees seem unaffected by extremely hot, dry sites. Catalpas are grown as balled-and-burlapped plants and in containers. The hole for planting should be no deeper than the depth of the ball of the plant and at least twice as wide. Remove the plants from their containers and slice any circling roots. Set the plant in the planting hole. Remove the burlap from the ball, and place it in the hole. Replace the soil and fill the hole with water. Make a saucer around the plant with any remaining soil.

Growing Tips
Water during extended dry spells. Dormant Catalpas are slow to leaf after transplanting. Be patient and do not overwater.

Care and Maintenance
Catalpas require very little care. Cut out dead or broken branches as they appear. These trees are very susceptible to verticillium wilt, a soil-borne fungus disease. Every effort should be made to avoid bringing this disease into contact with a Catalpa.

Companion Planting and Design
In spite of their coarseness, Catalpas make good street trees. They adapt well to our alkaline soils and will stand either wet or dry situations. They can withstand very hot and dry environments. There are several hybrid Catalpas that provide interest in the landscape. *Catalpa bignonioides* 'Nana' is a French selection that is grafted onto a 5-foot-tall standard trunk to produce a weeping, umbrella-like plant. These were very popular in the late 1800s and are in favor again in keeping with the current popularity of things Victorian.

Did You Know
The wood of Catalpa is very durable in contact with soil even though it is soft. It is used for fence posts and railroad ties.

These are old-fashioned trees, more closely associated with the South than the Midwest. The trees are contorted, with loose, coarse branches growing in no clear direction. The Catalpa is a tree for all seasons, however. It leafs out late, after danger of frost. (Some gardeners swear it is not safe to set out tender plants until the Catalpa leaves are at least the size of a man's hand.) Leaves are a pale green, large and heart-shaped. The flowers, which appear in late June or early July, cover the tree with purple-fringed white "orchids." When they drop, they create a summer snow on the lawn. Long seedpods appear after the flowers and remain on the tree all winter. The long, crooked branches are fascinating in winter.

Other Name
Northern Catalpa

Bloom Period and Color
June blooms in white "orchids" with purple fringes.

Mature Height × Spread
50 to 60 feet × 30 feet

Crabapple
Malus sp. and cv.

Few trees suitable for the northern climate compare to the beauty of Crabapples in full bloom. They are spectacular, with color ranging from white to pink, rose, and carmine. Fruits can be inconspicuous or sizable and provide fall color as well as food for wildlife. Crabapples have been hybridized indiscriminately for centuries. The primary objective for this effort was the profusion of flowers, flower size, and color. Within the last three or four decades, there has been emphasis on screening the current cultivars and hybridizing for disease resistance. New cultivars are increasingly disease resistant. The list of cultivars is quite long and confusing. Buy plants from a reliable grower who knows what cultivar was planted and can guarantee what you buy.

Bloom Period and Color
Spring blooms in white, pink, rose, deep red, carmine.

Mature Height × Spread
6 to 25 feet × 25 or more feet

When, Where, and How to Plant
Crabapples are easily transplanted. Plant containerized plants at any time. Crabapples are well adapted to the heavy soils of Illinois. If drainage is adequate, any soil will do. Plant in full sun and allow enough room for the plants to develop fully; otherwise plants will need a lot of pruning. Crabapples are sold bareroot, balled-and-burlapped, and in containers. The hole for planting should be shallower than the depth of the ball and at least twice as wide. Soak bareroot plants for several hours before planting. Remove plants from containers and slice any circling roots. Set each plant in the hole, keeping it slightly higher than it grew in the nursery. The result of deep planting or poor drainage is root rot and plant loss. Remove the burlap from balled-and-burlapped plants and place it in the hole. Replace the soil and fill the hole with water. Make a saucer around the plant with any remaining soil.

Growing Tips
Crabapples will need regular watering the first year after planting.

Care and Maintenance
Properly sited Crabapples need little pruning. Prune immediately after bloom. Remove vertical shoots growing through the center of the tree. If the plant was grafted to a rootstock, there will be suckers to remove. Spray them with diquat as they begin to grow, keeping the Diquat off the desirable foliage. Follow label directions. Many pests affect Crabapples: flat-headed apple borers, scales, aphids, fire blight, other cankers, cedar-apple rust, and the ever-present apple scab. Non-disease-resistant cultivars will require spraying in spring for apple scab and rust diseases. Select cultivars with resistance. Selecting own-root plants eliminates any suckering problem. If fruit-drop is a problem, select a cultivar with tiny fruit.

Companion Planting and Design
Crabapples are prized for their flowers produced in abundance in spring. Use them as specimens, borders, and around one-story buildings.

Did You Know
Illinois is a leader in developing disease-resistant Crabapple varieties.

Douglasfir
Pseudotsuga menziesii

When, Where, and How to Plant
Douglasfirs transplant well balled and burlapped, or from containers. Fall planting before October 1 is best to give the plants time to become established before the onset of winter. These large trees need plenty of room. They prefer moist but well-drained acidic soil, full sun, and protection from winds. Dig the planting holes at the same depth and twice as wide as the root ball. Set the plants at the same depth they were growing. Remove the burlap and twine and stuff it down in the hole. Backfill with the same soil that was dug out of the planting hole. Soak thoroughly to settle the soil. Container-grown plants are grown in artificial soil mix. Shake as much off the ball as you can without damaging the roots, mixing it with the soil from the hole before backfilling.

Growing Tips
Water the trees as needed during the first season, and during droughty summers thereafter. They do best in areas of high humidity and moderate temperatures, and do not like droughty or rocky soils. Mulching with shredded bark helps. Do not use them for windbreaks.

Care and Maintenance
Douglasfirs need little care once well established. Several insect and disease pests can attack Douglasfirs. Keeping the trees protected from environmental stress and vigorously growing will allow them to ward off the worst of the infestations. Control needle blights with fungicides applied at bud break; control caterpillars with *Bacillus thuringiensis*.

Companion Planting and Design
Douglasfirs will readily overcome a small city lot. Don't plant one in the front yard where you will be obliged to crawl around it after a few years. Use Douglasfirs in groupings or masses. They are suited for large plantings where there is room for them, and where they are protected from winds, especially in the winter.

Did You Know
Douglasfirs are excellent Christmas trees—fragrant and fresh indoors without needle-drop for weeks. Hybridizers have created improved types with better color and density that stay fresh longer indoors.

The majestic Douglasfirs are huge forest trees of the Pacific Northwest and the Rocky Mountains. Plants in native stands often reach 250 to 300 feet in height, and have been the mainstays of the timber industry, producing tough wood for construction and for manufacture of plywood. The trees are magnificent landscape plants as well, with soft blue-green foliage and relaxed form. When buying these trees, try to determine where the seed they were grown from originated. Plants from the Rocky Mountains, Pseudotsuga menziesii glauca, are more blue, shorter, and hardier than the West Coast types. Several selections have been made to improve the density and color of these trees, and for smaller sizes to fit city lots. 'Fletcheri' is the most compact, reaching 6 feet.

Other Name
Pseudotsuga taxifolia

Bloom Period and Color
May, yellow catkins.

Mature Height × Spread
50 feet (300 feet in the wild) × 20 to 40 feet

Eastern Hemlock

Tsuga canadensis

Eastern Hemlock is one of the most beautiful of the needle-leaf evergreens. In forest settings it is soft and graceful, with glossy, dark green foliage. In the home garden it can be allowed to grow if there is room, but is easily trimmed to keep it within the size limitations. Thus, it is one of the most useful of the evergreens and should be more widely planted. According to some sources, Hemlocks need acidic soils, but I see them thriving in the alkaline soils of our area. They seem to tolerate almost any situation except drought, drying winds, or the toughest of inner-city conditions. They are susceptible to quite a few insects and diseases. In spite of their problems, if they are given decent care, they are reliable, handsome landscape plants.

Other Name
Canadian Hemlock

Bloom Period and Color
Spring, yellow-green, inconspicuous.

Mature Height × Spread
40 to 70 feet × 25 feet

When, Where, and How to Plant
Plant balled and burlapped either in spring or fall. Container-grown plants can be planted all season. In either case plant them by about October 15 so they have time to become established before the onset of winter. A cool, well-drained but moist soil is preferred. These plants need protection from sweeping winds. They will deteriorate quickly in exposed situations. Dig the planting holes at the same depth and twice as wide as the root ball. Set the plants at the same depth they were growing. Remove the burlap and twine and stuff it down in the hole. Backfill with the same soil that was dug out of the planting hole. Soak thoroughly to settle the soil. Container-grown plants are grown in artificial soil mix. Shake as much off the ball as you can without damaging the roots, mixing it with the soil from the hole before backfilling.

Growing Tips
Water as needed during dry periods. Hemlocks are very susceptible to drought, high temperatures, and drying winds, developing brown needles and dead twigs. Mulch newly-planted Hemlocks with shredded bark to keep the soil cool and moist.

Care and Maintenance
Hemlocks tolerate heavy pruning and can be kept at heights of 3 to 5 feet quite easily. They make excellent hedges. Prune in spring or summer. Remove individual shoots with hand clippers to preserve the pleasing softness. If sheared, trim hedges back to size before growth begins, and shear during the season, leaving at least half of the new growth on the plant. Protection from drying winds and droughty soils is a must. Insects and diseases are less troublesome if the plants are not under stress.

Companion Planting and Design
Hemlocks can be used as specimens, in groupings, for screens, and for hedges. They are excellent backdrops for shade gardens, and around water features.

Did You Know
Hemlocks have been hybridized extensively. There are dwarf, rounded, weeping, fastigiate, and even prostrate forms for nearly any use.

Flowering Dogwood

Cornus florida

When, Where, and How to Plant

Flowering Dogwoods are available balled and burlapped and in containers. Plant balled-and-burlapped plants in spring or fall. Container-grown plants can be planted all season. Flowering Dogwood is an understory tree and adapted to shaded locations. It prefers a cool, moist, acidic soil, but can be found growing and doing well in hot, dry places. The hole for planting should be shallower than the depth of the ball, and at least twice as wide. Remove plants from their containers and slice any circling roots. Set the plant in the hole, keeping it slightly higher than it grew in the nursery. The result of deep planting or poor drainage will be root rot and plant loss. Remove the burlap from balled-and-burlapped plants and place it in the hole. Replace the soil and fill the hole with water. Make a saucer around the plant with any remaining soil.

Growing Tips

Flowering Dogwood requires little care once established. Provide water in extended droughts. Water regularly the first year after planting.

Care and Maintenance

Pruning, if needed, should be done immediately after flowering. Dogwood anthracnose, a disease of Flowering Dogwoods, has been traced to the eastern states. It causes the progressive death of stems and eventually the entire tree. The disease is prevalent in wet springs and more commonly affects plants under stress. Several fungicides are effective for prevention. Apply fungicide just before flowers open and repeat as long as wet weather persists. Flowering Dogwood blooms reliably in the southern half of the state. In the north, blooming has been variable. This could be attributed to differences in ecotypes. Those grown from seed or cuttings of northern types tend to be hardier.

Companion Planting and Design

Dogwoods have four-season interest: spring flowers, summer and fall foliage, fruit, and winter silhouette.

Did You Know

There are many selections of Flowering Dogwoods. Finding a particular one may be difficult. Local nurseries generally grow one or two types suited to your local conditions.

Flowering Dogwood is one of the most beautiful and best known of the flowering trees. In April, the woods come alive with its flower clusters (actually showy bracts surrounding inconspicuous flowers). It has white or pink blooms in spring; bright, clear green leaves all summer; and finishes the fall in a blaze of red. Flowering Dogwood is a small deciduous tree with horizontal branching that gives it a layered or stratified effect, especially when in bloom. While it is a woodland plant, it is well adapted to residential landscapes, particularly in wooded areas. There are many selections of Flowering Dogwood. Select plants grown from seed or cuttings collected locally. There is a wide variation in hardiness and flowering if regional types are grown outside their normal ranges.

Bloom Period and Color
Early spring blooms in white or pink bracts surrounding small green flowers.

Mature Height × Spread
30 feet × 30 or more feet

Ginkgo
Ginkgo biloba

Ginkgo is probably the most ancient tree now under cultivation. Fossil records show that it was a native plant in North America when the dinosaurs roamed. No one knows where the plants we grow today originated; there are none in the wild. They were brought to this country in 1784 from eastern China. Ginkgo is unusual in other ways. The leaves are shaped like a fan, yet the tree is more closely related to a Pine than to any broadleaf tree. There is only one species, but there are many cultivars. Female trees tend to be broad; male trees are more upright. Although the Ginkgo is a wonderful tree, there are some drawbacks. The female trees produce a fruit that is messy and foul smelling.

Bloom Period and Color
Spring blooms in green (insignificant).

Mature Height × Spread
40 to 50 feet × 40 feet

When, Where, and How to Plant
Gingko transplants easily. Spring or fall planting is equally successful. Containerized plants can be planted anytime. Deep, moist soil is preferred, but these trees are very adaptable and will accept almost any situation. They tolerate alkaline or acidic soils, sand or clay, if there is adequate drainage. They thrive in full sun and are excellent for parkways or yards. Ginkgo is relatively salt-tolerant. The Ginkgo is grown as a balled-and-burlapped plant and in containers. The hole for planting should be no greater than the depth of the ball of the plant and at least twice as wide. Remove the plants from containers and slice any circling roots. Set the plant in the planting hole. Remove the burlap from a balled-and-burlapped plant and place it in the hole. Replace the soil and fill the hole with water. Make a saucer around the plant with any remaining soil.

Growing Tips
Water regularly the first year after planting.

Care and Maintenance
There are no insects or diseases affecting these trees. Any pruning for shaping should be done in spring.

Companion Planting and Design
This is as good a tree as can be found for city plantings because of its tolerant nature. Ginkgo is equally suited for the open spaces where it can develop to its full potential. One of the most magnificent specimens I have ever seen is a female tree in the back yard over a big home, spreading over the house and yard like a huge umbrella, gorgeous in fall. Outstanding! (It doesn't fruit every year, and there are some things that can be done to lessen fruiting.)

Did You Know
There are many male selections of this tree. Most are propagated vegetatively. It is difficult to tell male from female seedling trees because they do not fruit until quite old. Males are generally narrower, but the best way to get what you are looking for is to buy a named cultivar.

Hackberry
Celtis occidentalis

When, Where, and How to Plant
Hackberries can be planted in either spring or fall. They tolerate almost any situation. Hackberries are excellent street trees because they will stand salting and compaction. Sun or shade and plenty of room are all they need. Hackberries are grown bareroot, as balled-and-burlapped plants, or in containers. The hole for planting should be no deeper than the depth of the ball of the plant and at least twice as wide. Soak roots of bareroot plants in a bucket of water for several hours before planting. Remove the plants from their containers and slice any circling roots. Set the plant in the planting hole at the same depth it grew in the nursery. Remove the burlap from a balled-and-burlapped plant and place it in the hole. Replace the soil and fill the hole with water. Make a saucer around the plant with any remaining soil.

Growing Tips
Hackberries take little if any care. They are native plants, and well suited to the climate and soils of Illinois. Newly planted Hackberries appreciate water every week or two in dry weather. Water mature trees in extended droughts every three weeks, applying an inch over the entire area under the tree.

Care and Maintenance
Hackberries tend to be messy trees. They drop berries and sticks from the witches'-brooms that require raking. They are susceptible to numerous insects, the nipplegall being the most troublesome. Insects causing the galls leave the tree in fall and may migrate indoors seeking winter quarters. They don't bite, eat, or reproduce indoors. Swat them and vacuum them up. Although beset with a myriad of problems, these trees simply shrug them off and grow on.

Companion Planting and Design
Use as a street tree or for shade in large areas. These trees will withstand tough city conditions and dry soils.

Did You Know
Three Hackberry cultivars have been developed for Illinois conditions. 'Chicagoland', 'Prairie Pride', and 'Windy City' have better form and resist witches'-brooms.

The Hackberry is a large deciduous tree, a native of the bottomlands from which our most adaptable tree species have been selected. It tolerates wet or dry, acid or alkaline, sunny or shaded, urbanized or rural situations equally well. These are the attributes that made the American Elm so useful. With the loss of the Elms, Hackberry seems to be a logical replacement, but an unsightly condition called "witches'-brooms" affects many Hackberries. This is caused by a mite and mildew growing on the buds. It results in masses of twiggy growth at the tips of branches, but it doesn't seem to bother the tree at all. Hackberries will thrive in rough conditions. Cultivars resistant to the witches'-brooms with superior habits have been introduced.

Bloom Period and Color
Spring blooms (insignificant).

Mature Height × Spread
50 to 60 feet × 40 feet

Hawthorn

Crataegus sp.

When plowed ground returns to nature, Hawthorns are often the first trees to take root. They appear as solitary plants or in groves. These rugged little trees are dense, twiggy, and armed with thorns. They bear attractive flowers and fruits, tolerate heat and cold, wet and dry, excellent and poor soils, urban and rural situations . . . all of the conditions we find in Illinois. As landscape plants, Hawthorns are durable and attractive when cared for adequately. They can make effective barriers because of their thorns. 'Cockspur Thorn', Crataegus crus-galli, is a rounded plant with shiny, green foliage reaching 20 feet. Washington Hawthorn, C. phaenopyrum, is vase-shaped and 20 feet tall with red fruit. These plants have strong, 3-inch thorns and should not be used where little children might encounter them.

Bloom Period and Color
Spring blooms in white.

Mature Height × Spread
20 to 30 feet × 30 feet

When, Where, and How to Plant

Plant Hawthorns in spring or fall. Hawthorns grown in containers can be planted anytime the soil is workable. Hawthorns tolerate many conditions but appreciate a rich, deep soil. Hawthorns are grown as balled-and-burlapped plants and in containers. The hole for planting should be about the depth of the ball of the plant and at least twice as wide. Remove the plants from their containers and slice any circling roots. Set the plant in the planting hole. Remove the burlap from a balled-and-burlapped plant, and place it in the hole. Replace the soil and fill the hole with water. Make a saucer around the plant with any remaining soil.

Growing Tips

Water to provide an inch per week in hot weather. Fertilize in fall or early spring with a complete fertilizer such as 10-10-10 at 1 pound per 100 square feet.

Care and Maintenance

Hawthorns require little care, but are susceptible to several insect pests and a disease that spots the leaves. The worst of the insects are leaf miners, which turn leaves brown with little tunnels running through them. Treat plants with acephate in May when the first brown spots appear. Control cedar-hawthorn rust (orange spots on the leaves) and cedar quince rust (fuzzy growth on fruit and tips of stems) with mancozeb, Daconil, or Bayleton as leaves open, and several more times if the weather is wet. Read and follow directions on the labels. Trim Hawthorns in winter to remove damaged branches, suckers, water shoots, and overly long branches.

Companion Planting and Design

Use as specimens or in the shrub border. Make sure they are not where children might accidentally run into them. (Thornless cultivars are available.)

Did You Know

Hawthorns have been bred and selected for better flowers and for disease resistance. 'Paul's Scarlet' is the showiest of all with double red flowers, but it is very susceptible to leafspot diseases that can cause the tree to be without leaves by midsummer.

Honeylocust
Gleditsia triacanthos inermis

When, Where, and How to Plant
Honeylocust is easily transplanted and can be moved in either spring or fall. Honeylocust can be planted in any soil, sun or shade, in the parkway, or as a lawn tree. Its filtered shade will not affect the lawn or flower plantings. Honeylocust plants are sold bareroot, balled and burlapped, or in containers. Set the plant slightly higher than it grew in the nursery. Deep planting or poor drainage may result in ganoderma root rot and plant loss.

Growing Tips
Honeylocusts will stand a drought, but they do better with a little water. Water as needed to prevent wilting.

Care and Maintenance
Prune to a single stem while the tree is small. These trees tend to develop in a zigzag manner, often with no central leader, in open situations. (In forest settings they grow straight up, seeking the light.) Once the trunk has developed to a satisfactory height, allow the plant to assume its normal growth pattern. Honeylocust is tolerant of pruning and can even be sheared. Honeylocust plant bugs feed on developing leaves in spring, distorting them and rendering the tree leafless for a few weeks. Carbaryl or acephate spray or patience will solve the problem. Mimosa webworm is serious in the southern part of the state. *Bacillis thuringensis* will control it. Honeylocust mite (not an insect) turns leaves bronze in late summer; use insecticidal soap when injury is first noticed. Read and follow directions on insecticide labels. Ganoderma root rot is a secondary invader that affects damaged plants; in the home lawn, the most common sources of this damage are wet soils and the lawn mower. There is no cure for the disease once it begins.

Companion Planting and Design
Honeylocust is an excellent lawn and street tree. It stands city conditions and dry soils. It does well in tree pit sidewalk cutouts in business districts. The tiny leaflets do not require raking up. They blow away.

Did You Know
Common Honeylocust trees have multitudes of big sharp thorns.

The loss of the Elms initiated a quest for the perfect tree to replace them. One of the first candidates was Thornless Honeylocust. This is a delightful large tree with finely cut foliage. It is broad and round-topped with a decidedly layered effect. Some newer selections develop a vase shape, reminiscent of Elms. The fine foliage allows filtered light to reach the ground and grass grows easily in its shade. It tolerates wet or dry, acid or alkaline, sunny or shaded, urbanized or rural situations well. Honeylocust is salt-tolerant, which has endeared it to urban landscape architects. It is so widely used that should a disease as devastating as Dutch elm afflict these trees, the effects on the shade tree population would be detrimental indeed.

Bloom Period and Color
May-June blooms in green.

Mature Height × Spread
70 feet × 30 feet

177

Hornbeam

Carpinus caroliniana

An interesting smaller tree, Hornbeam is a tough native of the bottomlands. It tolerates wet or dry, acid or alkaline, sunny or shaded situations. These are the attributes that make many native plants so useful in our landscapes. This is a particularly useful plant in a shaded site where overhanging trees could create a challenge to landscape designers. Hornbeam will stand the shade and relish the moist soil normal in these sites. Hornbeam is interesting in all seasons. The catkins are light green as leaves begin to open. Foliage is somewhat small and allows the interesting structure of the plant to show through. Fall color is yellow to orange. In winter, the beautiful smooth, gray bark on multiple, muscular trunks lends contrast to the white snow.

Other Name
Blue Beech

Bloom Period and Color
Spring blooms in light green.

Mature Height × Spread
20 feet × 20 feet

When, Where, and How to Plant

Balled-and-burlapped Hornbeam transplants well when small. Plant in spring. Plant in sun to partial shade. Hornbeam prefers well-drained but moist soil. It tolerates alkalinity and other difficult situations. Hornbeam will spread 20 feet, so place it no closer than 10 feet from a structure. Hornbeams are grown as balled-and-burlapped plants. These trees are shallowly rooted, needing a well-aerated soil. Dig the hole for planting them a little more shallow than they grew in the nursery and at least twice as wide. Set the plant in the planting hole; remove the burlap and place it in the hole. Replace the soil and fill the hole with water. Make a saucer around the plant with any remaining soil.

Growing Tips

Water during extended dry periods.

Care and Maintenance

There are no serious pests that affect Hornbeam. It is tolerant of pruning but seldom needs any.

Companion Planting and Design

Hornbeams tolerate the shade of the older tree-lined neighborhoods. They also are at home in the alkaline soils so common in urban areas. Use them where their interesting four-season character can be appreciated.

Did You Know

European Hornbeam, *C. betulus,* has received more attention in the nursery trade than the American species. It may be somewhat less hardy than *C. caroliniana,* but hardy enough for all parts of Illinois. It is a more refined plant, but with similar bark and muscled trunk. The wood of both the native species and the related European Hornbeam is hard and heavy. The name, Hornbeam, seems to have come from using the wood for the beam used across the horns of oxen to harness them. Axles, spokes of wagons, and other agricultural implements, were sometimes made of the tough Hornbeam wood. Closely related is Hophornbeam, or Ironwood, *Ostrya virginiana.* It has a similar habit and interesting fruits resembling hops. It is used in the same manner and will tolerate some of the same conditions as the above varieties.

Horsechestnut

Aesculus sp.

When, Where, and How to Plant
Horsechestnut trees are grown as balled-and-burlapped or as container plants. Horsechestnut is usually planted balled and burlapped in spring. Container plants can be planted at any time during the season. These plants prefer a moist situation in sun or shade. Some perfectly healthy examples, however, are found in heavy, dry locations. These trees have fibrous descending roots that need well-aerated soil. Dig the hole for planting them twice as wide and a little less deep than they grew in the nursery. Set the plant in the planting hole. Remove the burlap and place it in the hole. Replace the soil and fill the hole with water. Make a saucer around the plant with any remaining soil.

Growing Tips
Horsechestnut resents dry soils. Provide an inch of water per week in dry weather. Young trees will benefit from fertilizer. Apply 10-10-10 at the rate of 1 pound per 100 square feet of ground beneath the trees.

Care and Maintenance
Horsechestnut is free from insect pests, but is often afflicted by the foliar disease, blotch. The nuts can be troublesome if they litter the driveway. Leaves are large and fall all at once. Some pruning of young plants to train them may be necessary. Be certain to maintain a single leader.

Companion Planting and Design
These trees are probably too large for most small residential properties, and they create a dense shade. Use them in parks, along broad streets, on industrial campuses, or in large yards for specimens and shade.

Did You Know
The blooms of this tree are spectacular, but blotch disease limits its use. The hybrid Red Horsechestnut is a smaller and more rounded tree, but is nearly free of the disease.

A cross between Red Buckeye, A. pavia, and Horsechestnut, A. hippocastanum, produced Red Horsechestnut, Aesculus × carnea, with red blooms and good blotch resistance. The Horsechestnut is a handsome, dense, deciduous tree, showy in flower. As its buds open in spring, there is a succession of developing flower clusters at the ends of the twigs, followed by the unfolding of hand-like leaves. It produces gorgeous, upright spikes (panicles) of blooms in late spring. The palmate leaves, compound and light green as they open, are favorites of schoolchildren making leaf collections. The fruits are spiny nuts that are attractive food for squirrels and wildlife. Horsechestnuts are useful as street trees and for tree lawns where there is ample room. 'Baumannii', the Baumann Horsechestnut, has double blooms and no fruit.

Other Name
Buckeye

Bloom Period and Color
June blooms in white, pink.

Mature Height × Spread
40 feet × 40 feet

Hybrid Elm

Ulmus hybrids

Elm trees once lined almost every street throughout the Midwest. In the middle of the last century, Dutch elm disease decimated the plantings. Only pockets of Elms remain where communities have gone to great efforts to preserve them. They are still fondly remembered by people who grew up sheltered by these trees. Within the last decade, cultivars and hybrids bred with natural resistance to the disease have been introduced and are being planted in many communities. The best of these cultivars and hybrids have form similar to the American Elm which was the best of the Elms. Many of these varieties are being evaluated through the Chicagoland Grows program which has released several into the trade.

Bloom Period and Color
Early spring or summer, green, not conspicuous.

Mature Height × **Spread**
40 to 60 feet tall × nearly as wide

When, Where, and How to Plant
Plant balled-and-burlapped plants in spring or fall. Container-grown plants can be planted at any time. These are large trees and need room. Tolerant of soil pH, they can stand emersion in spring, but do best in a fairly well-drained soil. Set plants at the same depth they grew in the nursery or in the container. Be sure to remove the burlap and twine, or untie it and shove it down in the planting hole. Cut any girdling roots on container-grown plants. Make a saucer around the plant with any remaining soil. These trees will need to be watered the first season following transplanting.

Growing Tips
Water the trees the first season if weather is dry. Soak thoroughly and then allow them to dry before soaking again.

Care and Maintenance
These hybrid trees do not grow nice straight trunks and need trimming and training as they grow. Many insects and diseases do attack these trees, but usually cause no serious harm. Elm leaf beetles, gypsy moths, Japanese beetles and elm leafspot may damage the leaves. If the trees are healthy, they can live very nicely with these parasites. If the trees are weakened, the pests may damage or kill them. Ignore them, or treat as necessary. Trimming will be necessary every few years to keep the plants shapely and to remove any damaged or crowded branches.

Companion Planting and Design
Elms are shade trees for the parkway or for large yards. Use where they have lots of room to grow. Use them to frame the house or as backdrops. Our community has planted Regal Elms as street trees for several years. So far they are disease-free and doing well, some in adverse conditions.

Did You Know
Most hybrid Elms are crosses between American Elms and Asian species that resist Dutch elm disease and elm yellows. Many of the crosses including the newest one, Triumph TM, result from many years of research by Dr. George Ware of Morton Arboretum in Lisle, Illinois.

Japanese Tree Lilac
Syringa reticulata

When, Where, and How to Plant

Like other Lilacs, these trees move with ease in either spring or fall. Plant container-grown plants at any time. Japanese Tree Lilac tolerates almost any soil that has adequate drainage. It does not seem to be pH sensitive and grows well in the alkalinity of urban soils in northern Illinois. It prefers full sun but tolerates some shade. Flowering, however, may be diminished. Japanese Tree Lilacs are grown as balled-and-burlapped plants and in containers. The hole for planting should be no deeper than the depth of the ball of the plant and at least twice as wide. Roots of these plants are fibrous and shallow. Set the plant in the planting hole; remove the burlap and shove it down in the hole. Replace the soil and fill the hole with water. Make a saucer around the plant with any remaining soil.

Growing Tips

Japanese Lilacs will need regular watering the first year after planting.

Care and Maintenance

Japanese Tree Lilacs are relatively care-free. They can be pruned immediately after flowering. Use a pole pruner to keep them in bounds and to remove the faded flowers that turn brown and tend to hang on the tree. If planted in a tight location, heavy pruning can restrain them. The Japanese Tree Lilac is subject to many of the pests affecting others of the genus but it seems to be more vigorous, having little difficulty with borers or scale. If flowers remain on the plants, heavy seed loads will develop and drop. The result is a proliferation of seedlings although some propagators report difficulty with germinating the seed. They can be hoed or pulled easily.

Companion Planting and Design

The shade and dense shallow roots make planting ground covers beneath these trees difficult. Try Vinca, or annuals such as Impatiens. European Ginger does well under them as long as it receives enough water.

Did You Know

This tree shrugs off most common Lilac problems.

The Japanese Tree Lilac differs from most other Lilacs—it is more correctly a single stem or multi-stemmed tree than a bush. It flowers a full month later than other Lilacs with creamy-white blooms borne in foot-long, upright panicles covering the plants. The flowers are less fragrant than other Lilacs with an aroma resembling Privet. Leaves are typically heart-shaped and the bark is cherry-like, smooth and reddish, and marked with horizontal white lenticels. It is striking in winter. The cultivar 'Ivory Silk' is compact and flowers heavily. 'Ivory Silk' and the species are the only ones listed by most Illinois nurseries. Syringa pekinensis, Peking Lilac, is a similar species. Little hybridizing has been done on Japanese Tree Lilac, although a tree form, 'Summer Charm', was introduced by Wandell Nurseries, Urbana.

Bloom Period and Color
June blooms in white.

Mature Height × Spread
20 feet × 20 feet

Katsuratree
Cercidiphyllum japonicum

Katsuratree is a magnificent pyramidal tree with apricot fall color. It is rare to see a mature one, but most tree aficionados seem to know the location of at least one spectacular specimen. Two places in Illinois are the Morton Arboretum and the campus of the University of Illinois at Urbana-Champaign. Katsura starts out as a strongly upright tree, becoming broad with age. The tree has often been planted too close to buildings, requiring drastic pruning or removal.

Bloom Period and Color
Insignificant.

Mature Height × Spread
40 to 50 feet × 30 to 50 feet

When, Where, and How to Plant
Katsura is difficult to transplant. Plant it only in early spring, balled and burlapped, or as a container plant. Plant in a rich, moist soil with good drainage. Tolerant of either acid or alkaline soils, these trees do best and color up more intensely in full sun. Be sure to provide enough room for this tree. It is often as wide as it is high. The rather open crown allows some light and air. Katsuratrees are grown as balled-and-burlapped or container plants. The trees have shallow roots, needing well-aerated soil. Roots form a mat at the soil surface. Dig the hole for planting twice as wide and a little less deep than the depth of the ball. Set the plant in the planting hole. Remove the burlap and place it in the hole. Replace the soil and fill the hole with water. Make a saucer around the plant with any remaining soil.

Growing Tips
Supplemental watering is essential during the first few seasons until the tree develops a good root system. Apply an inch of water every week or two in dry spells.

Care and Maintenance
Katsuratree is relatively trouble-free. There are no insects or diseases that seriously affect the tree. Exposed bark may be subject to scalding. Be careful when pruning not to expose bark to the sun too suddenly. Try to orient the tree so that the south side remains south in its new location. Getting the tree established is sometimes difficult.

Companion Planting and Design
Katsuratree is an excellent street tree where there is room, and a magnificent specimen tree. It is suited for parks, residences, and office campuses. Use it where it has room to develop.

Did You Know
Katsuratree has the reputation for being difficult to grow. The secret is adequate water as it is trying to get started. Soak it and let it dry before watering again.

Kentucky Coffeetree
Gymnocladus dioicus

When, Where, and How to Plant
This tree may be planted balled and burlapped in either spring or fall. Container plants may be planted at any time. Full sun and a well-drained, moist soil are preferred, but Coffeetree is quite adaptable. Kentucky Coffeetree is a large plant that needs room to develop to its full size. Set balled-and-burlapped plants at the same depth they grew in the nursery. Be sure to remove the burlap and twine. Be sure to cut any girdling roots on container-grown plants and mix some of the container soil with that in the planting hole to avoid soil incompatibility problems. Roots are fleshy, with a few fibers growing downward.

Growing Tips
It requires regular watering the first season after planting. Soak thoroughly every week or two, especially in dry weather.

Care and Maintenance
Kentucky Coffeetree is relatively maintenance-free. Few insects or diseases affect it. It is a somewhat messy tree at times, though the leaflets that drop from the leaves in fall are small and no problem. They can be shredded as the lawn is mowed and disappear. The rachises (stems) of the leaves persist and usually fall in late winter and the pods fall in spring. This can mean cleaning up several times. If that coincides with other cleanup times or with mowing the lawn, it need not be an overwhelming chore.

Companion Planting and Design
This is a large and rather coarse tree. It makes an excellent street tree, and specimen for large lawns. The foliage allows light to penetrate so lawns do well beneath it. It is a tough tree and can stand the rigors of urban areas, not minding the alkaline Midwest soils.

Did You Know
Kentucky Coffeetrees are not well known in the landscape industry, but that is changing. Size may have something to do with it, but with the huge homes being built lately, they should become quite popular. Municipalities are beginning to plant them as street trees in good numbers.

Kentucky Coffeetree is large with foliage that is doubly pinnately compound. The leaves are large, sometimes 3 feet long with leaflets about 3 inches long and half as wide. The effect is quite airy in summer. It is one of the last trees to leaf out in spring. In winter, the structure shows large spreading limbs rather bereft of branches, quite coarse but bold. The seedpods, a foot long, hang on female trees all winter to rustle in the wind. Kentucky Coffeetree is suited for larger sites, parkways, large lawns, and parks. Kentucky Coffeetree tolerates wet or dry, acid or chalky, sunny or shaded, urbanized or rural situations well. The seeds of Kentucky Coffeetree, although used in pioneer days as a coffee substitute, are considered poisonous. Speculation is that roasting eliminates the toxic substance but don't try it unless you know how to use them.

Bloom Period and Color
Deciduous. May to June blooms of large, fragrant, lovely white panicles.

Mature Height × Spread
60 to 70 feet × 90 feet

Larch
Larix decidua

Larches are unusual conifers that lose their leaves in fall. (Most conifers are evergreen, but Larches are deciduous.) In the spring, soft, light-green leaves join tiny pink-and-yellow "flowers." Later, leaves are deeper green but retain their soft appearance. Fall color can be spectacular, depending on the weather and site. Larches are graceful pyramidal trees with sweeping, pendulous branches. They provide light shade and do not interfere with the lawn beneath them. In the fall, the leaves that drop filter into the lawn and disappear without raking. Larches are planted throughout our community as parkway and lawn trees. Many have been in place for over seventy-five years and remain healthy. 'Fastigiata' is narrow with short ascending branches and is a good replacement for Lombardy Poplars.

Other Name
European Larch

Bloom Period and Color
Deciduous.

Mature Height × Spread
50 to 100 feet × 25 feet

When, Where, and How to Plant
Plant Larches in spring when fully dormant. Fall planting can be successful if not followed by a particularly harsh winter. Container-grown plants can be planted anytime during the season. Larches require cool, moist soils and good drainage. They tolerate periodic inundation and perform well for pondside planting. Full sun and additional organic matter create ideal conditions. Set balled-and-burlapped plants at the same depth they grew in the nursery. Be sure to remove the burlap and twine. Cut any girdling roots on container-grown plants. Mix some of the container soil with that in the planting hole to avoid soil incompatibility.

Growing Tips
Water as needed to keep them from wilting. Larches are trees of the moist forest.

Care and Maintenance
Larches require very little care once they are established. There are few pests that bother them. Prune in midsummer.

Companion Planting and Design
Many Larches are planted around the water features that, because of the necessity of retention ponds, have become quite common. Larches appreciate the moist soils, and their form makes them excellent pondside additions. They are used as street trees and as shade trees, especially useful on the south sides of homes where the lack of leaves in winter allows the sun to warm the home and melt the snow.

Did You Know
Deciduous conifers, those that lose their leaves in winter, are quite unusual. The form is that of an "evergreen," so the uninitiated may think the poor thing has died when it drops its leaves. We have received many calls from new owners of these plants, especially city folks who have just moved to the "country." Other deciduous conifers include Bald Cypress, Dawn Redwood, and American Tamarack. American Tamarack, *Larix laricina,* is the native Larch, common throughout the northern Midwest. It grows best if left in its natural "moose meadows." Tamarack does not tolerate any pollution or any shade, so is not suited for landscape use.

Linden
Tilia sp.

When, Where, and How to Plant

Lindens transplant easily. They may be planted in spring or fall. Container-grown plants may be planted any time during the season. Lindens prefer a deep, moist, well-drained soil, but will grow in most Illinois soil. They inhabit limey sites in the wild. Full sun or partial shade is satisfactory. Set balled-and-burlapped plants at the same depth they grew in the nursery. Be sure to remove the burlap and twine, or untie it and place it in the planting hole. Cut any girdling roots on container-grown plants. Make a saucer around the plant with any remaining soil.

Growing Tips

Water plants regularly the first season after transplanting. Lindens are shallow-rooted, and suckering from the roots can be troublesome. If roots are nicked by a mower, they will produce shoots and suckers in the lawn.

Care and Maintenance

Lindens require very little care. Pruning to shape them while they are young is helpful. These plants take pruning very gracefully and can be sheared into hedges, a practice common in Europe. There is a long list of insects and diseases, but fortunately, Lindens aren't often stricken. Wood rot, which hollows out the center of the tree, is fairly common. The condition usually does not affect the longevity or sturdiness of the tree. If cultivars are grafted on seedling rootstock, the rootstock may sucker. Trim off, or apply a burn-off herbicide such as Diquat.

Companion Planting and Design

Lindens are stately trees for streets, lawns, or parks. They are often used in sidewalk cutouts in municipal business districts. They do tolerate the tough conditions, but not as well as some other trees. Grafted Lindens have been troublesome because of graft incompatibility, reducing their useful lives. Own-root trees eliminate that problem.

Did You Know

Lindens are often called "Bee Trees." The trees have fragrant flowers in spring which attract wild bees, and hollow Lindens are often inhabited by bees that build their hives in the cavity.

Lindens are some of our most valuable shade trees, and there has been extensive selection to improve them. Lindens are excellent for planting in the lawn, as street trees, in malls, in sidewalk tree pits, in parking lots, or wherever shade is desired. The larger species are especially good in the industrial parks where trees of grand scale are needed. Lindens are attractive trees with handsome foliage and inconspicuous, beautifully scented flowers. They have good neat form for the most part and stay fairly clean. Tilia americana, American Linden, Basswood, or Bee Tree, is a large tree with large leaves. The species is excellent for park-like settings or street trees. The cultivars 'Redmond', 'Rosehill', and 'Greenspire' Littleleaf Linden are more suitable for streets or lawns.

Bloom Period and Color
Late June, July blooms in cream-yellow.

Mature Height × Spread
50 feet × 30 feet

Magnolia

Magnolia sp.

Magnolias are small- to medium-sized trees, often grown for their large, spectacular, fragrant flowers. Several Magnolia species are hardy enough for Illinois gardens. The Star Magnolia, M. stellata, blooms in early spring before the leaves emerge. The flowers are fragrant with strap-like white petals. The plant is a small, often multi-stemmed tree growing to about 20 feet. The Saucer Magnolia flowers later with large, saucer-shaped blooms, white on the inside, maroon on the reverse. The tree may grow to 20 or 30 feet with a spread as wide as it is tall. Magnolia grandiflora, the Southern Magnolia, is widely planted in the south and reportedly hardy in Zone 5. It is recommended only in the southern part of the state (Zones 6 and 7).

Bloom Period and Color
April, May, June, blooms in white tinged with pink or maroon.

Mature Height × Spread
15 to 30 feet × 30 feet

When, Where, and How to Plant

These plants do not move gracefully. Buy them in containers or balled and burlapped and plant them in spring. Plant in a sunny spot with good air circulation. Soil must be moist but well drained and with a pH that is neutral or lower. Star Magnolia will turn yellow if planted in an alkaline soil. Set balled-and-burlapped plants at the same depth they grew in the nursery. Be sure to remove the burlap and twine. Cut any girdling roots on container-grown plants. Mix some of the container soil with that in the planting hole to avoid any soil incompatibility problems. Magnolias have fleshy roots and care must be taken to minimize damage to them. Damaged roots will rot, and recovery from transplanting will be jeopardized.

Growing Tips

Water in dry periods is essential. Soak thoroughly and let dry before watering again.

Care and Maintenance

Magnolias are clean plants that require very little care. Pruning should be minimal. If pruning is needed, it should be done as soon as possible following flowering to assure that flower buds are set for the next year. Recently, magnolia scale, a large showy insect, has become troublesome in many plantings. Treat with insecticidal soap or Orthene in late September or early spring when buds are opening.

Companion Planting and Design

Magnolias are grown for the magnificent blooms early in the season. Plant smaller types as accents or in the shrub border. Larger types are sizeable trees and need room. They can be used as specimens, lawn trees, in groupings around large buildings, or as screens.

Did You Know

Magnolias have fleshy root systems with few lateral roots. The roots are shallow and easily damaged. There are some named selections of Saucer and Star Magnolias. In most of Illinois, the later flowering varieties are to be preferred. Late frosts decimate the blooms about a third of the time. Consider planting in a protected location preferably where it is cooler so flowering is delayed.

Maple

Acer sp.

When, Where, and How to Plant

Maples transplant easily in spring or fall. If container-grown or dug while dormant, they may be planted all season. Most Maples will tolerate any decent garden soil. The pH may be acidic or alkaline, though Red Maples will lose color and become chlorotic in limey soil. They do best in full sun, but will grow in filtered or even quite dense shade. Maples require room. Some produce shallow roots and dense shade, preventing the growth of grass. Set balled-and-burlapped plants a little higher than they grew in the nursery. These are shallowly rooted plants that suffer from collar rot at the soil line if planted too deeply.

Growing Tips

Maples are shallowly rooted and can benefit from water during extended dry weather. Apply a measured inch every week or two to the entire area beneath the branch spread. Chlorotic Red or Silver Maples may be helped by application of chelated iron to the soil in late fall or early spring.

Care and Maintenance

Prune to develop single leaders. Maples are best pruned in winter to reduce bleeding. Many pests affect Maples. Cottony maple scale on Silver Maples generally attracts enough natural predators that it disappears after a few years. Spray if needed with dormant oil in late winter or Malathion in early summer. Norway and Sugar Maples allowed to wilt severely in high temperatures may suffer the loss of branches. Apply an inch of water per week in dry weather.

Companion Planting and Design

Plant Sugar and Red Maples for their spectacular fall color and their excellent form. With a backdrop of Spruces or White Pines the colors will stand out even more. Norway and Silver Maples are fast-growing and provide quick shade, but Norway Maples make shallow roots. Silver Maples may be brittle and buggy.

Did You Know

All Maples can grow girdling roots which encircle the trunk at or just below the soil, killing the trees.

Spectacular fall color! That is reason enough to plant Maples. Maples are some of the best trees for shade in the lawn or garden, for the street, or for specimens in larger spaces. They are tidy in form, easily transplanted, and undemanding. Some even produce colorful flowers in spring. The characteristic shape of a Sugar Maple or Norway Maple leaf, palmately veined with three or five pointed lobes, is familiar to even the youngest school child. Sugar Maple, A. saccharum, lights up the land in fall. The crown is somewhat open, allowing light to grass underneath. This upland tree can be grown in any well-drained soil. Norway Maple, A. platanoides, has become the most widely planted Maple lately, surpassing the Silver Maple.

Bloom Period and Color
Spring blooms in yellow, red, green.

Mature Height × Spread
40 to 60 feet × 25 to 40 feet

Oak

Quercus sp.

Oaks are among our finest trees; the White Oak is our state tree. Big, beautiful trees, they are most prized by tree aficionados. Oaks are generally slow growing, although Red Oaks may grow up to 2 feet per year in optimum settings. They are excellent street, parkway, and lawn trees, suited to acidic soils, but, except for Pin Oak, seem to do very well in the chalky soils of Illinois when there is adequate drainage. This may be due to the symbiotic association with fungi called mycorrhizae that serve as the functioning roots of Oaks in these soils. Construction often results in killing of the mycorrhizae, followed by decline and death of the old trees. New trees on these sites grow well, as they adjust to the conditions when young.

Bloom Period and Color
Inconspicuous.

Mature Height × Spread
40 to 80 feet × 25 to 80 feet

When, Where, and How to Plant
Oaks are best planted in spring. Dig when leaves are the size of a mouse's ear, and relocate promptly. Oaks will tolerate most well-drained soils. Full or partial sun is best. Plant in parkways, tree lawns, or other large areas for shade. Groves of Oaks are appealing for large industrial park sites. Set balled-and-burlapped plants a little higher than they grew in the nursery. These are shallowly rooted plants. If planted too deeply, some may suffer from collar rot that will girdle them at the soil line when they approach mature size. Transplant trees when young.

Growing Tips
Oaks are shallowly rooted—they benefit from water during extended dry weather. Apply a measured inch every week or two to the entire area beneath the branch spread. Chlorotic trees may be helped by application of chelated iron to the soil in late fall or early spring.

Care and Maintenance
Oaks require very little care once established. Prune to a single leader. Many insects and diseases will live on Oaks. If the trees are healthy, they will live in comfortable association with these parasites. If the trees are weakened, the pests may damage or kill the trees. Leaf miner and anthracnose will turn leaves blotchy-brown some seasons. Unless this happens every year, no treatment is needed. Consult a certified arborist for treatment. Avoid pruning in spring and summer to reduce chances of oak wilt.

Companion Planting and Design
Oaks in nature grow in association with other trees such as Hickories, Sugar Maples, American Ash, and understory plants such as Redbuds, Flowering Dogwoods, or Ironwood. Mix them in landscape plantings for interest, and to reduce chances of catastrophic diseases.

Did You Know
Oak wilt is a fungus disease that is spread by sap beetles. It can be transmitted from tree to tree through grafted roots. If an Oak suddenly dies, consult a certified arborist or your county extension office for advice. Most old Oaks die from changes in their environment, not from oak wilt.

Pine

Pinus sp.

When, Where, and How to Plant

Balled-and-burlapped plants are best moved in spring but can be moved in the fall. Plant container plants any time during the season. Pines develop taproots and wide-spreading laterals. They need deep, well-drained soil, either heavy or light. Some will tolerate compact soils. Full sun to partial shade is satisfactory. Protect from winter sun and wind. Pines move easily if root-pruned in the nursery. Many are container grown. Set balled-and-burlapped plants at the same depth they grew in the nursery. Remove the burlap and twine, or untie it and place it in the planting hole. If planting potted or canned plants, mix some container soil with that in the planting hole to avoid any soil incompatibility problems. Replace the soil and fill the hole with water. Make a saucer around the plant with any remaining soil.

Growing Tips

Water newly set Pines freely during the first year.

Care and Maintenance

Prune out dead branches and maintain a single leader. Zimmerman pine moth will bore into the trunk at the branch whorls of Austrian and Scotch Pines. Treat with Cygon in April and August. Treat for sphaeropsis tip blight with copper or thiophanate-methyl in spring. Follow label directions.

Companion Planting and Design

Pines make excellent screens, backdrops for small flowering trees or shrubs, and fine specimens. They are large plants and should be used with care in small properties. They can be used in mass plantings, but their interesting forms and branching will be hidden. The trend to much larger homes and properties allows greater use of these magnificent plants.

Did You Know

Many horticultural forms of Pines are available. Some are natural dwarfs or bush forms such as Swiss Mountain Pine (*P. mugo*). Others are selections such as Contorted White Pine or pyramidal Austrian Pine. The most comprehensive collection of unusual Pines (and other evergreens too) in Illinois is Rich's Foxwillow Pines in Woodstock. Their catalog lists nearly 100 Pines of every imaginable form.

Pines are forest plants. They are upright in forest situations and tend to be conical in open spaces. In the landscape, they are often used as screens and seldom achieve mature size. With their persistent needles and good green color, Pines are excellent evergreen landscape conifers. Unfortunately, pine wilt disease has decimated some plantings of Scotch and Austrian Pines. With careful selection and care, however, Pines can still serve well. Pinus strobus, White Pine, has a soft texture and graceful form. It grows best on moist, well-drained sites and will even grow in sand if there is enough water. High pH and wet soils are not satisfactory. The White Pine can be damaged by road salt leaching into the soil or salt spray on the foliage.

Bloom Period and Color
Evergreen foliage.

Mature Height × Spread
50 feet × 25 to 35 feet

Redbud
Cercis canadensis

Redbud is a native plant of the hardwood forests and will grow from Minnesota to Florida. Moist woods are full of Redbud and Dogwood blooms in the spring. They are breathtaking after a dreary winter. The foliage of Redbud is dark green, and the individual leaves are heart-shaped. Fall color can be quite good on some cultivars. Redbuds for landscape use are almost always multi-stem. They adjust well in the landscape where a small tree is desired. A Redbud can serve as an anchor for foundation plantings. The blossoms cover the stems in spring, and the leafy canopy provides welcome relief from the harshness of the city. Cercis canadensis alba is white. 'Royal White' has pure white flowers larger than those of alba.

Other Name
Eastern Redbud

Bloom Period and Color
April blooms in pink and white.

Mature Height × Spread
15 to 20 feet × 15 to 20 feet

When, Where, and How to Plant
Redbuds are best planted in the spring so they can become established before the onset of winter. Redbuds tolerate all kinds of soils as long as they are moist and well drained. Full sun or partial or full shade is satisfactory. In shade, there may be losses of interior small twigs from insufficient light, and growth will be slower. Set balled-and-burlapped plants at the same depth they grew in the nursery. Be sure to remove the burlap and twine. Cut any girdling roots on container-grown plants. If planting potted or canned plants, mix some container soil with that in the planting hole to avoid any soil incompatibility problems. Replace the soil and fill the hole with water. Make a saucer around the plant with any remaining soil. Water Redbuds during the first season after transplanting.

Growing Tips
Verticillium wilt is a serious disease and can kill Redbuds; avoid bringing the disease in on soil or on other plants. Redbuds can defend themselves from the disease if they are well watered and vigorously growing. It may be helpful to use organic mulch that stimulates antagonistic soil organisms that attack the fungus.

Care and Maintenance
Redbuds need very little care. There are some insects that can become troublesome, but rarely do they require treatment. Pruning to shape and to keep the plants in bounds may be necessary.

Companion Planting and Design
Redbuds are understory trees and do best in protected locations. They have wonderful horizontal branching and should be planted where there is enough room for them to display their natural form. Use them in woodland settings, shrub borders, and as specimens.

Did You Know
Redbuds grow from Minnesota to Florida. Plants from southern climes will not survive up north. Be careful where you buy plants. Ask where the seed was collected. Plants grown from locally collected seed by local growers are more likely to be hardy in your area.

Spruce
Picea sp.

When, Where, and How to Plant
Spruces are best planted in the spring. Plant container plants any time during the season. Spruces prefer rich, moist, well-drained soil. They are not particular about pH. Best in full sun, they will grow in partial shade but may become thin, losing leaves and lower branches. Set balled-and-burlapped plants slightly less deeply than they grew in the nursery. Remove the burlap and twine. Cut any circling roots on container-grown plants.

Growing Tips
Watering is important in dry periods.

Care and Maintenance
Spruces tolerate pruning well. They can be sheared after new growth has hardened off in spring. Some can be hedged effectively. To retard plants so they don't rapidly outgrow their situations, clip off half of the new growth on selected branches each spring. Plants will become dense, and size will increase at half the normal rate. Several diseases and insects affect the Spruces. Cytospora canker attacks large trees under stress, killing individual branches throughout the plants. Ultimately the affected plant is of no aesthetic value and should be removed. Spruce gall adelgids cause distorted tips on branches. Control with malathion, following label directions, in spring as new growth begins.

Companion Planting and Design
Use care in selecting and placing these plants in the landscape. They are beautiful if properly used. Blue Spruces are formal plants suitable as specimens. Norway Spruces, *P. abies,* are best used as windbreaks or screen. Norways are not specimen type plants. With age, something approaching thirty years, they lose their looks and form. Use them as temporary plants, and expect to cut them out and replace them. A dwarf suitable for foundation plantings is Black Hills Spruce, *P. glauca densata.* It grows very slowly to about 15 feet, has a very soft texture and good conical form.

Did You Know
The most comprehensive collection of unusual Spruces (and other evergreens too) in Illinois is Rich's Foxwillow Pines in Woodstock. Their catalog lists 60 or 70 Spruces of every imaginable form.

Spruces are evergreen trees of considerable importance in landscaping. They are strongly conical with stiff or descending branches. Their form is lovely while young, but some do not grow old gracefully. Spruces are used as screens, in masses, and as individual specimens, sometimes not very wisely. These are large trees. Appropriately used, they are assets; poorly used, they are liabilities. Dwarf varieties will fit small sites. Colorado Blue Spruce, Picea pungens, is a magnificent tree, variously green to silver-blue with a stiff, upright, conical form. These trees are beautiful in masses where they can develop to their full size. As screens, they are rather formal and strikingly beautiful. Allow plenty of room since the spread will be as much as 40 feet at the base.

Bloom Period and Color
Evergreen foliage.

Mature Height × Spread
40 to 50 feet × 20 to 25 feet

Sweet Gum
Liquidambar styraciflua

Sweet Gum has a neat, symmetrical outline and the potential for great size. It is pyramidal when young, becoming rounded at maturity. Sweet Gum has glossy, green, star-shaped leaves in summer and fall color that rivals Red and Sugar Maples. There is a lot of variability in color from one year to another, and between individual plants. Quite a bit of selection has been done for improving the color and hardiness. They are not reliably hardy north of Interstate 72. Sweet Gum is native to bottomlands and swamps. One cultivar, 'Moraine', is an improvement over the species. The named cultivar has more reliable color in fall. Nursery catalogs list only the species, so finding anything else may be difficult.

Bloom Period and Color
Late spring in green (not showy).

Mature Height × Spread
40 to 50 feet × 35 feet

Zones
5b – 6

When, Where, and How to Plant
Sweet Gum should be planted in spring only. Container plants are slightly more tolerant and can be planted in spring or early summer. Sweet Gum performs best if planted in a moist, deep, slightly acid soil. It will tolerate different soil types as long as they are moist and well drained. A pH at neutral or lower is preferred. Chlorosis will develop in alkaline soils. The roots of Sweet Gum need a lot of room to develop. Set balled-and-burlapped plants at the same depth they grew in the nursery. The roots are fleshy and take a long time to recover from transplanting injury. If container-grown plants were grown in an artificial soil, shake some off the ball and mix it with the soil in the planting hole. Make sure the soil is well watered for it to settle around the roots.

Growing Tips
Water the tree the first season after planting, but avoid inundation.

Care and Maintenance
Pruning may be needed as the tree develops to maintain a central leader. Slow recovery from transplanting may result in dead twigs that need to be removed. Once the tree is established and growing, there is little care required. Water the tree the first season after planting, and weekly during dry weather. Golfball-sized fruit that falls in lawns should be raked up.

Companion Planting and Design
Sweet Gums are large trees with a very neat form and outline. They are excellent specimen trees, but are well suited as a street or lawn trees as well. They do not tolerate the alkaline soils and pollution of highly urbanized sites.

Did You Know
A small wild population of Sweet Gums has become established in central DuPage County in northern Illinois. Numerous large and small trees are mixed with Oaks in a kettlehole woods west of Argonne National Laboratory. They are in a low, protected area, but survived the terrible winters of the mid-70s. Hardiness seems to involve more than just cold tolerance.

Tuliptree
Liriodendron tulipifera

When, Where, and How to Plant

Transplant balled and burlapped trees in spring. Container plants can be transplanted in spring or early summer. Deep, well-drained soil with a pH of neutral or lower is preferred. These plants need full sun and plenty of room for roots. Protection from wind or planting in groves will reduce storm damage. Set plants at the same depth they grew in the nursery. Be sure to remove the burlap and twine or untie it and place it in the planting hole. Cut any girdling roots on container-grown plants. This tree transplants with difficulty. Water as needed to prevent wilting. Do not overwater.

Growing Tips

A physiological condition, yellows, causes sudden yellowing and dropping of leaves and can be troublesome for newly planted trees or during droughts. Regular watering usually prevents this condition.

Care and Maintenance

Tuliptrees are slow to recover from transplanting. They have fleshy, poorly branched root systems. Prune to maintain a single leader as high as possible. Trees with multiple trunks are more easily damaged in storms.

Companion Planting and Design

Tuliptrees are not for the small city lot. They are big trees and need room to develop to their full potential. They are suitable for broad parkways, large lawns, office parks and natural areas. In forest plantings, the trees are associated with Sugar Maple, American Linden, and American Beech. These are all trees of the wooded uplands.

Did You Know

Tuliptrees were so important to the colonists that they introduced them into Europe. Pioneers hollowed out the huge logs to make lightweight dugout canoes. The wood is knot-free and used to make furniture, toys, musical instruments, crates, and for pulpwood. It is one of the principal commercial hardwoods. Large numbers of board feet of lumber can be cut from one tree. In the eastern forest plantings the trees reach 200 feet in height, and 200 years of age. *Liriodendron* comes from the Greek, *lirion,* "lily," and *dendron,* "tree."

The Tuliptree is large with high branches that spread with age. It needs a lot of room to develop to its full potential. In the wild, it may reach 100 feet or more and be free of branches for half its height. Pyramidal in its youth, Tuliptree eventually develops a framework of several large branches high in the tree. For all of its massive size, Tuliptree can be brittle and may break up in storms or under snow load. The leaves of the tree are tulip-shaped in profile and the flowers resemble Tulips as well. Fall color is clear bright yellow. If you have room for this magnificent tree, it will provide unique bloom, foliage, and color for decades.

Other Name
Yellow Poplar

Bloom Period and Color
May blooms in greenish-yellow with orange clusters.

Mature Height × Spread
60 to 70 feet × 35 to 40 feet

Turfgrasses *for Illinois*

Nearly every home and business has a lawn. In terms of the dollars spent on installation and care, turfgrasses are the number-one agricultural enterprise in Illinois. The lawn is one of the most important parts of the landscape. It ties the entire landscape together. It provides the setting for the home, business, or office building. It connects the grounds with surrounding features, walks, streets, or neighboring properties. The lawn can enhance the appeal of the entire property, making it friendly and inviting.

On a more practical level, lawns reduce the dust and dirt that get into the home or office. They absorb noise. Lawns reduce erosion and runoff in storms, reduce glare from the summer sun, and absorb heat. If you walk barefoot from a sandy beach or from a blacktop parking lot onto a well-kept lawn, the temperature difference is immediately noticeable.

A well-maintained lawn is an asset, while a poorly maintained, weedy lawn can be an eyesore, a detriment to any neighborhood. Maintaining a nice lawn requires some work, and it requires some skill as well. No longer is it simply a matter of cutting the grass if it gets too tall. When I was growing up, mowing was the only lawn-care chore. Watering was a luxury, and it was usually a by-product of a children's game of running under the sprinkler.

How Grass Grows

Turfgrasses are complex little plants, not just tufts of green poking out of the ground. A grass plant grows from a structure called a crown that is just below the soil surface. Leaves arise from the crown and roots grow from the bottom of the crown into the soil. If the grass is not mowed, it elongates into a stalk called a culm. At the top of the culm are flowers and, eventually, seeds.

Some grasses grow horizontal stems from their crowns. When underground, they are called rhizomes; if they lie along the top of the ground, they are called stolons. Sometimes more than one culm will grow from a crown, making a bunch grass. Other structures, auricles and ligules, are helpful in identifying the various species. These structures are quite tiny, and those of us who spend a lot of time examining grasses develop green knees and elbows from crouching down to investigate. Different kinds of grasses grow in different ways, so it is important to know which one you are growing.

Most lawns in Illinois are cool-season grasses, though some warm-season grasses may be grown in the southern part of the state, in the transition zone. The basic care for all grasses is just about the same. Timing and mowing heights will differ.

Establishing a Lawn

Prepare the site by leveling it to the proper grade. Do a good job, because you will live with any imperfections. Kill the vegetation with glyphosate. Apply lime, sulfur, superphosphate, and potash according to soil test recommendations. Disk or till to prepare a finely pulverized seedbed. Up to this point, it makes no difference whether you choose to seed, hydroseed, or sod the lawn. The preparation is the same.

Sodding: Buy sod grown on a soil as nearly like that on your site as you can find. The sod should be thinly cut, fresh, dark green, and absolutely free of weeds. Moisten the soil and apply a starter fertilizer to provide 0.5 pounds of nitrogen per 1000 square feet of lawn. Roll out the sod, staggering the ends and making sure that the rolls are butted tightly against each other. Roll to firm the sod to the soil. Water daily to keep the sod wet for two weeks, or until it begins to knit. Then reduce the watering frequency. Do not let the sod wilt. Mow when the grass is 33 percent higher than the cutting height.

Seeding: Buy top-quality seed; do not look for bargains at this point in the process. Sow the seed with a drop spreader, half back and forth in one direction, and the other half at a right angle to this direction. Be sure to overlap the wheel tracks. Gently rake the seed into the soil. I use a wire grass rake, upside down, and just drag it back and forth over the seed. This covers the seed with about 1/4 inch of soil. Roll with a medium roller. If seeding in spring, cover with 2 inches of lightly laid straw to provide about 50 percent shade. Hydroseeding applies seed and mulch in one operation. Water frequently to keep the seed from drying, but do not soak it to the point of runoff.

Mowing: Mow the grass often enough to remove only $^1/_3$ to $^1/_2$ of the blades. Mowing will be necessary more often in cool, moist weather, sometimes more often than once a week. Set the mower at the correct height for the kind of grass. The cool-season grasses should be kept mowed at $2^1/_2$ inches high; that means mowing before they reach 4 inches. The warm-season grasses are cut at $^1/_2$ to 1 inch, mowed before they reach 1 to 2 inches.

Watering: Many lawns are watered more often than they need to be. The grass does not need to be watered until it wilts. Wilted grass turns a hazy purplish color, and footprints don't spring back after you walk across it. Apply a measured inch of water. Use a coffee can under the sprinkler to measure the amount. When there is an inch of water in the bottom of the can, move the sprinkler.

Automatic sprinkler systems must be set to apply an inch of water per cycle. After watering, turn the water off, and do not water again until the grass wilts. Running the sprinkler a few minutes every day

does not sufficiently water the grass. Running the sprinkler hours every night will force the root system to the surface and eventually drown the grass.

Fertilizing: Fertilizer should be applied just before the maximum growth of the grass plant. For cool-season grasses, that is in late August; for warm-season grasses, it is late spring. Apply 1 pound of nitrogen per 1000 square feet of lawn. If applying a slow-release fertilizer, double the rate. If applying fertilizer to a cool-season grass before or during hot weather, apply it at half rate.

Cool-season grasses may benefit from a second application if fertilized in late fall, with another application in midspring.

Weed control: Apply crabgrass preventer when the Honeysuckles are in bloom. Apply a broadleaf herbicide when the weeds are vigorously growing, either spring or fall.

Insect control: Control grubs (annual white grub, white grub, Japanese beetle, and

billbug) with Merit applied in June or July. Control ataeneus grubs with Merit applied in May. After application immediately apply $^1/_2$ inch of water to wash the Merit into the root zone before the material dries on the surface.

Control sod webworm with diazinon applied two weeks after the small adult moths are noticed flying over the lawn at dusk. Do not water the diazinon into the lawn.

Control greenbugs with insecticidal soap. Carefully read and follow the directions on the labels of all pesticides. Keep the materials out of the reach of children.

Disease control: Most turf diseases are due to cultural problems. Summer patch, necrotic ringspot, and other ring and spot diseases are due to fungi that attack plants under stress. Stress often comes from compaction or layering of the soil due to accumulated thatch. To repair, core-aerify the lawn to produce a hole every 2 inches, thirty-six holes per square foot. Some lawn-care companies and landscapers are reluctant to do a proper job of this; make sure they do by checking the placement of the holes before you pay them.

Minor accumulations of thatch, $^1/_4$ to $^1/_2$ inch, can be controlled by power raking. Mildew and leaf spot diseases are controlled by planting resistant cultivars. Dollar spot is a disease of hungry grass. Rust is controlled by fertilizing and by mowing frequently enough that the rust never matures.

Turfgrass repair: In spring or fall, small damaged spots in the lawn can be scratched up with a garden rake or cultivator, then seeded. Larger areas can be cut out and the soil scratched up and sodded. Make sure the sod was grown on a soil like the one in your yard.

Thin lawns or lawns badly damaged by insects, diseases, drought, or winter desiccation can be slit-seeded. Have the seeder run at two directions, with a difference of 45 degrees, to avoid the appearance of rows.

Lawns infested with quackgrass or other perennial weedy grasses can be killed off with glysophate in mid-August and slit-seeded a week later. If Perennial Ryegrass is included in the seed mix, the new grass will be green and growing before the old grass turns brown.

If you are planting Kentucky Bluegrass, always plant a blend of different cultivars, and incorporate 10 to 20 percent turf-type Perennial Ryegrass for increased site tolerance and disease resistance.

Bentgrass
Agrostis sp.

Two species of Bentgrass are used for ornamental turf in Illinois: Creeping Bentgrass, A. palustris, and Colonial Bentgrass, A. tenuis. These are temperate-zone plants, and they perform best in 80° temperatures, though Creeping Bentgrass is more tolerant of high temperatures than is Colonial. The Bentgrasses are high-maintenance plants, used for high-quality lawns and for sports turf. Creeping Bentgrass is a stoloniferous, spreading grass and the more demanding of the two kinds of Bentgrass. Colonial Bentgrass unfortunately was sometimes combined with Bluegrass and Ryegrass in seed mixtures for shady lawns. It tolerates shade, but it will overcome other grasses in the same population. It is a different color than the other grasses and is really not compatible. Grow Colonial in the cooler areas of the state.

Other Names
Creeping Bentgrass, Colonial Bentgrass

Color and Texture
Light green with fine texture.

Mowing Height
$1/2$ to $3/4$ inch

Zones
All, but better in Zones 4b, 5, and 6a

When, Where, and How to Plant
Plant Bentgrasses in late summer or fall. Seeding until June 1 is successful if crabgrass, which germinates at the same time, can be controlled. These grasses are generally not for typical lawns but are used for golf courses, bowling greens, tennis courts, and other closely mowed sports turf. Where a high-quality turf is needed and where the owner is willing to expend the energy, Bentgrass is an option. Bentgrasses are started from seed or sprigs, and occasionally from sod or hydroseeding. The soil must be pulverized, then graded to eliminate any high or low spots. Sow seed at the rate of 2 pounds per 1000 square feet of lawn. Sprigs are planted at a rate of 5 to 10 bushels per 1000 square feet. Gently rake the seed into the top $1/4$ inch of soil. Plant sprigs in furrows or work into the soil mechanically. Install sod over well-prepared soil, butting the joints together. Water every day until the grass has knitted to the ground.

Growing Tips
Apply water as needed to prevent wilting. Fertilize to maintain good color and a moderate rate of growth. Bentgrass requires 5 to 6 pounds of nitrogen fertilizer per 1000 square feet of turf per season and must be mowed every other day. Water to provide $1 1/2$ inches per week

Care and Maintenance
Bentgrass is aggressive and will invade neighboring areas. Mow at $1/2$ to 2 inches and remove no more than $1/4$ to $1/3$ of the leaf area each time you mow. Diseases appear in inclement weather; be prepared to spray to keep them from destroying the turf. Slice and topdress to prevent puffiness and core-aerate to eliminate layering.

Companion Planting and Design
The Bentgrasses do not blend well with any other turfgrasses. At one time they were included in shady grass seed mixes, but their performance was poor, and that was quickly discontinued.

Did You Know
Bentgrasses are not for the average home lawn.

Bermudagrass
Cynodon dactylon

When, Where, and How to Plant

Bermudagrass is started in the spring. Plant it in full sun. It will not tolerate shade. Start Bermudagrass from sod, plugs, or sprigs. Sod provides an instant lawn. Prepare the soil as for seeding, pulverizing it finely. Lay the strips of sod, being careful to butt the seams tightly together. Plugs are planted in holes punched in the soil surface. A bulb planter can be used to punch the holes. A plug is dropped in a hole and a little soil is pushed over it and stepped on to firm. Sprigs can be planted individually by plowing a furrow and dropping a sprig every couple of feet, or with a sprig planter. Thoroughly water the lawn after planting, and keep it moist until plants have rooted. Hybrid Bermudagrass cannot be grown from seed.

Growing Tips

This is a drought-tolerant grass; water as needed to maintain the level of growth you want. Apply nitrogen fertilizer monthly.

Care and Maintenance

Mow Bermudagrass at a height of 1 to 1^1/2 inches. Bermudagrass produces thatch with a vengeance—thoroughly core-aerate monthly. Slicing and power raking may be necessary if a heavy thatch does develop. Bermuda is a soft grass, not stiff like Zoysia. It is a tough grass with good wear resistance. Mow with a sharp mower. A reel type is best. Sharpen a rotary mower every few times the grass is mowed.

Companion Planting and Design

Bermudagrass is a tough and invasive grass. It does not blend well with other grasses, but can benefit from overseeding with Ryegrass while it is dormant in winter.

Did You Know

Bermudagrass is being hybridized for increased cold-tolerance, but it probably will never replace Kentucky Blue.

Bermudagrass is a highly variable, Zone 6b, warm-weather grass. It is aggressive and will establish very quickly. The common seed-grown types are weeds throughout the South. Hybrid Bermudagrass is the best-quality turfgrass for the southern states, and it is the kind that should be planted in Illinois. Hybrid Bermudagrass is hardy in southern Illinois, and its range is extended by hybridization for increased cold tolerance. Bermudagrass has excellent heat tolerance; it survives cold by going dormant. It turns brown in early fall and greens up in mid-spring. Two Bermudagrasses with superior cold hardiness are Midway and Midiron. Suppliers at garden centers in the southern part of the state will normally handle cultivars that will stand conditions in that area. Check with them to see what is new.

Other Name
Hybrid Bermudagrass

Color and Texture
Bright to dull green with medium to fine texture.

Mowing Height
^{1}/2 to 1^1/2 inches

Zone
6b

Creeping Red Fescue
Festuca rubra

Creeping Red Fescue is a grass for infertile soils and shaded sites. It is not a particularly aggressive grass, and will not stand a lot of traffic. It will stand short periods of drought, but it does not like hot weather. Although it is a soft grass with very fine, needle-like leaves, its color and growth characteristics are very similar to those of Kentucky Bluegrasses and Perennial Rye. These three kinds are often included in mixtures. In shade or on poor soils, the Fescue will outgrow the Kentucky Blue and Rye, eventually predominating. In the southern part of the state where summer temperatures will force it into dormancy, it is suitable only for shade areas. Creeping Red Fescue spreads by means of short rhizomes.

Color and Texture
Dark green with very fine texture.

Mowing Height
$2^1/2$ inches

When, Where, and How to Plant
Creeping Red Fescue is best planted in late summer or fall. The cooler weather and increased chances of moisture provide good conditions for germination and growth. Weeds are less likely to germinate and to compete with the developing grass. Plant Creeping Red Fescue in areas where shade or infertile soil would make the growth of Kentucky Bluegrass and Perennial Rye difficult. Creeping Red Fescue is available as seed, not as sod; rhizome development is not sufficient to develop a sod that will stay together for harvesting. Some Fescue sod has been grown on mesh to overcome that problem. Level and work the soil to produce a fine seedbed. Sow seed at 4 pounds per 1000 square feet of lawn. Cover lightly with soil.

Growing Tips
Apply water as needed to prevent wilting. Red Fescue kept constantly wet will be destroyed by fungal diseases. Creeping Red Fescue is a low-fertility species. Avoid fertilizing it in the shade unless it is consistently off color and stops growing. Overfertilization will result in a reduced root volume and declining turf. Enough fertilizer to provide about $1/2$ pound of nitrogen per 1000 square feet of turf in early fall should suffice.

Care and Maintenance
Creeping Red Fescue has poor wear resistance. Mow at $2^1/2$ inches and often enough to remove only $1/3$ to $1/4$ of the leaf area. This grass is susceptible to several diseases. Leaf spot, melting out, brown patch, and the summer ring and patch diseases can damage it. Normally, proper watering practices and fertilizer applications will keep the diseases in check.

Companion Planting and Design
Use Creeping Red Fescue with Kentucky Bluegrasses and Perennial Ryegrass in shady sites.

Did You Know
Fine-leaf Fescues, including Hard Fescue, Sheep Fescue, and others, are being bred for roadsides and other low use areas. They are short and tough, needing no supplemental watering or fertilizing, and little if any mowing. They are not suited for lawns, however.

Kentucky Bluegrass
Poa pratensis

When, Where, and How to Plant

Seed in late summer to early fall. Spring seeding until June 1 is successful if crabgrass can be controlled. Install sod whenever the soils are not frozen and there is sufficient water available. Some Kentucky Blue selections tolerate shaded conditions better than others. Kentucky Bluegrass lawns may be started from seed, sod, or hydro seeded. The soil should be finely pulverized and graded. Sow seed at the rate of 2 pounds per 1000 square feet of lawn and cover lightly. If seeding in spring, cover with straw to provide 50 percent shade. Water daily or more often to keep seed moist until germination. Reduce frequency of watering after the grass has come up. Lay sod over prepared soil, butting the joints together. Water every day until the grass has knitted to the ground.

Growing Tips

Fertilize in fall, also early and late spring to maintain a moderate green color. Water to apply 1 inch per week. Apply a measured inch, and do not water again until the grass wilts.

Care and Maintenance

Mow at $2^1/2$ inches and often enough to remove no more than $1/3$ to $1/4$ of the leaf area. Practice proper maintenance and use resistant varieties to control disease. Sodded lawns may deteriorate if the soil on which the sod was grown is different from that on which the sod is installed. Remedy by thorough core-aeration to produce a hole every 2 inches, thirty-six holes per square foot, repeated until rooting has occurred. High-quality Bluegrass lawns have moderate wear resistance and require cultivation to control thatch. Low-maintenance common Bluegrass lawns can be grown without the benefit of added water and fertilizer.

Companion Planting and Design

Kentucky Bluegrasses blend well with turf-type Perennial Ryegrasses and the better Creeping Red Fescues. They grow at the same rate and the colors are compatible.

Did You Know

You can use quick-germinating Ryegrasses as nurse grasses to protect the Kentucky Bluegrass as it germinates. Add Creeping Red Fescue in the shade.

Kentucky Bluegrass is the most widely planted turfgrass in Illinois. It is a medium-textured grass, attractive and well adapted to the climate. It is a native of central Europe, which has a climate much like ours, though the summers are not as hot as those in most of Illinois. The grass has become naturalized throughout the "Bluegrass area" of central Kentucky and has resulted in the common name Kentucky Bluegrass. The USDA Yearbook of Agriculture indicates that farmers 200 years ago considered the Bluegrass turf more valuable than crops that could be grown on the land, and they were reluctant to break the sod. Disease-resistant Kentucky Bluegrass varieties include Adelphi, America, Denim, Glade, Midnight, Touchdown, and A-34 in the shade.

Color and Texture
Dark green with medium to coarse texture.

Mowing Height
$2^1/2$ inches

Perennial Ryegrass
Lolium perenne

Perennial Ryegrass is well adapted to the climate of Illinois. Common Perennial Ryegrass is a coarse, tough grass. Germination from seed is very rapid, sometimes four or five days. It has been used as a nurse grass to provide cover while slower-developing Kentucky Bluegrasses or Fescues germinate. The coarse common Ryes persisted as weeds in the Bluegrass lawns; they were hard to mow and never attractive. As a result of hybridization, turf-type Ryegrasses fully compatible with the finer Bluegrasses are available. Newer selections have better high- and low-temperature tolerance as well. The Perennial Rye provides a greater range of disease resistance, and often persists after something has killed the Bluegrasses. The improved Perennial Ryegrasses have better growth characteristics and better disease resistance than the species.

Color and Texture
Dark green with medium texture.

Mowing Height
2^1/$_2$ inches

When, Where, and How to Plant
Perennial Rye is best planted in fall before October 1, or after November 15, or in early spring. Worn or damaged areas can be seeded any time during the season. Perennial Rye can be sown in sun or shade. The soil should be well drained and not compacted. Perennial Ryegrass may be seeded or hydroseeded. The soil should be finely pulverized and graded. Sow the seed at the rate of 5 to 10 pounds per 1000 square feet of lawn and cover lightly with soil. If seeding in spring, cover with straw to provide 50 percent shade; hydro-seeding will also provide shade. Water daily or more often if necessary to keep seed moist until germination has taken place. Reduce the frequency of watering after the grass is up.

Growing Tips
To maintain a moderate green color, fertilize in fall, and also in early and late spring. Water to apply a measured inch each time, and do not water again until the grass wilts.

Care and Maintenance
Perennial Rye has good wear resistance and should be mowed at 2^1/$_2$ inches, often enough to remove no more than ^{1}/$_3$ to ^{1}/$_4$ of the leaf area. These grasses have different disease resistance than the Kentucky Bluegrasses and add a different dimension of resistance to the lawn. Most diseases are controlled by keeping the grass growing vigorously. Fungicides are rarely needed.

Companion Planting and Design
Sow with Kentucky Bluegrass to provide quick cover to protect the slower Bluegrass seedlings as they germinate. Use in combination with Kentucky Bluegrass to develop added disease resistance.

Did You Know
Newer selections of Perennial Ryegrass are well suited for use as permanent lawn grasses. By the end of the season, Perennial Ryegrass seeded to repair damaged athletic fields is often the only grass left. Most people can't tell it from Bluegrasses. Annual Ryegrass is used exclusively as a nurse grass. It is coarse, light green, and lives only one season.

Tall Fescue

Festuca elatior arundinacea

When, Where, and How to Plant

Plant Tall Fescue in fall or spring. For increasing the plant population as an established turf, it may be sown all season long. Tall Fescue can be planted in sun or filtered shade. Plant it where it will be allowed to grow naturally—it will crowd out other weedy plants. Heavily seeded Tall Fescue lawns make a satisfactory turf. This grass does not develop a rhizome system and cannot be grown as sod. Some growers have resorted to growing it on mesh so that it can be handled without falling apart. It is usually seeded. Soil should be finely pulverized and graded. Sow seed at the rate of 2 pounds per 1000 square feet of lawn. Cover lightly with soil. Water as needed to keep the seed moist until germination takes place.

Growing Tips

Fertilize to maintain a moderate to light-green color. Tall Fescue tolerates drought and does not require the heavy watering needed by the finer grasses. Apply an inch of water when the grass has wilted.

Care and Maintenance

Tall Fescue has good wear resistance. Mow at a height of 3 to $3^1/2$ inches, often enough to remove no more than $1/3$ to $1/4$ of the leaf area each time. Keep the mower sharpened; a dull mower will have a tough time cutting this grass. Some Tall Fescue strains contain endophytes that provide some resistance to insect damage. Where these are available, it is suggested they be incorporated into the seed mixture.

Companion Planting and Design

Tall Fescue is not compatible with other turfgrass varieties. It grows much faster and is a lighter green color. If grown in a Kentucky Bluegrass lawn it will appear as coarse, lighter green bunches.

Did You Know

Tall Fescue is often recommended for athletic fields. It does not develop rhizomes that can grow into damaged areas, so it does not repair itself. Newer selections do have narrower leaves and better color, more suitable for lawns.

Tall Fescue is a tough wide-bladed grass. It flourishes with neglect. It tolerates drought or periodic inundation, and will grow without supplemental fertilization. It does not develop rhizomes and will not fill bare areas. To successfully sustain a planting of Tall Fescue, plan to overseed constantly so that new plants will be growing into the population to replace damaged or missing plants. Tall Fescue can make a satisfactory turf and is well adapted to the southern part of the state, Zone 6. It can stand high summer temperatures better than some other temperate-climate grasses. Kentucky 31 Fescue must not be confused with Kentucky Bluegrass. It grows twice as fast, is much coarser, and is considered a weed in a Bluegrass lawn.

Color and Texture
Medium green with coarse to medium texture.

Mowing Height
3 to $3^1/2$ inches

Zoysiagrass

Zoysia japonica

Zoysiagrass will grow throughout Illinois. Once established, it does not take a lot of care, and it looks nice all summer. It does have some peculiarities. It is a warm-season turfgrass that survives our winters by going completely dormant, turning brown in mid-fall when temperatures are in the mid-50-degree range. It is very slow to green up in the spring and stays brown into May, a time when the cool-season turfgrasses look their best. Zoysiagrass is expensive to install. It is started from plugs, which take several years to fill in. Sod is prohibitively expensive. Zoysiagrass has stiff blades that spread by means of above-ground stolons. The grass is aggressive and will invade beds and borders. Zoysiagrass is a tough, durable grass, resisting salt damage.

Color and Texture
Light green with coarse texture.

Mowing Height
1/2 to 1 inch

When, Where, and How to Plant
Plant Zoysiagrass about the time it is greening up in spring. This grass does best in full sun, but will grow reasonably well in shade. It is tolerant of heat and drought. The soil should be finely pulverized and graded. An even surface is essential because this grass must be mowed quite short. If the ground is uneven, scalping will be a problem. Plant plugs in holes punched in the soil surface (a bulb planter can be used to punch the holes). The plug is dropped in the hole, a little soil is pushed over it, and it is stepped on to firm. Space the plugs at about 12 inches; at that spacing, the grass will be established in two to three years. Closer planting will fill in more quickly.

Growing Tips
Fertilize as necessary to maintain color. Water during extended droughts.

Care and Maintenance
Following installation, provide weed control to keep weeds from taking over the planting. If all vegetation was killed off prior to planting, preemergent herbicides can be used to prevent weeds. Mow Zoysiagrass at 1/2 to 1 inch tall, mowing often enough to remove only 1/3 to 1/4 of the leaf area. Because of the density of the grass, a heavy reel-type mower is best. A rotary mower will ride up on the grass, giving a very uneven cut. Zoysiagrass has good wear resistance and develops dense thatch, requiring core-aeration or power raking. A large volume of material for disposal will result from power raking. During the time Zoysiagrass is brown and dry, some gardeners have been known to burn off the lawn as a thatch control measure.

Companion Planting and Design
Annual Ryegrass can be overseeded in fall to provide a green lawn while the Zoysiagrass is dormant. It will die out when the Zoysiagrass resumes growth in spring.

Did You Know
To have a green lawn all year, some people paint the dormant Zoysiagrass green in fall.

Vines *for Illinois*

Vines are useful in any garden. They can be used strictly as ornamentals, or for utilitarian purposes. They may be grown on fences, trellises, pergolas, arbors, or gazebos. In these places, they are pleasing to look at, and may give you some privacy as well. If they are flowering vines, the blooms themselves may be sufficient reason to plant the vines.

Vines can be grown up the sides of buildings, and may reach several stories high. It is not unusual to see Boston Ivy or Climbing Hydrangea covering the side of a 6-story building. Some college campuses are noted for their ivy-covered buildings. Almost every campus has at least a few. The modern glass and steel buildings aren't too well suited to this treatment, but there seems to be a trend lately toward traditional brick and mortar buildings. Many apartments and condominiums in our area are being built of masonry and vines are being grown on them.

Some vines are better suited to the north sides of structures than almost any other woody plant. They do well in the shade, they don't take a lot of ground space, and some need protection from winter sun. These are perfect for such places.

Vines grow in three different ways. Some climb by means of little root-like holdfasts that attach themselves to the support. Boston Ivy climbs this way. Clematis and Grape Vines climb by winding tendrils or petioles around the supports. The Wisteria stems themselves twine around their support. Before selecting vines, it is important to know how they climb, so the right kind of support structure can be provided. If you are going to grow a twining Bittersweet up a wall, you will need to provide something for it to twine around, for instance.

The supports for the vines must be strong enough to hold them up. It will surprise you how heavy some vines can be. Be sure the structure you grow the vine on won't be damaged by it either. A Boston Ivy growing on one of the newer stucco-over-Styrofoam buildings will quickly pull the stucco off.

Wood-sided houses and fences need to be painted every few years. Vines clinging to them can complicate the process, and the adhesive pads left by some vines are difficult to remove. Providing the vines with something else to cling to, such as a plastic sheet for Boston Ivy, or a trellis for twining types, allows the vines to be taken down and replaced after the work is done. A handy neighbor has devised a trellis, hinged at the bottom and hooked at the top, which is easily lowered and replaced without any damage to the vines.

Using Vines in the Garden

Vines growing up trees can also be very attractive. It is an excellent use of vines, but there are some cautions. If the vine encircles the tree, unwind it every year so it doesn't girdle the tree. It won't strangle the tree, but if it encircles a small tree, the expanding tree trunk will eventually grow to where the vine is. As it tries to grow around the vine, it will be girdled, unable to expand any farther. (Circling roots and twine left when planting the tree can do the same thing.) If the vine is not removed, the tree will be strangled at that point. Wintercreeper growing on Maple trees does this all too often. Don't let that discourage you from growing vines on trees. But, do it right.

It isn't necessary to limit your vine planting to one kind. Mixing vines can make the planting more interesting and add color. Inter-planting Boston Ivy and its relative Virginia Creeper, *Parthenocissus quinquefolia*, creates a different texture. Adding Clematis or Morning Glories (see the description in the chapter on annuals) to English Ivy, for instance, will provide attractive blooms. Planting several different Clematis varieties on the same support will add color and may increase the bloom time. Don't let yourself be trapped by convention. Let your imagination run. Even if you make a mistake, it is easily corrected. Gardening should be, first of all, fun.

Care for Vines

A major necessity for healthy and vigorous vines is regular pruning. The old wood needs to be removed, forcing new stems to grow. Each type of vine will have certain needs, and some experimenting will be necessary to figure out how to handle your vines. Don't be afraid to do some cutting. Plants do grow back and vines grow back fast.

We see plantings of vines that have been beautiful for many, many years. They often have large, old stems in them, but many times the vines are not the same ones that were set there at the beginning. To keep some types of vines vigorous and young, interplant with new plants every year or so, and remove the old ones. Seeds can be collected from some kinds of vines, and seedlings started in Styrofoam cups. Small container-grown plants of other vines can be bought from local suppliers. A landmark planting of English Ivy in an indoor tennis court, and the vines at Wrigley Field are maintained this way. However, some vines, like Wisteria, will grow to extremely old age with proper care.

Nine interesting vines are described in the following pages. These are only a few, really just a sampling, of those that can be grown in Illinois. Try some of these, and take a look at others too. You will find them at botanical gardens and arboreta, labeled with the names. Once you recognize them, notice which ones are growing in your area, and how they grow.

American Bittersweet

Celastus scandens

American Bittersweet is a hardy vine that climbs by twining; it will grow to a height of 20 feet or more if provided with adequate support. It is a native plant, so it is perfectly able to contend with Illinois conditions. It will grow just about wherever it gets a start, and it can become a tangle of vines if allowed to grow wild. Bittersweet will climb shrubs and trees, some with large trunks. The vines twine tightly and are very sturdy. If allowed to encircle a tree, a vine can eventually girdle it. Bittersweet vines have male and female flowers on separate plants, requiring at least one of each to produce fruit. There are no cultivars of C. scandens.

Bloom Period and Color
June blooms in yellow, greenish, followed by attractive bright orange fruits.

Mature Height × Spread
20 feet × twining. Can grow 50 feet or more along a fence.

When, Where, and How to Plant
Plant American Bittersweet in either spring or fall. Plant containerized plants at any time during the season. Bittersweet will grow in full or partial sun, but fruit production is better in full sun. The soil can be any decent garden loam. Actually, these plants will grow in just about any soil. Many producers plant a vegetatively produced male and a female plant in each container. If plants are sold separately, make sure you buy a male plant and a female plant. Dig the planting holes the same depth and twice as wide as the containers in which the plants were grown. Plant a male and a female plant in the same hole to make sure there will be good pollination. One or two pairs of plants are usually sufficient for most homes. These are big plants!

Growing Tips
Try not to fertilize Bittersweet plants or they will grow even more aggressively. Keeping the soil a little dry and withholding fertilizer will slow down the plant and improve fruit production.

Care and Maintenance
Prune American Bittersweet heavily to keep it contained; prune in fall as stems with the colorful berrylike fruits are collected, and if needed, in spring after the first flush of growth. Do not be afraid to cut! If you do it "wrong," the plant will grow back anyway, and you will have another chance to do it right. Control Euonymous scale with acephate applied about the time Catalpas are in bloom. Repeat two or three times. Follow label directions.

Companion Planting and Design
Use it as a screen, along the side of the house, or to soften the effects of utility poles or rough fences. Grow Bittersweet up a trellis for cutting. Its stems with their colorful fruits are excellent for flower arrangements.

Did You Know
Don't let this vine encircle a small tree or shrub. It may eventually girdle the plant just the same as would a wire wrapped around it.

Boston Ivy
Parthenocissus tricuspidata

When, Where, and How to Plant

Boston Ivy seeds need cold to break their dormancy. Plant in the fall in nursery beds—or plant them in a moist, artificial soil mix, keeping them in the refrigerator for about three months, and germinating them at 70°F under lights indoors. Transplant to pots and then outdoors when the soil is dry enough to work. Containerized plants may be planted anytime during the season. Plant at the bases of walls, fences, or trellises, around rock gardens, and as a ground cover plant. Set plants from small pots in holes the same as you do when planting annuals. Water them thoroughly after planting. Plants are available in 1- and 2-gallon cans from nurseries and garden centers. Dig planting holes as deep and twice as wide as the containers. Set the plants at the same depth they were growing at the nursery. Water thoroughly to settle the soil.

Growing Tips

Boston Ivy may need some help getting started up a wall or other support. Fasteners are available from garden stores, or staple a twist-tie to the structure and fasten the vine with it. Rather than allowing the vine to cling to the building, construct a support of wire mesh or netting for the plant to grow on. It will protect the structure, and if there is a need to remove the vine for repairs or painting, the support can be cut loose and reinstalled when the work is done.

Care and Maintenance

Japanese Beetles and leaf spot diseases can damage Boston Ivy plantings. Control the Japanese beetles with Tempo or Sevin or Orthene (acephate). Treat the leaf spot with Bordeaux mixture, maneb, or Zyban. Follow label directions carefully.

Companion Planting and Design

Use as a tough, low-maintenance covering for walls, fences, trellises, and embankments.

Did You Know

Start new plants by collecting the berries in fall, storing them in the refrigerator over winter, and sowing them in Styrofoam cups in spring. Plant out when seedlings have two leaves.

Boston Ivy is the plant of ivy-covered walls, a sturdy vine with attractive foliage. The leaves have three-pointed lobes on the upper part of the plant; lower down are leaves with three leaflets. The vine climbs and attaches itself with tendrils, each with an adhesive "foot." Boston Ivy will easily climb a five-story building in just a few years. It tolerates city conditions very well and will grow in any of the city soils. The walls of the "Friendly Confines," Wrigley Field, are covered with Boston Ivy. It is probably the most scrutinized and meticulously maintained Boston Ivy anywhere. Parthenocissus quinquefolia, Virginia Creeper, is a more aggresive plant. It can become weedy in the garden. Its crimson red fall color is outstanding.

Bloom Period and Color

Spring blooms in green (inconspicuous). Deciduous, with red fall color.

Mature Height × Spread

50 feet × twining. Can extend 50 feet along a fence.

Clematis

Clematis × jackmanii

Flowers of the Clematis are among the most beautiful in the garden. Although they are undeniably gorgeous, these vines are conspicuously absent from most gardens in Illinois. They are relatively easy to grow if given a proper location and some support. Clematis vines require attention to detail. This means planting them where they get full sun or filtered shade, in a cool, moist soil. In the hottest parts of the state, some relief from the midday sun will keep them flowering. One apparent problem with growing Clematis is figuring out where to put it; it can go anywhere other vines can be grown. Grow it on a fence, up the side of the garage, on a pile of rocks, over an arbor, or over the swing.

Bloom Period and Color
June until frost blooms in red, white, yellow, purple, violet-purple, rose, pink, blue.

Mature Height × Spread
5 to 15 feet × vining. Can spread 20 feet along a fence.

When, Where, and How to Plant
Plant Clematis in spring, or all summer from containers. Plant on anything that will support them. Soil should be deep and well drained but moist. The pH should be neutral or a little above. Plant in full sun or partial shade (full shade results in fewer flowers). Prepare the soil by spading it over and adding organic matter. Provide adequate drainage. Set the plants at the depth they were growing in the nursery. Plants are available in containers, or as bareroot plants from mail-order catalogs. Soak the ground thoroughly after planting to settle the soil around the roots.

Growing Tips
Water the plants during dry weather. A mulch to keep the soil cool is probably helpful as well.

Care and Maintenance
These plants will need some temporary support to keep them off the ground as they are becoming established; a bamboo stick will suffice. Once they begin to grow, use the permanent support. Clematis are divided into two kinds: those blooming midspring on stems that grew the previous year (old wood), and those that bloom on stems growing the current year (new wood). Prune those blooming on old wood when they finish flowering. Remove spent blooms, and reduce the length of the stems to force new growth. Prune those blooming on new wood in early spring before growth begins. Cut back severely to force vigorous growth. A fungal disease is devastating to Clematis in wet seasons, especially in wet soils. Ascochyta leaf spot and stem rot will kill plants at the soil line. Treat with wettable sulfur. Spray the foliage and stems every week as long as wet weather lasts. Improve drainage if needed.

Companion Planting and Design
These plants can be used anywhere any other vine can be grown.

Did You Know
Some of the most beautiful Clematis I've seen grew on a split rail fence at a horse farm—a plant every couple of yards, literally covering the fence.

Climbing Hydrangea
Hydrangea anomala petiolaris

When, Where, and How to Plant

Plant container-grown Climbing Hydrangeas in the spring. They may also be planted all season with care. (The roots are slow to recover from injury.) Plant in a rich, moist, well-drained soil. The plants will grow in full sun, but in exposed locations they may be winter-injured. They will grow in full shade, but will be slower to develop. Prepare the soil by spading, incorporating organic matter. Dig the planting holes the same depth and twice as wide as the containers in which the plants were grown. Carefully remove the plants from the containers to avoid injuring the roots. Set the plants at the same depth they were growing in the nursery. If the soil in the containers is a light artificial mix, either shake some of it off the roots or get extra from the nursery and mix it with the soil that will go back into the planting hole. This will create a gradual change from the soil on the plant to the soil around it.

Growing Tips

These are slow to recover from transplanting—make sure they have enough water, but be careful not to drown them.

Care and Maintenance

It is essential that some means of support be provided for this plant. It is a woody vine, and the weight of a mature plant will be surprising, especially if it comes tumbling down and must be raised and resupported. Make sure your building will not be damaged by these plants. The plants can climb trees without harm unless they encircle them, risking girdling. They can climb utility poles, but they may be damaged by linemen if there is a need to climb the pole.

Companion Planting and Design

Climbing Hydrangea is a large plant. According to some, it is the best of the clinging vines. Use it for massive effect on walls, arbors, or any free structure.

Did You Know

These plants are often listed as *Hydrangea petiolaris* in catalogs.

Climbing Hydrangea is a fine plant. It is not for the timid, however. It will grow to an immense size, easily reaching the tops of 6-story buildings. The plant clings by means of aerial rootlets. It will cling tenaciously, and will destroy wood or old masonry surface if allowed to get a good hold. This vine does not adhere closely to the wall supporting it but stands out, sometimes shelflike, creating greater relief than the flat effect of Boston Ivy, for instance. The attractive foliage is a glossy dark green, as well. The red exfoliating bark is interesting in winter. The flowers are fragrant 6-inch clusters of lacy blooms held away from the foliage on long stems.

Bloom Period and Color
Late June blooms in white.

Mature Height × Spread
60 to 80 feet × climbing

Dropmore Honeysuckle

Lonicera sempervirens × hirsuta

Dropmore Honeysuckle is a twining vine that produces fragrant red flowers throughout the summer months. This plant climbs by twisting around its supporting structure. It is a vine that can be used as an accent in any garden—it is not so aggressive that it can't be kept under control. Dropmore Honeysuckle can be trained quite easily with a little pruning and some tying of stems to get it started. This Honeysuckle leafs out early with attractive foliage and is one of the earliest plants to show color in the spring. The flowers are spectacular and continue for much of the summer. The fragrance is particularly noticeable on a warm, still evening. Fruit is produced in fall—it is a bright-red berry, quite nice when plentiful.

Other Name
Lonicera × brownii 'Dropmore Scarlet'

Bloom Period and Color
June to August blooms in red.

Mature Height × Spread
20 feet × twining. Will extend as much as 20 feet along a fence.

When, Where, and How to Plant

Dropmore Honeysuckle is best planted in spring; the plants are available in 5-gallon cans. Containerized plants may be planted throughout the season, if care is taken not to injure the roots. Plant in full sun or light shade in a moist, well-drained soil. These plants will grow well in the shade, but there they will flower sparsely or sometimes not at all. Dig the planting holes as deep and twice as wide as the containers. Set the plants at the same depth they were growing in the containers. Roots are slow to recover from transplanting. Space the plants so that they have room to grow. Usually one plant to a trellis is sufficient, and one plant every 5 feet on a fence should be enough.

Growing Tips

These plants may have difficulty starting up the support. Use twist ties to hold them up while they gain a foothold. Mulch to keep the soil moist but not wet. Provide water in dry weather to keep the plants flowering.

Care and Maintenance

These plants will make a tangle that needs to be pruned vigorously to keep it in some semblance of order. Pruning is the major maintenance chore associated with these Honeysuckles; it should be done as soon as the plants have finished flowering. Remove overly long stems, and shoots going in the wrong direction. Removal of the oldest canes all the way to the main stem will stimulate vigorous new growth. This plant flowers on old wood, so vigorous growth will increase the chances of flowers. Aphids have been problems with the *L. sempervirens* Honeysuckles. Control them with acephate (Orthene), following label directions.

Companion Planting and Design

Use on fences, on trellises, on banks, over low piles of rocks in the garden—any place that can display the flowers.

Did You Know

This plant was developed in Dropmore, Manitoba, so you can rely on its hardiness.

English Ivy

Hedera helix

When, Where, and How to Plant

Plant from pots or flats in spring so the plants can become well established before they must stand the rigors of winter. Growing best in shade, English Ivy needs protection from sun, especially in winter. It prefers a cool, rich, well-drained soil, but will tolerate almost any situation. It tolerates dry sites when well established. It tends to be shallowly rooted. Prepare the planting area by tilling or cultivating, incorporating organic matter if the soil is heavy. Set plants at the same depth they grew in their containers. Space them 12 inches or more apart along the wall or other support, depending on how quickly you need cover. If the plants were grown in a light, artificial soil mix, shake as much of it as you can off the roots before planting, and plant 2 inches deeper than previously.

Growing Tips

Root rot will develop in wet sites. Provide adequate drainage, and water thoroughly but infrequently.

Care and Maintenance

English Ivy will grow rapidly once established. English Ivies climb and cling by aerial rootlets, and they will hold tenaciously. They may damage wood or old masonry. Provide some means of support. The weight of a mature plant will be surprising, especially if it comes tumbling down and must be raised and resupported. Prune to remove old and damaged wood. The largest plants will lose lower leaves, leaving the lower part of a wall bare. Setting new plants into the planting every few years and removing the older plants will ensure continuing healthy vines. Aphids and mites can be troublesome, but insecticidal soap will control both. Leaf spot diseases develop in wet seasons; use Bordeaux mixture, triforine, or maneb fungicides.

Companion Planting and Design

English Ivy is excellent for covering walls, arbors, or any free structure. It resents winter sun, so use it on the north sides or where shaded by large trees or other buildings.

Did You Know

'Thorndale' is the hardiest English Ivy cultivar.

English Ivy is a beautiful evergreen vine—the plant most people envision as Ivy. If well supported, this plant can grow as high as the support allows. This vine is especially good for shaded spots in the garden. It prefers to be protected from winter sun, and will remain evergreen. It mutates freely, and literally thousands of selections have been made, usually for leaf size, color, shape, or local adaptations. Some of these selections are strictly Southern adaptations. Some selections made in the North have resulted in hardier cultivars that will tolerate our winters. These plants are well suited for growing on masonry walls, on fences, up trunks of trees, or on the sides of buildings. They can be enticed to cover arbors and pergolas.

Bloom Period and Color
Insignificant.

Mature Height × Spread
90 feet × climbing.

Japanese Wisteria
Wisteria floribunda

Japanese Wisteria is one of the loveliest flowering vines. This is a stout vine that climbs by twisting around its support. The twist always turns clockwise. If grown as a tree form, Wisteria develops a twisted trunk that may be several inches in diameter. Wisterias are heavy and will pull down inadequate structures. When I was a youngster, our family had a home with a large porch festooned with Wisteria. The plant was supported on heavy wires securely fastened into the concrete structure. I remember how heavy the plant was when it was necessary to remove it for painting. It took many of us to lift it back into place. Our Wisteria bloomed profusely every spring, with a heady fragrance that filled the evening air.

Bloom Period and Color
Spring blooms in pink, purple, white.

Mature Height × Spread
20 to 30 feet × climbing

When, Where, and How to Plant
Plant Japanese Wisteria from containers in the spring. These vines will grow up anything if given the chance. They look lovely growing up a tree, but they will eventually strangle it. Train Wisteria on fences, arbors, pergolas, and porches where a support system has been devised. Wisteria does best in full sun and any good garden soil. Wisterias are available in 5- to 6-gallon containers. Dig the planting hole the same depth and twice the diameter of the container, and set the plant at the same depth it was growing. Water thoroughly to settle the soil. Wisteria plants are large; a plant every 10 to 20 feet along a support will be more than adequate.

Growing Tips
Wisteria plants need good drainage, and must have sufficient water during flowering time. Do not overstimulate Wisteria plants with nitrogen or they will never bloom. Unless the plant is obviously deficient of nitrogen, it is better not to use any. Potassium fertilizer counteracts nitrogen's effects (excessive vegetative growth). Phosphorus fertilizer will sometimes stimulate flowering.

Care and Maintenance
Prune to keep the plant in bounds. Cut back vigorous growth to only three or four buds immediately after flowers drop. Remove any suckers from the bottom of the plant. Some Wisterias are very difficult to get to flower. Excessive vegetative growth is usually the cause. Plants usually begin flowering three to five years after being planted. If blooming does not start, deeply cultivate the plant to sever surface roots. This will shock the plant into reduced vegetative growth and may cause it to bloom. Plants in full sun will usually develop the excess stored sugars needed for blooming sooner than plants in shade.

Companion Planting and Design
These magnificent vines are at their best where the hanging clusters of blooms can be appreciated.

Did You Know
These plants resent TLC. They respond by producing lots of foliage and no flowers. Prune and fertilize cautiously.

Trumpet Vine
Campis radicans

When, Where, and How to Plant

Planting Trumpet Vine in spring or fall is probably best. Plant containerized plants all season. Plant in any soil. The pH is not important. It grows best in sun or light shade. The plant will grow in shade, but flowering will be diminished. Use these plants where quick cover is needed on fences, as screening, or to cover utility poles, retaining walls, ornamental arbors, or trellises. Avoid planting where its aggressive character will allow it to invade other plantings, such as in perennial gardens. Dig the planting holes the same depth and twice as wide as the ball of the plant. Set the plant at the depth it was growing in the nursery. Water the plant well following planting to settle the soil around the roots.

Growing Tips

The plant is vigorous enough without fertilizing.

Care and Maintenance

It is extremely important to gain control over this plant from the beginning. If it is allowed to get a head start, it will be difficult to control, and there will be a tangle of strong vines to unwind. Pruning is the key to handling Trumpet Vine. It flowers on new wood, the stems growing during the current season. Prune old canes to a few buds in fall after leaves have dropped, or in spring. You will be surprised at how fast the vine grows to a large size each year. If the plant is cut back severely every spring, blooming will be enhanced. Deadheading the blooms will prolong the flowering well into late summer. Many insects and diseases will reside on these plants, but the plants are so vigorous they will outgrow the pests.

Companion Planting and Design

These rambunctious plants need to be grown where they have adequate support and where they can be kept from growing over anything in their path.

Did You Know

Trumpet Vine can be trained into a tree form.

Trumpet Vine is an aggressively hardy plant that will grow over anything in its way. It is a native American plant, perfectly able to handle the typical Illinois weather. It spreads by means of suckering from roots, or from root segments left in the ground. Trumpet Vine makes a dense cover on fences, trellises, and pergolas, or as a screen on a staunch support. The vine climbs by means of rootlike holdfasts that are not strong. The vines are very heavy, and they will break loose from supports in storms. They may need tying to keep them attached. Their bright flowers are the primary reason for growing Trumpet Vines. The flowers are trumpet-shaped, three inches long, and one and one-half inches wide at the mouth.

Bloom Period and Color

Summer blooms in red, orange, yellow.

Mature Height × Spread

30 feet × twining. Will extend as much as 30 feet along a support.

Wintercreeper

Euonymus fortunei 'Vegetus'

Wintercreeper is a strong vine that will climb walls, fences, trees, and posts; it will easily reach the top of a two-story house. This plant is a true vine, climbing by means of aerial rootlets which attach strongly to the support. Wintercreeper is one of only a few evergreen vines that will tolerate Illinois winters. If growing in an exposed situation, it will turn light green or yellow for the winter. Some years the leaves are dropped if conditions are too severe. The stems of the plant generally remain viable in such years, and refoliate normally the next spring. The best of the Wintercreeper for vining is E. fortunei 'Vegetus'. It has medium-green foliage and is a vigorous plant once it has become established.

Bloom Period and Color
Early summer blooms in green (inconspicuous).

Mature Height × Spread
40 to 50 feet × climbing to 70 feet.

When, Where, and How to Plant

Transplant in spring to allow it to become established before contending with winter. Wintercreeper isn't particular about soils as long as it doesn't stand in water. These plants are well suited for growing on masonry walls, on fences, up trunks of trees, or on the sides of buildings. They can be enticed to cover arbors and pergolas. Euonymus plants are grown in quart- to 5-gallon-sized containers, and as balled-and-burlapped plants. The hole for planting should be no deeper than the depth of the ball of the plant, and at least twice as wide. Set the plant in the planting hole. Remove the burlap from a balled-and-burlapped plant, and stuff it down in the hole. Replace half the soil and fill the hole with water. Replace the remaining soil, and fill the hole with water again. Make a saucer around the plant with any remaining soil. Space the plants 3 to 5 feet apart.

Growing Tips

Water early in the day and keep moisture off the leaves. Applying a balanced fertilizer as the leaves begin to develop in spring will aid in recovery from winter damage.

Care and Maintenance

Prune annually in spring, removing any winter-damaged branches. These vines may be cut to a few buds on a branch, and will regrow vigorously. Crown gall causes large growths on the stems and roots and can kill the plants. Mildew and anthracnose disfigure leaves. Black vine weevils eat notches out of the margins of leaves and feed on the roots. Euonymus scale is the most damaging. Spray with acephate about the time Catalpas are in bloom to control. Repeat two or three times. Follow label directions.

Companion Planting and Design

Use on walls, trellises, pergolas, or wherever a climbing plant is needed. The color is lighter than most other vines, and variegated forms are commonly available.

Did You Know

These plants will grow to a height of 60 or 70 feet on a wall.

Water and Bog Plants *for Illinois*

Within the last decade, water features have become the most popular new item in gardening. There is something about water that soothes and satisfies the soul. Whether it is sitting beside a quiet pool, hiking to a secluded waterfall, sailing on a big lake, or enjoying the fountain in the park . . . water comforts.

Water features can be as simple as a birdbath or a tub with a few water plants. A more elaborate choice is a backyard pond. The necessity of detention and retention ponds in new residential developments, the presence of barrow pits where soil for road construction was taken, and the accessibility of lake-front building sites have resulted in many urban dwellers with ponds and lakes outside their front doors.

Backyard pond construction and maintenance have been simplified by the equipment and supplies now available from stores specializing in water gardens. This does not mean you can build a pond and forget it. Water gardens constitute a very sophisticated kind of gardening, and do require some work. If done properly, though, they can provide tremendous enjoyment. Plants, fish, even frogs, birds, and other animals will take up residence in a healthy pond. The movement of the water and the other creatures will assure something different to see whenever you have time to enjoy your water garden.

Planning a Pond

A successful pond takes planning. Before investing a lot of time in planning, check with your local authorities for any regulations that may affect your design. Some towns require a fence if the pond is over a certain size and depth. Locate your pond where it gets at least six hours of light a day. And it needs to be in the area of your yard where you can most enjoy it. Avoid overhanging trees that will drop leaves into the pond. The area should be dry so that the pond will not sink, or if the water table rises, the liner won't be forced up by water pressure from below. It is helpful to locate the pond in the lowest part of the yard, if that fits the other requirements, because it will look more natural.

If the spot collects runoff or tends to flood, some provision will need to be made to keep floodwater, with its dirt and chemicals, out of the pond.

The pond doesn't need to be too large. A three-foot pond will support a water lily, oxygenator plants, and some fish, such as koi. The pond can be from 12 inches to several feet deep. A three-foot-deep pond will not freeze solid and will allow fish and some plants to be overwintered in it. If your pond is shallower than that, some provision will need to be made for the koi, and for tender plants such as lotuses or tropical water lilies, which may need to be overwintered indoors. If you plan to stock your pond with koi or other fish, you may need to provide protection from scavengers. Neighborhood cats, raccoons, and even blue herons will find the fish in your pond easy pickings unless it is deep enough for the fish to get away.

Ponds can be constructed from many materials. The easiest to build are of preformed plastic or fiberglass. Using flexible liners in holes dug in the ground allows the possibility of creating freeform ponds of any shape or size. Many water garden firms offer catalogs listing all kinds, descriptions, and dimensions of pond liners.

Pond plants consist of submerged oxygenators, free-floating plants, emergent plants, and marginals. Oxygenators generally root in the pond bottom (hydrosol), remove carbon dioxide and pollutants from the water, and release oxygen. Free-floating plants do not root into the hydrosol, but drift around with the breezes, providing shade to prevent buildup of algae, and shelter for the small animals and fish. Emergent plants are larger—rooted into the hydrosol and reaching the surface. They provide shade, and usually attractive foliage and flowers. Marginal plants grow in the boggy soil at the edge of the pond and include many plants described elsewhere in this book. Blue Flag Iris, Astilbe, Hosta, Japanese Silver Grass, Eastern Hemlock, Red Twig Dogwood, and many others are adapted to moist areas.

For a balanced pond, oxygenator plants should occupy about 30 percent of the water volume. They can be aggressive, though, and readily take over the pond. Grow them in containers and remove a few if they become overabundant. Free-floating plants and emergent plants should cover 50 to 60 percent of the surface of the pond. Free-floating plants can provide temporary cover until the larger plants develop. When the larger plants are developed, some of the free-floating plants should be removed.

Other creatures needed for the health of your pond are scavengers such as fish, snails, and tadpoles. One animal per square foot of pond is about right. They clean up leftover fish food, algae, and decaying material or detritus. A properly balanced pond will clear up on its own a few days after planting. If it does cloud up, don't empty the pond. Let the inhabitants do their jobs and it should clear up on its own.

Ponds are delightful additions to any garden—large or small. Try various combinations of plants until you get the effect you want. They are always works in progress, so if something doesn't look just right, change it. The most important step is to get started. You will be glad you did.

Arrowhead

Sagittaria latifolia

Arrowhead is a common plant of wet areas. The characteristic arrowhead-shaped leaves are some of the first recognized by youngsters just learning about native plants. The plants grow at the water's edge in lakes throughout the state and are completely hardy if wintered below the water surface or underground. Where it is contained, it needs to be protected for the winter. The plants form little, bright white flowers in summer. They have three petals, quite similar to Trilliums, but borne in whorls along upright stems. Arrowhead spreads by means of underground runners which can be undesirable in small gardens. Its spread can be controlled by planting it in a container, and it can make an attractive addition to the pond margin.

Other Name
Duck Potato

Bloom Period and Color
Mid-to-late summer. White.

Mature Height × Spread
20 inches × 20 inches

When, Where, and How to Plant

Arrowhead is a native plant of the water's edge. It can be planted in shallow water or in ground that remains saturated all season. The plants can be aggressive, and unless there is a lot of room, might best be planted in large containers where they can be controlled. Set the containers in saturated soil in or around the pond. Fill the containers halfway with heavy garden soil. Buy fertilizer tablets specifically designed for pond use. They are slow-release materials and will not stimulate the growth of algae in your pond. Push fertilizer tablets into the soil. Set the rhizomes so the tips are level with the rim, and fill the rest of the way with soil. Make sure growing tips are exposed.

Growing Tips

Grown in containers, these plants will need winter care. If the plants can be submerged into the pond where they will not freeze, they can be overwintered outdoors. Otherwise, move them indoors for the winter. Remove the plants before they freeze. Cut off dead foliage. Store them in their containers in trays of water, or lift the tubers and store them in containers of damp sand.

Care and Maintenance

Arrowheads need little care. Keep the plants trimmed of any dead leaves and flowers so they do not foul the pond. These plants get big. Before they are set into the garden in spring, they can be divided, and replanted into the containers. Discard the extra tubers or offer them to another pond gardener.

Companion Planting and Design

In nature, these plants are found growing in muddy marshes, pools, and bogs with other marginal plants such as Swamp Milkweed, Pickerel Weed, Blue Flag Iris, and Cattails. These plants can be incorporated to make a realistic and attractive margin to the pond.

Did You Know

The tubers of Arrowhead were harvested in fall, cooked, and used by Native Americans for food.

Canadian Pondweed

Elodea canadensis

When, Where, and How to Plant

Plant oxygenator plants as soon as the pond has been filled. Canadian Pondweed will root into the bottom of the pond if there is sufficient hydrosol. However, it is easier to plant them in containers. Then, if the plants become too numerous, some of the containers are easily removed from the pond. Fill a small container (a 6-inch clay pot will suffice) with heavy clay soil. Bunch plants together, each bunch containing six to twelve stems. Stick a bunch into the soil in each pot, and set the pots in the pond. The plants will quickly root into the soil. Start with one pot for every square yard of surface water in small ponds, less in larger ones. As the plants grow, remove some of the pots. Try to maintain enough plants to occupy no more than 1/3 of the volume of the pond.

Growing Tips

Canadian Pondweed needs little if any care once it is planted. Remove any stems that break loose from the bottom. It needs a water depth of at least 3 feet.

Care and Maintenance

It is important to keep the numbers of the plants under control. If the plants begin to grow overly long, lift the pots and trim the stems to the right length—with the tips of the stems and leaves lying flat on the water surface. A sturdy wire fork can be made for lifting the pots to make the job easier. Excess Pondweeds can be added to the compost pile or dug into the garden. Any dead stems must be removed from the plants as they appear.

Companion Planting and Design

Canadian Pondweeds are planted in combination with deep water plants such as Water Lilies, and floating plants such as Water Hyacinth, to maintain the correct amount of vegetation for oxygenation, to shade the surface, and for shelter in the pond.

Did You Know

Elodea crispa is a similar submerged oxygenating plant often sold for ponds. It is actually *Lagarosiphon major*, Curly Water Thyme.

Canadian Pondweeds are common plants found in lakes and streams throughout North America. They are excellent oxygenators and are used widely in aquariums and ponds. They provide shelter for fish and other pond inhabitants. In nature, the plants can become aggressive and may need to be controlled. In a pond, control consists of removing some of the plants if they become too numerous. Canadian Pondweed grows completely submerged except for the tips of the stems which may float lying flat on the surface of the water. Stems are slender and covered with whorls of small 1/6-inch by 1/2-inch leaves. They are evergreen and completely hardy so they may be left in the pond over winter where they will provide oxygen if there is enough light for photosynthesis—even if the pond ices over.

Other Name

American Elodia

Bloom Period and Color

Summer, white, insignificant.

Mature Height × Spread

3 to 13 feet long depending on water depth

Cattail

Typha angustifolia

Cattails are familiar to nearly everyone. The interesting spikes are used as floral accessories for fall arrangements. The large Cattail, Typha latifolia, is a huge plant and not adapted to small water gardens. The Dwarf Cattails are especially useful in ponds. They are aggressive plants and must be contained so they don't take over the garden. The plants spread by means of underground rhizomes. These can be restricted by planting in a sturdy container. Small Cattails are available from pond supply stores along with many other kinds of aquatic plants. Many sales yards actually sell from ponds in which the plants are growing. This is a good way to be sure what you are getting. Unless you have a huge pond, do not try to grow Wild Cattails. They take over very quickly.

Other Names
Reedmace, Miniature Reedmace, Bulrush

Bloom Period and Color
Summer. Tan to brown in spikes.

Mature Height × Spread
2 to 6 feet tall, spreading if not controlled

When, Where, and How to Plant
Cattails are planted in spring. Plant them at the edge of the pond, in marshy soil, or in the pond on a shelf. Cattails are best planted in containers that will restrict their spreading into other parts of the garden. Use containers constructed of fine mesh so the plants do not send rhizomes out of the sides of the containers. Pond suppliers have several kinds of baskets that will fit any need. Fill the containers halfway with heavy garden soil. Set the rhizomes so the tips are level with the rim, and fill the rest of the way with soil. Make sure growing tips are exposed. Set the containers so the plant crowns are even with the soil surface or at the surface of the water.

Growing Tips
Cattails are so vigorous that they should not be fertilized or they will quickly outgrow their site. They do need to be kept submerged in water or in soggy soil. This may require watering if weather is dry.

Care and Maintenance
Cattails need little care once they are established. If the plants are growing in containers, they will need some preparation for winter. Set the containers so the plants will be submerged all winter, or bury the containers and mulch to keep them from desiccating or heaving. Divide and repot the plants in spring to reduce the size. Discard the extra plants. Few pests attack these plants.

Companion Planting and Design
The long, strap-like leaves add a vertical dimension to the garden in contrast to the flat, round leaves of many pond plants like the Water Lilies.

Did You Know
Cattails are considered weeds in most lakes and streams. Be careful not to let them get out of control or escape from your garden.

Frogs-bit

Hydrocharis morsus-ranae

When, Where, and How to Plant

These tiny plants are introduced into the pond as soon as it has been filled. Starts are available from pond supply stores. They are simply dumped into the pond.

Growing Tips

In a tough winter, Frogs-bit depends on turions for survival. Turions are swollen buds produced by a small number of water plants such as Frogs-bit. They are hardy, over-wintering in the mud at the bottom of a pond, assuring survival even if severe conditions kill the parent plants. If your pond is shallow, collect turions in fall, storing them indoors in soil submerged in 3 or 4 inches of water. When the turions float to the surface in spring, pot them up in heavy soil, keeping them submerged indoors until the pots can be set in the pond.

Care and Maintenance

Frogs-bit is a self-sufficient plant that takes little care in the pond. If the surface of the pond is more than 50 to 60 percent covered by foliage, remove some of the plants by skimming them from the surface. Remove plants damaged by snails before the leaves die and drop to the bottom of the pond. Dead vegetation in the water competes for vital oxygen needed by fish and to keep the water clear. In the winter, the plants develop turions, which sink to the bottom and rise in spring to start new plants. Should it be necessary to drain and clean the pond in spring before the turions have begun to grow, be sure to save some of the mud from the bottom of the pond and to reintroduce it as the pond is refilled.

Companion Planting and Design

Frogs-bit is used to provide the 50 to 60 percent cover necessary for a healthy pond. It should supplement larger plants with floating leaves such as Lilies and Lotuses. More aggressive floating plants can be added in spring to hasten the coverage.

Did You Know

The American Frogs-bit is a different genus and species, *Limnobium spongia*. It is not suitable for ornamental ponds.

Frogs-bit is a free-floating plant, similar to a Miniature Waterlily. It produces a rosette of shiny, kidney-shaped leaves and white flowers with yellow centers, an unusually attractive plant. Hydrocharis in Greek means "graceful water plant." The miniature size makes this plant especially valuable in smaller backyard ponds. A native of Europe and Asia, it is found in still, shallow waters, and may root into the mud. It provides excellent shelter for small animals in the pond, but may be damaged by snails. The plants form runners which give rise to offsets to form new plants. Frogs-bit is more civilized, its rate of spread being not as great as that of other floating plants.

Bloom Period and Color
Summer, white.

Mature Height × Spread
2 to 4 inches × nearly 2 inches high

Ivy-Leafed Duckweed

Lemna trisulca

Duckweeds are common inhabitants of natural ponds. They are the smallest flowering plants, consisting of one or two tiny leaves, a single root, and a single flower. They are free-floating plants and help provide the 50 to 60 percent cover needed for healthy ponds. They are especially valuable for temporary cover until the larger plants can provide enough shade. Duckweeds reproduce by growing another leaf out of the side of a mature leaf, and can multiply rapidly. In winter, they sink to the bottom of the pond and rise again in spring. Common Duckweed and other Duckweed species, common in natural ponds, are probably too aggressive for most backyard ponds. Ivy-Leafed Duckweed is much easier to control.

Other Name
Star Duckweed

Bloom Period and Color
Spring. Tiny, white.

Mature Height × Spread
Less than 1 mm. × ¹/₂ inch

When, Where, and How to Plant
Ivy-leafed Duckweed can be introduced into the pond as soon as it has been filled. The starter plants are available from pond suppliers, and are simply dumped into the pond. Make sure the supplier is selling you Ivy-Leafed Duckweed, not the common type.

Growing Tips
Ivy-Leafed Duckweed takes no care once it is introduced into the pond. It grows on its own once water temperatures are high enough.

Care and Maintenance
The care of these tiny plants consists of keeping the numbers under control. If allowed to proliferate on its own, it would soon cover the surface of the pond with a carpet of green. Excess population of the plants will begin to die off and settle to the bottom of the pond where they will decompose, using up the vital oxygen. When the surface of the pond is about 50 percent covered by Duckweeds and other floating leaves, skim off the excess Duckweed with a net. It may be necessary to skim the pond several times in the early part of the season when the plants are actively growing. The plants will reappear each spring on their own. There is no need to replant each season.

Companion Planting and Design
Use free floating plants such as Duckweed in combination with submerged oxygenating plants and emergent plants to provide a balanced environment for the fish and other animals in your pond.

Did You Know
Sometimes ponds become infested with the common Duckweeds brought in by birds or animals that may visit after swimming in natural ponds. Common Duckweeds will grow well in backyard ponds, but are so prolific that they can cover the surface in a matter of days. Whereas the tiny fronds or leaves of Common Duckweed are rotund, the fronds of Ivy-Leafed Duckweed are elliptical, much longer than they are wide. With a hand lens, it is easy to tell the difference between the two. You can check this out at your pond store. If your pond becomes contaminated with the common kind, remove all the Duckweed and start over.

Lotus
Nelumbo sp.

When, Where, and How to Plant
Plant Lotuses in large containers so they can be kept under control. Fill containers halfway with heavy garden soil and push fertilizer tablets into the soil. Use only tablets designed for pond use. They are slow-release materials and will not stimulate growth of algae in your pond. Set rhizomes so tips are level with the rim. Fill the rest of the way with soil. Make sure the growing tips are exposed. Cover the surface with 1/2 inch of pea gravel to prevent fish from rooting soil out of the container and fouling the water. Set the containers so crowns are 2 to 6 inches below the surface depending on the variety. The warmth at the surface will hasten their development in the spring. As they begin to develop, set them lower in the water.

Growing Tips
Lotuses are heavy feeders, but be sure to use the slow-release fertilizer tablets designed for ponds. These will not add to nutrients in the water which cause algae problems.

Care and Maintenance
Lotuses allowed to root into the hydrosol will take over. Control by trimming, or by removing some from the pond. Removing all dead leaves and flowers is essential before they foul the water. Lotuses need winter protection. Set them into the deepest part of the pond. If the pond is shallow, store Lotuses indoors. Lift them before they freeze. Cut off stems and foliage. Store them in their containers in trays of water. Or, remove the rhizomes and store them in damp sand. Divide plants as needed before replanting in spring. Check during the winter to make sure plants are not drying out. Cover tops of containers with plastic wrap if you are having trouble keeping them moist.

Companion Planting and Design
Lotuses provide shade needed to eliminate algae bloom, and are used for protection by small animals. Use free floating plants to provide 50 to 60 percent shade until the larger plants grow enough. Then remove some of the free floating plants.

Did You Know
The pods left after the petals fall from the flowers are the Lotuses used by florists for dried arrangements.

Lotuses are magnificent emergent pond plants. The American Lotus is native to North America and is ideal for pond culture. Many Lotuses have intense fragrances, striking foliage, and exquisite flowers up to a foot in diameter. Asian Lotuses have been cultivated for thousands of years. Young plants develop rosettes of leaves at the surface of the water. As they develop, the leaves are lifted as much as 6 feet on stout stems, terminating in the superb blooms. These plants need hot weather for the best performance. In cooler areas they will be late to bloom. A couple of weeks of 90° weather in July will see them at their best.

Other Names
American Lotus, Sacred Lotus

Bloom Period and Color
Midsummer. White, yellow, orange, pink, red.

Mature Height × Spread
1 to 6 feet above the water × 2 to 4 feet

Zones
All (4b to 6b), but needs winter protection.

Pickerel Weed

Pontederia cordata

Some aquatic plants are beautiful whether they are in bloom or not. Pickerel Weed has exquisite elongated heart-shaped leaves with swirled markings. These plants are well suited to the pond margin, or can be set in saturated soil next to the pond edge. The flowers arise in spikes from the whorl of leaves. This is a native plant and can be grown in boggy soil where it will grow and flower without any attention at all. It is usually grown in a container, but it is not invasive, which is a real plus for gardeners, as most pond and bog plants need to be contained so they don't take over.

Bloom Period and Color
Late summer. Blue.

Mature Height × Spread
2 feet × 2 feet or more

Zones
All (4b to 6b), but will need winter protection in the North.

When, Where, and How to Plant
Pickerel Weed is best planted in spring. Plants are available from pond supply stores all season in containers and can be planted throughout the summer if they are to be lifted for the winter. Plant in full sun at the margin or in boggy areas next to the pond. Usually, they are best planted in large containers. Set the containers up to the rims in saturated soil in or around the pond. Water depth over the crowns can be up to 3 or 4 inches. Fill the containers halfway with heavy garden soil. Push fertilizer tablets into the soil. Use only fertilizer tablets designed for pond use. They are slow-release materials and will not stimulate algae growth. Set the rhizomes so the tips are level with the rim, and fill the rest of the way with soil. Make sure growing tips are exposed.

Growing Tips
Buy containerized plants or divide plants in the spring. Fertilize containerized plants in spring with fertilizer tabs.

Care and Maintenance
Pickerel Weeds need no special care during the season except to keep the soil around the plants saturated. The plants are completely hardy when growing in their natural habitats. However, grown in containers they will need care to survive the winter. If the plants can be submerged into the pond where they will not freeze, they can be over-wintered outdoors. Otherwise, move them indoors for the winter before they freeze. Cut off dead foliage. Store them in their containers in trays of water, or lift out the tubers and store them in containers of damp sand.

Companion Planting and Design
Pickerel Weed is a robust plant best for growing at the edge of the pond. Its vertical pointed leaves and beautiful purple spikes mix well with pond-side grasses, the flat round leaves of Water Lilies, or Water Plantain.

Did You Know
The seeds of Pickerel Weed were used by Native Americans as cereal or ground into flour for bread.

Water Hyacinth

Eichhornia crassipes

When, Where, and How to Plant

Water Hyacinth plants are available from suppliers in late spring and summer. They may not be suitable for the smallest ponds, but are essential in ponds of any larger size. Introduce them by floating them into the pond as soon as the water warms in late spring.

Growing Tips

When too crowded, the plants become elongated and unsightly. Thin out the planting by making divisions and discarding the remainder.

Care and Maintenance

The plants are not hardy at all and must be lifted for the winter. This is a hardship, but also an advantage. The plants never become so prolific as to completely take over the pond, and cannot exist in nature where they freeze in winter. Before the weather turns cold in autumn, lift the plants and move them indoors. They should be kept moist on a layer of damp peatmoss, and in a cool bright place. In spring when danger of frost has passed, refloat the plants in the pond. If the cover begins to exceed 60 percent, remove some of the Hyacinths. Often other pond gardeners will be happy to receive a few plants for a start. Where the weather is mild and no frost occurs, these plants will literally choke ponds and rivers. In Florida, the plants are capable of obstructing waterways so boats cannot get through.

Companion Planting and Design

Use Water Hyacinths to provide some of the 50 to 60 percent cover needed for shelter and for protection of the pond animals. Combine with other free floating plants and emergent plants. The low, somewhat rounded form of Water Hyacinths combines well with the upright Pickerel Weeds and narrow-leaved Dwarf Cattails. The Hyacinths multiply quickly and can afford temporary essential cover until the larger emergent plants produce enough leaves to provide the protection animals need.

Did You Know

These plants are so desirable in ornamental ponds that some hybridizing has been done to produce better colors and form.

Water Hyacinth is the tropical that chokes rivers in the South. But, it is prized by northerners who appreciate its magnificent flowers and unusual bladders that allow the plants to float freely. It is well-suited to parts of the country where water freezes in the winter, as that kills the tender plants before they take over. The bladders are actually enlarged petioles that also keep the plants upright. Flowers are produced all summer in spikes up to 15 inches high. As the plants begin to flower, they develop anchoring roots that will anchor the plants into the hydrosol if the water is sufficiently shallow, maybe a foot or so deep. The roots provide excellent shelter for the small animals in the pond.

Bloom Period and Color
Summer. Lilac with yellow eye.

Mature Height × Spread
15 inches × 18 inches

Water Lettuce

Pistia stratiotes

Water Lettuce is a small tender floating plant. It can provide quick cover in water gardens, and is familiar to anyone who has seen it in the Everglades where it covers ponds in the summer. They truly look like fields of Lettuce. The Water Lettuce has deeply veined, velvety, light green leaves clustered like heads of Leaf Lettuce. In warm climates, it can quickly get out of hand, but in the cool north, it is easily controlled. It is not hardy and will not survive the winter. This means any problems it may cause through overabundance are automatically corrected. The plants develop runners on which new plants develop, and plants in all stages of growth can be seen at any time of the season.

Bloom Period and Color
Summer. Small, white, inconspicuous in the cluster of leaves.

Mature Height × Spread
6 inches × 6 inches

When, Where, How to Plant
Set plants in the pond in spring after the water has warmed to 70°. It is a free-floating plant and needs no container. Water depth is not important.

Growing Tips
Water Lettuce is a tender plant and will not over-winter outdoors.

Care and Maintenance
Water Lettuce is an aggressive plant. It may grow too rapidly for small ponds, but is very useful where it can provide quick cover for the pond animals. There are no pests that will keep it under control, so you will need to make sure it does not get out of hand. The plants grow well free floating, but are more vigorous if allowed to root into the hydrosol. Keeping the water more than $2^1/2$ to 3 feet deep keeps the plants from rooting so they will not take over as quickly. If plants do begin to cover more than 50 to 60 percent of the surface of the pond, lift out some of the Water Lettuce plants. Water Lettuce should be lifted from the pond when the water temperature falls to 70° in autumn. Keep the plants in pans of water or on a layer of damp peatmoss, and in a cool, bright place. In spring, when danger of frost has passed, refloat the plants in the pond. They can be used for temporary essential cover until the larger emergent plants produce enough leaves to provide protection for the pond animals.

Companion Planting and Design
Combine with other free floating and emergent plants to provide some of the 50 to 60 percent cover needed for shelter and for protection of the pond animals. The plants multiply quickly and can afford temporary essential cover until the larger emergent plants produce enough leaves to provide the protection the animals need.

Did You Know
The roots of floating plants absorb nutrients and fish wastes that could contribute to growth of algae and clouding of the water in the pond.

Water Lily

Nymphaea sp.

When, Where, and How to Plant

Plant in spring, as soon as the water warms up. These plants should be planted in larger containers. Fill the containers halfway with heavy garden soil. Push fertilizer tablets into the soil. Set the rhizomes so the tips are level with the rim, and fill the rest of the way with soil. Make sure growing tips are exposed. Cover with 1/2 inch of pea gravel to prevent soil from getting rooted out by fish and fouling the water. Thoroughly saturate the soil. Then, set the containers so the plant crowns are at the minimum distance below the surface of the water. The warmth at the surface will hasten their development in the spring. As they begin to develop, they may be set lower in the water.

Growing Tips

Large plants such as Water Lilies need proper amounts of fertilizer to thrive. Use special, pelletized, slow-release fertilizers so they do not increase the nutrients in the water, resulting in algae problems. Don't use any fertilizers unless specially made for water plants.

Care and Maintenance

Removing dead or dying plant material is essential before it fouls the water. Keep plants in the proper balance with the needs of the pond. Too few or too many will result in degradation of the water. Some plants may need to be removed if they become too abundant. Lilies need preparation for winter. Remove Tropical Water Lilies before they freeze. Cut off dead foliage. Store them in their containers in trays of water, or lift the rhizomes and store them in containers of damp sand. Set hardy Water Lilies off their shelves or supports into the deepest part of the pond. If the pond is shallow, even hardy kinds should be stored indoors. Divide the plants as needed before replanting them in spring.

Companion Planting and Design

Use in combination with floating plants to provide the needed 60 percent shade.

Did You Know

Tropical Water Lilies add delightful fragrance to the pond, especially at night.

Water Lilies are emergent plants growing from the hydrosol. Leaves and flowers float on the surface, shading the water so sunlight does not simulate algae, and protecting fish and the small animals from predators. The lovely, fragrant flowers are essential in the water garden. Even the smallest pond can support one Lily. These large plants do need from 1 to 3 feet of water to thrive. In deeper water they may be left in the pond for the winter.

Other Name
Pond Lilies

Bloom Period and Color
Summer. White, yellow, pink, red, blue, copper, orange, and changeable colors.

Mature Height × Spread
Flowers borne just above leaves, maybe 6 to 12 inches high × leaves spread 12 to 36 inches

Zones
All (4b to 6b), but Tropicals are not hardy.

Water Milfoil

Myriophyllum sp.

Water Milfoil and Parrot Feather are two of the better oxygenators. They have delicate feathery leaves along hollow vertical stems. Fish will utilize the protection of the foliage for spawning. The tiny flowers are held above the water in spikes. These plants are very common in aquariums and are easily handled without getting out of hand. They grow to a length of about 3 feet, and are adapted to smaller, shallower ponds. Parrot Feather (M. aquaticum) is semi-hardy in northern waters, but if the pond does not freeze solid will survive most winters without the need to winter it indoors. Water Milfoil (M. verticillatum and others) is fully hardy. These are native plants common in lakes and ponds throughout Illinois and the rest of the Midwest. Avoid M. spicatum, a terrible weed if it escapes into natural areas.

Other Name
Parrot Feather

Bloom Period and Color
Summer. Yellow, inconspicuous.

Mature Height × Spread
3 feet long × spreading about the same

When, Where, and How to Plant
Plant as soon as the pond has been filled. Water Milfoil stems will root into the bottom of the pond if there is sufficient hydrosol. However, it is easier to plant them in containers. When plants become too numerous, some of the containers are easily removed from the pond. Fill a small container (a 6-inch clay pot will suffice) with heavy clay soil. Make bunches of the plants, each containing six to twelve stems. Stick a bunch into the soil in each pot, and set the pots in the pond. The plants will quickly root into the soil. Start with one pot for every square yard of surface water in small ponds, less in larger ones. As the plants grow, remove some of the pots. Try to maintain enough plants to occupy no more than $1/3$ of the volume of the pond.

Growing Tips
Water Milfoil takes virtually no care. In natural lakes and ponds, Water Milfoil is found in combination with Pondweeds and Coontails, as well as with other water plants not as well suited for small ponds. Plant a mixture of different oxygenators in your pond for interest, and for varied habitat for the animals in your pond.

Care and Maintenance
It is important to keep the volume of submerged plants under control. They should occupy no more than 30 percent of the water volume. Skim off any pieces of the plants that break off and float to the surface. Promptly remove any dead stems.

Companion Planting and Design
Plant Water Milfoil and Parrot Feather in combination with deep water plants, such as Water Lilies or Lotuses, and floating plants to maintain the correct amount of vegetation for oxygenation, to shade the surface, and for shelter in the pond.

Did You Know
Parrot Feather can be grown in a watertight hanging basket, and if water can be kept standing on the surface, the plant will gracefully hang over the edges of the basket.

Wildflowers *for Illinois*

On that first warm day of spring, they poke their heads through the sod . . . the Bird's-foot Violets, Spring Beauties, and Pasque Flowers. The Illinois woodlands and prairies burst forth with a palette of color, as they have each spring for centuries. The progression of blooms continues through the season with Goldenrod, Rattlesnake Master, Joe-Pye Weed, and towering Sunflowers. These are the wildflowers of our state. They bloom by the roadside, in abandoned fields, in woodlands, and even vacant lots.

Considering Wildflowers for the Garden

In the past, some gardeners took notice of these plants. The flowers were nice, but they were just weeds. They didn't belong in the garden. Maybe they were too common. But in Europe, wildflowers native to North America were actually highly valued, and our "weeds" became garden flowers. Lately, almost as if shaken awake, we have begun appreciating them more. These weeds have become treasured wildflowers, and are appearing in gardens all over America. Actually, many of them have been in our gardens for years as well-known perennials: Gaillardia, Coneflower, Phlox, Columbine, and others. Many gardeners might even be unaware that these are the same plants as those along the road.

Wildflowers are being planted in gardens, in restored prairies, in urban woodlands, parks, nature centers, and once again, along the roadsides. This renewed interest in wildflowers is none too soon. Diminishing habitat is being strengthened by restorations of wild areas. Once again the prairie is blossoming with the flowers that always should have been there. A huge development northwest of Chicago is landscaped mostly with wildflowers. Rural estates are planting prairies. The forest preserve district of Lake County is developing and maintaining many acres of wildflower plantings. Golf courses are helping, too, by establishing natural areas.

Using Wildflowers in the Garden

Wildflowers are perfect additions to the garden because they often take less work. They are well adapted to the climate, and to the soils. Even disturbed soils will support wildflowers if there is some drainage. Many of the wildflowers are available in garden centers and nurseries. These plants are often the same ones sold as perennials. Some are

cultivars and, if allowed to spread untended in the natural garden, they can revert to their original forms. Phlox will do this in a couple of seasons or so. The seeds they drop are no longer the same genetically as the parent plant. And, sometimes these are not quite as colorful as the cultivars. But, you may find that like their wild relatives they are more resilient, and might even persist in difficult circumstances better than their hybrid relatives.

Wildflower nurseries and specialists are to be found all over Illinois. A prairie plant association is flourishing in the state. Restored prairies, and preserved woodlands are good places to learn about these plants. They have certain needs that determine where they will grow best. Once those are provided, the wildflowers do just what they are intended to do . . . grow. If you have a spot for wildflowers, or even if you have room for just one special kind, plant it. You will find that if you select the right one, it will grow without much trouble, flowering happily year after year.

Types of Wildflowers

There are two general types of wildflowers, those that grow in the open prairie, and woodland plants. Some will grow in the transition area between the two. While some wildflowers are annual or biennial, the ones in the following plant profiles are perennials. Some will reseed themselves, too.

Sometimes wildflowers can be collected from areas scheduled for development. When you notice a site scheduled for development, get in touch with the developer for permission to collect some of the plants. Railroad right-of-ways where plants are to be sprayed with herbicide or continually mowed are sources. Fellow gardeners may have extras when dividing their plants.

When acquiring wildflowers, make sure not to stray too far from home. Some wildflowers are native to large areas of North America. While these plants may look the same, they may be quite local in their adaptations. Plants grown from seed collected in central Texas where summers are hot and winters mild, may not survive in Elizabeth, Illinois, where summers are moderate, and winters can be character-builders.

Because of space limitations, the wildflowers we profile here are just a few of the many that will grow happily in Illinois. For more descriptions, check your local library or neighborhood bookstore. Also, you can glean a lot of good information on the web.

A fun way to learn more about wildflowers is to visit one of the restored prairies. There are many in the state. The Chicago Botanic Garden, in Glencoe, and the Morton Arboretum, in Lisle, both maintain restored prairies. At the Botanic Garden, several types have been established so you can see which kinds of plants prefer certain environments. Check in your area for local and state parks that maintain prairies. County forest preserves are very active in promoting prairie plantings also. Our local park district has recently begun a prairie restoration project, and has involved both children and adults in planting and caring for it.

The knowledge you gain from helping care for the plants in your public areas can translate into making your garden even better. Besides that, you will meet some very nice people who are interested in the same things that interest you . . . wildflowers.

Wildflowers of the Open Prairie*

Black-eyed Susan—*Rudbeckia hirta*

Blue Boneset—*Eupatorium coelestinum*

Blue Flag Iris—I*ris virginica*

Big Bluestem—*Andropogon gerardii*

Little Bluestem—*Schizachyrium scoparium*

Butterfly Weed—*Asclepias tuberosa*

Common Purple Coneflower—*Echinacea pallida*

Goldenrod—*Solidago* sp.

Lead Plant—*Amorpha canescens*

Milkweed—*Asclepias* sp.

Prairie Smoke—*Geum triflorum*

Prairie Violet—*Viola pedatifida*

Puccoon—*Lithospermum canescens*

Pussytoes—*Antennaria plantaginifolia*

Queen of the Prairie—*Filipendula rubra*

Rattlesnake Master—*Eryngium yuccifolium*

Shooting Star—*Dodecatheon meadia*

Wild Strawberry—*Fragaria virginiana*

Yellow Star-grass—*Hypoxis hirsuta*

Woodland Wildflowers*

Blue Flag Iris—*Iris virginica*

Goldenrod—*Solidago* sp.

Jack-in-the-Pulpit—*Arisaema triphyllum*

Joe-Pye Weed—*Eupatorium purpureum*

May Apple—*Podophyllum peltatum*

Prairie Phlox—*Phlox pilosa*

Spring Beauty—*Claytonia virginica*

Trillium—*Trillium* sp.

Virginia Bluebells—*Mertensia virginica*

Wild Columbine—*Aquilegia canadensis*

Wild Geranium—*Geranium maculatum*

Wild Strawberry—*Fragaria virginiana*

*Some plants appear on both lists

These lists include wildflowers not described in the plant profiles.

Black-Eyed Susan

Rudbeckia hirta

Black-Eyed Susans are among the most popular wild-flowers. They bloom throughout the summer, providing an unusually long floral display. More than one species of Rudbeckia grows as a wildflower. R. serotina and R. laciniata *are found in old pastures and prairie remnants throughout the state.* R. hirta pulcherima *is included in wildflower seed mixes. Some of these plants are considered weedy, and* R. serotina *is reported to be rather aggressive. Unless these flowers are grown in a small, confined garden, their aggressive nature should not be a disadvantage. Most seed mixes list only* R. hirta *and* R. subtomentosa, *the Sweet Black-Eyed Susan.* Rudbeckia hirta *is a short-lived perennial, or it may be biennial. It self-sows and should maintain itself in the wildflower garden.*

Other Name
Coneflower

Bloom Period and Color
June to September blooms in golden-yellow/brown disc.

Mature Height × Spread
3 feet × 3 feet

When, Where, and How to Plant
Potted plants are available for planting throughout the season. Seed can be sown in fall or spring. Plant in open areas with full sun on well-drained soils. These plants will tolerate dry weather better than they will wet soils. The seed may be sown in a small nursery bed. Set the seedlings in the garden when large enough to handle. In prairie plantings, the seed may be broadcast in combination with other wildflower seeds. Prepare the soil by tilling to a 4- to 6-inch depth. Plants may be set into the loosened soil by hand, spacing them about a foot apart. Seed can be broadcast and raked down into the soil an inch or so, or plant the seed in shallow furrows and cover lightly.

Growing Tips
Wildflowers are well adapted to the natural conditions and do not need to be fertilized or watered once established. As with many native plants, moist fertile soils result in plants that become overly lush and will tend to lodge. New transplants benefit from watering during the first season.

Care and Maintenance
Black-Eyed Susan, like most wildflowers that are perfectly adapted to their surroundings, needs no care. Mildew may be a problem late in the season. It is unattractive, but does the plants no harm. These plants are short-lived perennials, but they drop abundant seed and reliably reseed themselves. Perennial cultivars of Black-Eyed Susan can be divided in spring or fall.

Companion Planting and Design
Black-Eyed Susans are commonly included in prairie flower seed mixes with Coreopsis, Phlox, Asters, Goldenrod, and other common wildflowers. They bloom from early summer until frost and can be planted in restored prairie, wildflower gardens, or the perennial border.

Did You Know
Black-Eyed Susans were used extensively by Native Americans for various medicinal purposes.

Blue Boneset
Eupatorium coelestinum

When, Where, and How to Plant

Blue Boneset can be planted from seed scattered in fall, or from divisions made in early spring. A moist, well-drained soil is best, but this plant is undemanding, and any good soil will suffice. For a prairie planting, the existing soil will be satisfactory, and the plant will exist in damaged or reconstructed soils as well. Plant in the garden away from valuable perennials that may be invaded by the Blue Boneset. Seeds may be sown in a small nursery bed. Set the seedlings in the garden when large enough to handle. The seed may be broadcast in combination with other wildflower seeds in prairie plantings. Clear the area of any introduced grasses and broad-leaved weeds. The soil may be tilled for seeding. Divisions are planted 3 feet apart at the same depth they were growing. Each clump should have several old stems and some well-developed roots.

Growing Tips

Blue Boneset requires very little maintenance. In a natural setting, no care will be required.

Care and Maintenance

Burning to eliminate old tops and invading weedy plants may be advantageous. Dividing every year or two will keep it under control. In the garden, pinch or cut back during the summer to increase the numbers of shoots and flowers. Deadhead to keep the plants blooming longer, well into fall. Blue Boneset has been introduced as a perennial garden flower, and it has a place in the cutting garden as well where it will need to be staked. Growing it in full sun and keeping it on the dry side will help. In the northern part of the state, these plants may suffer some winterkill.

Companion Planting and Design

The blue flowers blend well with the yellows of Black-Eyed Susan and Goldenrod, or the whites of Asters or hardy Mums blooming at the same time of the season.

Did You Know

Boneset was a common but foul-tasting remedy for colds in the 18th century.

This is a wildflower of late summer that grows in waste places and prairie restorations. It is a plant that should be in every wildflower garden. It is easy to handle because of its relatively short height, and it has a good blue color. Blue Boneset is adapted to well-drained, somewhat dry, soils and low fertility. Under such conditions it stays in bounds and does not fall over in storms. In moist, fertile soils it is more vigorous, producing more and larger blooms. Under these conditions it will tend to lodge and will spread very quickly. In a naturalized planting with other prairie plants, and where soils are dry and low in fertility, this plant will stay shorter and be easier to control.

Other Name
Wild Ageratum

Bloom Period and Color
Late summer, fall blooms in violet-blue.

Mature Height × Spread
2 to 4 feet × 2 to 4 feet

Blue Flag Iris

Iris virginica

The native Irises are plants of the moist prairie and formerly could be found around the prairie potholes. As youngsters, we hiked and played in the open lands north of our home. They were full of potholes, and we picked Irises to take home every spring. The potholes are long gone, but the Irises are still around. They are residents of the many ornamental lakes and ponds that serve as retention basins in the new developments and the many office parks that have sprung up in ever-expanding suburbia. These plants are at home in moist places in the garden where other flowers have a tough time. Plant them where the sump pump or downspout keeps the ground damp.

Other Name
Blue Flag

Bloom Period and Color
Spring. Blue, purple.

Mature Height × Spread
24 to 30 inches × 24 to 30 inches

When, Where, and How to Plant
Containerized Blue Flag Irises can be planted anytime during the season. Often they are available from suppliers of pond and water feature plants. Divide plants in late summer after the foliage has begun to yellow. Plant in full to partial sun. These are marsh plants; they do best in moist or boggy soil. Dig planting holes as deep and twice as wide as the containers. Remove the plants from the containers and set them in the holes. Backfill with the soil from the hole and soak thoroughly. Select divisions with one or two fans of leaves. Set them on their sides with the leaves pointing up. The rhizomes should be at or just below the soil surface. Blue Flags will grow in marshes or bogs, and can be planted where as much as 2 or 3 inches of water stands in spring.

Growing Tips
These plants do best if the soil is kept evenly moist all summer. They are plants of the wet prairie. If growing in soggy soil or under a few inches of water, they essentially are pest-free. Although they prefer moist soils, these Irises can tolerate drier soils, but they will not stand a drought.

Care and Maintenance
Irises are self-sufficient. They take little care once they are established. But, like Bearded Irises, when they eventually become crowded, they do need to be divided. Lift the clumps, and cut away any damaged parts. Separate the clumps into segments, each with a fan of leaves, a piece of rhizome, and several feeder roots. Extra pieces will be sought eagerly by neighbors.

Companion Planting and Design
These lovely plants with their long sword-like leaves make good partners with Common Boneset, Swamp Milkweed, Common Arrowhead, and other plants of moist areas.

Did You Know
The rhizomes of these plants are poisonous, but they were used medicinally in small amounts by the Native Americans and pioneers to get rid of tapeworms and to treat goiters.

Bluestem
Andropogon sp.

When, Where, and How to Plant
Bluestems can be divided, or seed may be sown in spring. Plants are sold in containers and can be planted at any time during the season, the earlier the better. Plant in the garden where there is plenty of room, or in naturalized areas. The soil should be well drained, but any garden soil will suffice. Full sun is preferred. The seeds may be sown in a small nursery bed. Set the seedlings in the garden when they are large enough to handle. Seed may be broadcast in combination with other wildflower seeds in prairie plantings. For prairie seeding in seed mixes, prepare the area by disking or tilling. Sow the seed, and drag to cover it lightly; or conservation-drill the seed. As a constituent of a mix, the seed is often hydroseeded in prairie plantings. In the garden, dig planting holes the same depth as the plant ball and twice as wide. Set the plants at the same depth they were growing. Divided clumps should be reset at the same depth they grew. Water the plants to settle the soil around the roots. Seeded areas may be irrigated to get the seed to germinate.

Growing Tips
Once the plants are established, they need very little watering. Fertilizer is unnecessary. In fertile or moist soils Bluestems become rank and weak, and lodge, destroying their attractiveness. These plants are unaffected by either insect or disease problems.

Care and Maintenance
Plants should be cut down in fall or late winter before new growth begins. Divide garden plants when they become too crowded.

Companion Planting and Design
Use in naturalized plantings or as specimens.

Did You Know
Big Bluestem was the dominant constituent of the tall grass prairies. It is the "king of native grasses." As settlers moved into Illinois, they quickly learned that the best corn grew where the "Big Blue" grew. Today, the top producing land for corn is found in the counties where Big Bluestem once stood.

The Bluestems are plants of the prairie. Big Bluestem (Andropogon gerardii) grows into big clumps and will develop into a dense sod. Big Bluestems spread (slowly) by rhizomes and by seed. The root systems can be extensive and will grow down several feet into a deep soil. Little Bluestem (Schizachyrium scoparium) is found in the sand dunes along Lake Michigan and in dry prairie remnants. It is a bunch grass, an intermediate plant between the tall grasses and the short grasses of the drylands. In the sand dunes, it forms clumps, turning brown and lasting through the winter. It grows to about 3 feet tall in scattered bunches, so flowering plants will grow with it. The leaves of the plants are blue-green, and the stems are bluish at the joints.

Bloom Period and Color
August through September blooms in green to bronze or purplish.

Mature Height × Spread
2 to 10 feet × 3 feet

Butterfly Weed

Asclepias tuberosa

Butterfly Weed is aptly named. It is one of the plants sought by butterfly enthusiasts (our grandchildren among them), because its bright colors attract butterflies. Butterfly Weed is native to Illinois and is found along roadsides and in other waste places. It is a plant of dry, infertile soils. In a garden it will prosper from the improved soil conditions, but is not invasive, and even though it will grow larger, it will not fall over. Once established, this plant is indestructible. Small, first-year plants are shallowly rooted and may be heaved out of the ground the first winter. Just push them back down and they will grow as though nothing has happened. The plants grow deep taproots, but they will spread with time.

Bloom Period and Color
Late spring to midsummer blooms in orange, yellow, red.

Mature Height × Spread
3 feet × 1¹/2 feet

When, Where, and How to Plant
Root cuttings or seed may be planted in early spring. Potted plants may be set in the garden at any time during the season. Plant in full sun in any good garden soil (these plants can be planted in almost any kind of soil except a swamp—the deep taproots cannot survive in soggy soils). Butterfly Weed may be grown in the perennial garden or naturalized in prairie plantings. It can also be planted in a butterfly garden among other plants, or in the cutting garden. The seeds may be sown in a small nursery bed. Rub the fluff off the seeds and sow them in prepared soil. Set the seedlings in the garden when they are large enough to handle. In prairie plantings, the seed may be broadcast onto prepared soil; disk or till to prepare a seedbed. The seed is short-lived, so be sure you buy new seed. Dig holes for containerized plants the same depth as the plant ball and twice as wide. Set divisions at the same depth they were growing before. Water to settle the soil.

Growing Tips
The plants may benefit from a mulch in winter after the ground has frozen. Apply a 4- to 6-inch layer of straw to keep the plants from freezing and thawing all winter.

Care and Maintenance
No insect or disease pests will seriously affect Butterfly Weed. Avoid using insecticides that may harm the butterflies.

Companion Planting and Design
Butterfly Weed is excellent for fresh floral arrangements, and its flowers can be dried as well. It is especially attractive planted in groups along driveways or rustic walkways, much as Daylilies are used.

Did You Know
Butterfly Weed is a primary food source for monarch butterfly larvae. The insects ingest a toxin from the plants that makes them distasteful to predators. The flowers are nectar sources for many butterfly species. Removal of the first blooms as they fade will encourage another flush of flowers.

Common Purple Coneflower

Echinacea pallida

When, Where, and How to Plant
Seeds of Purple Coneflowers may be sown in the fall or in spring. Divisions or started plants may be planted in early spring. Plant in naturalized areas or wildflower gardens, in full sun or light shade. Soils may be light or heavy, but they must be well drained. These are upland plants and will not survive in wet soils. The seeds may be sown in a small nursery bed. Set the seedlings in the garden when they are large enough to handle. For seeding a prairie seed mix, prepare the soil by tilling or disking. Drill or broadcast the seed and drag to cover it lightly. Set divisions at the same depth they were growing before. Planting slightly high is preferable to planting too deeply.

Growing Tips
The plants should be watered thoroughly after planting and during the first season if there is extended dry weather. Seeded plantings will rarely need watering once the plants are up and growing. Wildflowers are well adapted to the natural conditions and do not need to be fertilized or watered once established. As with many native plants, moist, fertile soils result in plants that become overly lush and tend to lodge.

Care and Maintenance
Prairie plantings will benefit from burning every few years to reduce competition from introduced species and woody plants. Most prairie plants respond to burning with increased vigor and floriferousness.

Companion Planting and Design
Plant in naturalized areas and wildflower gardens, in combination with Goldenrod and Black-Eyed Susans and other fall blooming prairie plants.

Did You Know
The history of this plant includes many medicinal uses. Native Americans of the plains used ground roots as poultices for snakebites, bee stings, or dog bites. They chewed root shavings for toothaches. The juice seems to contain a topical anesthetic and was used by early settlers for relief from the pain of burns. In recent years, interest has grown regarding the medicinal properties of Echinacea and it is promoted as a remedy for a variety of ailments.

Purple Coneflower, Echinacea pallida, is a native of our Illinois prairie. Two Purple Coneflowers were once widespread throughout Illinois: Common, E. pallida, and Broadleaf, E. purpurea. For all practical purposes, they are both plants of drier soils and will grow in wildflower plantings. They are adapted to the small or large wildflower garden and are quite tidy in their habits. Restored prairie plantings often include Purple Coneflowers, because they are reliable and provide interesting form and color for several weeks in summer. They are adapted to our heavy, often alkaline soils and the vagaries of precipitation in our typical summer. Once established, they can stand drought and will keep on blooming. They are sturdy plants, but do not spread aggressively.

Other Name
Echinacea

Bloom Period and Color
June to October blooms in purple with brown center.

Mature Height × Spread
2 to 4 feet × 2 to 4 feet

Goldenrod
Solidago sp.

Goldenrod is a flower of late summer, offering its golden blooms as the season is winding down. For the wildflower purist, there are many species that can be grown in the garden or in prairie plantings. We can always enjoy the Goldenrods that we find growing along the roadsides and in other undisturbed places. Goldenrod plants growing in places scheduled for development can be moved to your garden without difficulty. (It is advisable to ask permission first.) If considering a plant rescue, be aware that there is at least one endangered Goldenrod in Illinois. Some cultivars and some hybrids have better form and color than the species.

Bloom Period and Color
Midsummer to late fall blooms in yellow.

Mature Height × Spread
2 to 6 feet × 1 to 3 feet

When, Where, and How to Plant
Goldenrod can be started from seed sown in fall or spring. Divide plants in spring before growth begins. Containerized plants can be planted at any time during the season. Goldenrods grow in any soil of average fertility and decent drainage, in full sun or partial shade. Higher fertility will result in taller, weaker plants. The plants are suited to the perennial border and the cutting garden, and some species are adapted to woodlands with light shade. Seed may be sown in naturalized settings. Several Goldenrods are often included in wildflower mixes. Disk or till the soil, and broadcast or drill the seed. The seeds may be sown in a small nursery bed. Once established, Goldenrod reseeds itself easily. Set the seedlings in the garden when large enough to handle. Plant divisions or container-grown plants at the same depth they were growing before. Dig the planting holes the same depth and twice as wide as the plant balls. Space the plants 1 1/2 to 2 feet apart in groups. The taller kinds will tend to support each other if closely planted.

Growing Tips
Wildflowers are well adapted to the natural conditions and do not need to be fertilized or watered once established. As with many native plants, moist fertile soils result in plants that become overly lush and will tend to lodge. New transplants benefit from watering during the first season.

Care and Maintenance
Once established in the garden, Goldenrod requires little care. The garden's higher fertility will encourage vigorous growth, and division will be necessary every few years.

Companion Planting and Design
Naturalized clumps are attractive along pathways; they combine well with other wildflowers blooming at the same time in naturalized areas.

Did You Know
Goldenrods respond well to burning, which eliminates old leaves and plants, non-native species, and woody plants that invade the planting. Fire stimulates the growth of native prairie plants and is necessary for seeds of some types to germinate.

Jack-in-the-Pulpit

Arisaema triphyllum

When, Where, and How to Plant

Jack-in-the-Pulpit can be started from seeds sown in the fall as soon as they are collected. Plants may be dug up and moved in spring just as the shoots appear and before the leaves emerge. Jack-in-the-Pulpits must be planted in moist soil. They can stand filtered or full shade. Use them in shade gardens, on the north sides of buildings where it stays dark and moist, in woodland gardens, or next to shaded water features. Seed is collected in fall as the berries turn red. The berries are attractive to birds, so get there early. Squeeze the berries open to get the seeds, and sow them immediately outdoors where you want them; or stratify the seeds in moist sphagnum moss for two months, and sow them indoors under lights. Germination takes three weeks. Set the plants out when the soil is dry enough to work. The corms are deeper than you think, so be careful not to cut the top off without the corm—take a big clump of soil. Wear gloves to handle the corms, or the calcium oxalate crystals will get into your skin and make you itch.

Growing Tips

Jack-in-the-Pulpits are plants of moist woodlands. They need moist conditions and should be watered to prevent drying. An inch per week should be sufficient. Apply fertilizer in spring as plants begin growth. Well watered and fertilized plantings develop large plants and spread quickly.

Care and Maintenance

Once in place, Jack-in-the-Pulpits do not like to be disturbed. Leave them alone. There are no pest problems associated with these plants.

Companion Planting and Design

These plants are well suited to dark wet places where other plants perform poorly. Interplant with Wild Geraniums, Trilliums, May Apples, Virginia Bluebells, and other wildflowers of the moist woodlands.

Did You Know

I still associate croaking of frogs, filtered sunlight through the leafing-out trees, and spring songs of birds with finding the first Jack-in-the-Pulpits in spring, the floor of the woods covered with their umbrella-like leaves.

Jack-in-the-Pulpit is a favorite woodland plant, eagerly sought out each spring by nature lovers as a true sign that spring is here. Jack-in-the-Pulpit is strictly a moist shade plant. If you have an area where nothing will grow because of the shade and wetness, Jack may solve your problem. Once these plants are happy, they will proliferate and become more attractive each year. They can cover an area with their big leaves, and, if kept moist, will last all summer. Two leaves on long petioles grow from the corm planted deep in the ground. As they reach full size, a third stalk bears the pulpit-shaped structure called a spathe. This is Jack, or as it is sometimes called, "the preacher."

Bloom Period and Color
Spring blooms in green with brown stripes.

Mature Height × Spread
1 to 2 feet × 6 inches to 1 foot

Joe-Pye Weed

Eupatorium purpureum

Joe-Pye Weed is such an unusual name that it is difficult to forget it. Most people remember the name long before they can recognize the plant. According to legend, Joe Pye was a Native American herb doctor in the Massachusetts Bay Colony. He used this plant to cure fevers. The plant is still used in parts of Appalachia for some disorders. This plant is too big for many gardens, but where there is room and where it can be kept under control, it will provide quite a display of purple blooms. While ignored here, Joe-Pye Weed was first popularized in Great Britain. The plants are just too common here, growing along roadsides—but the recent popularity of native plants has sparked interest in this plant as a garden flower.

Bloom Period and Color
Late July to September blooms in purple.

Mature Height × Spread
7 feet × 3 feet

When, Where, and How to Plant
Joe-Pye Weed is planted from seed sown in fall, or from divisions in spring. Plant container-grown plants at any time during the season. This plant will tolerate dry places but may scorch. It can be planted in full sun or semi-shaded sites. For prairie restoration and sowing a seed mix, prepare the soil by disking or tilling. Spread the seed and cover it lightly. The seeds may be sown in a small nursery bed. Set the seedlings in the garden when large enough to handle. Dig and divide clumps in spring. The roots are tough and fibrous; divide the clumps in half or in quarters. Dig planting holes the same depth as the balls of the plants or the clumps. Set the plants at the same depth they were growing.

Growing Tips
These plants will need to be watered to keep from wilting the first season after planting. They will tolerate droughty conditions if watered in dry weather.

Care and Maintenance
Joe-Pye Weed requires little care. Joe-Pye Weed can be grown in a small garden if it is cut down to 2 feet in June. It will respond with a lower, bushy plant and many flowers. The leaves of this plant give off a pleasant vanilla-like fragrance when crushed.

Companion Planting and Design
This is a plant that is too big for many gardens, but where there is room, it goes well with the Goldenrod and Rudbeckia in bloom at the same time. Use it in a wide border, with ornamental grasses, in naturalized areas, at the edges of woods, or near water features. It is a plant of the woodland border that will prosper in woods that have been burned off to reduce the underbrush.

Did You Know
Most prairie plants, including Joe-Pye Weed, benefit from burning, which eliminates the old tops and stimulates seed germination. Check with appropriate officials of your local municipality before considering a controlled burn on any property.

May Apple

Podophyllum peltatum

When, Where, and How to Plant

Divisions can be planted in late summer or spring. Plants can be used well in shady areas surrounded by concrete walks or driveways, and are especially good on banks. Shady slopes around buildings are impossible to keep sodded, and May Apples have been used successfully in these situations. They can be combined with taller Ferns for a pleasing contrast in texture. Few plants are as well adapted to a naturalized woodland setting as is the aggressive May Apple. Plant divisions in holes dug the same depth and twice as wide as the plant balls. Set the divisions at the same depth they were growing before. Backfill the holes and water to settle the soil around the roots. On banks or among tree roots, where planting is difficult, mulch them with shredded bark, and water until they have become established. If necessary, a few rocks will hold the plants in place until they take root. The berries may be collected as they ripen and the seeds rubbed out. Sow them immediately; they will germinate the next spring.

Growing Tips

Once established, May Apples need no care.

Care and Maintenance

Remove the large leaves after they ripen in fall, or burn off the area in spring. If the plants begin to grow out of their situation, remove them by digging up the wayward plants and disposing of them. No diseases or insect pests are known to affect May Apples—they are as trouble-free as any garden plant can be.

Companion Planting and Design

May Apples are quite aggressive and will easily overtake less aggressive plants. Combine them with larger Ferns or Jack-in-the-Pulpit.

Did You Know

May Apple was used for medicinal purposes by Native Americans and early settlers as a treatment for snakebite and as a cathartic. Modern medicine has extracted a resin effective in treating some kinds of skin problems and reported to have anti-tumor properties. The fruit loses its toxicity as it ripens, and pioneers used the berries for preserves. Don't try it unless you know how to use them.

May Apple is a plant of the moist woodlands. It grows from a large rootstock, appearing in early spring as one or two large umbrella-like leaves. It is very difficult to kill May Apples. I have dug them up and planted them in our yard in midsummer. They wilt for a few days, then resume growing as if they had never been moved. The flowers appear beneath the leaves and are hard to see unless a leaf is lifted. This is a very vigorous plant, and it will spread if not confined. It is a valuable plant where other things will not grow. The name May Apple refers to the fruit that appears in midsummer. The fruits are poisonous.

Other Name

Wild Mandrake

Bloom Period and Color

May blooms in white.

Mature Height × Spread

1 to 1 1/2 feet × 1 1/2 feet

Milkweed

Asclepias syriaca

Milkweeds are beautiful plants when in bloom. It is interesting to watch the seedpods as they open in fall, releasing their fluffy parachutes into the wind. The flowers are good for cutting, and the pods are wonderful in dried arrangements. Milkweeds attract butterflies; their flowers are sources of nectar; larvae feed on leaves. These are large plants with fleshy leaves, so the feeding of a few of these insects does little to harm their looks. In our neighborhood, a few Milkweeds grow in alleys, vacant lots, and other unmowed places. Swamp Milkweed, A. incarnata, is a plant from the edges of prairie potholes where water persisted until well into summer. It is so wide-ranging in its adaptation that it will grow in fairly dry, alkaline soils as well.

Bloom Period and Color
July and August blooms in pale pink to rose-purple.

Mature Height × Spread
5 feet × 2 feet

When, Where, and How to Plant
Milkweed crowns can be planted in spring or fall. Sow seeds as they develop in late summer. Plant in moist soil in full sun. These are large plants, so locate them at the back of the garden or in naturalized areas next to water features, ponds, or streams. Start a butterfly garden with Milkweed and other inviting species. Specialty wildflower growers start these plants in pots. Set the crowns at the same depth they were growing in their containers. The seeds may be sown in a small nursery bed. Rub the fluff off the seeds, and sow them in prepared soil. Set the seedlings in the garden when large enough to handle. The seed may be broadcast in combination with other wildflower seeds in prairie plantings. Drag the area to cover the seeds lightly. The plants will develop slowly, taking two seasons or more to flower. Swamp Milkweeds are difficult to divide because they develop taproots and don't spread. They can be transplanted, but be sure to dig deep enough to minimize root damage. Common Milkweed will spread and is easier to transplant from root divisions.

Growing Tips
Milkweeds are completely self-sufficient.

Care and Maintenance
Aphids are common on the plants, but are usually controlled naturally by ladybugs. Don't spray or dust the plants or the butterfly larvae will be killed.

Companion Planting and Design
Milkweeds fit in well with Joe-Pye Weed and other larger native plants. Use them in borders, natural gardens, and butterfly gardens.

Did You Know
Milkweed is a primary food source for monarch butterfly larvae. They ingest toxins from the plants, making them distasteful to many predators. Monarch eggs can be collected, the larvae reared in cages, allowed to pupate and emerge as adults in just a few weeks . . . an excellent summertime children's activity. Adults can be tagged* for release to track migration patterns. The flowers are nectar sources for great spangled fritillary butterflies.

*Contact: Dept. of Entomology, University of Kansas, Lawrence, for information.

Prairie Phlox

Phlox pilosa fulgida

When, Where, and How to Plant

Seed is available from suppliers of prairie or wild-flower seeds, and in prairie-seed mixes. Seed may be collected as it develops and before the capsules pop open. Divide plants in spring or late fall. Plant Prairie Phlox in full sun in a well-drained soil. Use them in the border, the wildflower garden, or in naturalized prairie plantings. Sow seed in fall as soon as it is collected, or in spring in prepared soil. Seeds may be sown in a small nursery bed. Prepare the soil by disking or tilling. Cover the seed lightly. Set the seedlings in the garden when large enough to handle. Plant divisions at the same depth they were growing. Dig the planting holes as deep and twice as wide as the rootball of the plant.

Growing Tips

Once established, Prairie Phlox requires no care. Wildflowers are well adapted to the natural conditions and do not need to be fertilized or watered once established. As with many native plants, moist, fertile soils result in plants that become overly lush and tend to lodge.

Care and Maintenance

In prairie plantings, burning every few years will prevent invasion by introduced species and woody plants, and it will stimulate the growth of native plants.

Companion Planting and Design

These flowers are used on many reclaimed sites, and are used on berms and in prairie plantings throughout the state. Some roadside plantings by the Illinois Department of Transportation have included Prairie Phlox. Prairie plantings in large industrial sites, such as the Sears Prairie Stone development in Northern Illinois, are brightened by these flowers in spring.

Did You Know

Prairie Phlox attracts butterflies. Many kinds of Phlox have upper stems that are covered with a sticky material thought to prevent non-pollinating insects from getting to the flowers. *Phlox divaricata* is a low-growing woodland plant; Sand Prairie Phlox, *Phlox pilosa*, inhabits dry upland sandy soils, but will stand moist soils, too.

Prairie Phlox is a delightful plant that blooms in mid- to late spring. It is similar to many other Phlox, with its heads of dainty blooms on tall, unbranched stems. Prairie Phlox is a more delicate flower than perennial Garden Phlox, P. paniculata. It has fewer flowers, and its colors tend to be more pastel. It is included in prairie plant seed mixes and used on many reclaimed sites. This Phlox is a plant of dry soils and will tolerate some drought. It will grow where the soils are more moist, but not in soggy soils. Prairie is not as spectacular as Garden Phlox, but it does not require as much care. Hybrid Garden Phlox, if allowed to drop seed, will revert to the species.

Bloom Period and Color

April to June blooms in pink, rose, violet.

Mature Height × Spread

15 to 30 inches × 15 inches

Trillium

Trillium sp.

Trilliums are identifiable to almost everyone. They are distinctive, with their single stem growing from a bulb. The stem is topped with a whorl of three leaves and a colorful flower with three petals. In some deciduous woodlands, the ground is covered with these lovely blooms in spring, just before the leaves in the canopy close out the sunlight. Trilliums are easy to grow in the wildflower garden. Plant them and leave them alone. They do not like to be disturbed; picking the flowers will remove leaves necessary for replenishing the bulbs. Those picked plants will not bloom the next spring, and may not survive the winter. Trilliums in the wild have been the targets of plant collectors, and some populations have been destroyed.

Other Name
Wake Robin

Bloom Period and Color
Spring blooms in red, white.

Mature Height × Spread
18 inches × 6 inches

When, Where, and How to Plant
Sow seed outdoors in summer as soon as the seed is ripe. Set out potted plants in early spring. Collect bulblets after the tops die down in summer. Trilliums often do not transplant well. Plant Trillium bulbs in moist woodlands that have a deep, humusy soil. Filtered sunlight is preferred, as it will allow the best replenishing of the bulbs. Sow seed in a prepared bed outdoors. Collect the seed as berries begin to ripen, but before they split. Check the seeds in a few berries, and collect them as soon as they turn dark. Sow immediately. If they dry out, they will not germinate. The seeds will germinate over the next two years. Move the tiny new bulbs to permanent locations after the tops dry down in late summer. Plants will flower in two or three years. Space the plants 2 feet apart.

Growing Tips
If these plants are in a spot that dries out in summer, water them as long as the leaves are still green. Trilliums usually grow where there is a lot of litter from fallen leaves. In the garden, mulch them with compost to keep the soil cool and moist.

Care and Maintenance
There are no insect or disease pests that affect Trilliums. Try to keep the leaves on the plants as long as possible in spring. The longer they last, the better your chances of having plenty of flowers the following year.

Companion Planting and Design
Trilliums are especially attractive in masses on the forest floor, or as specimens of the white-flowered species in the shade garden. Locate them where the absence of leaves later in the summer will not be noticed.

Did You Know
Trilliums have been used in folk medicine for centuries. Native Americans used them to treat arthritis. They pounded the joint with a stick imbedded with needles and rubbed a tea of powdered roots into the affected area. Some practitioners are using similar treatments with success today.

Virginia Bluebells
Mertensia virginica

When, Where, and How to Plant

Seed may be collected in spring as the fruits ripen. Tubers can be dug after the tops of the plants die down in early summer. They are offered for sale along with spring bulbs in fall. Plant in filtered shade where soils are cool and moist, shaded rock gardens, perennial borders, naturalized woodlands, or shaded grassy areas that are not mowed. These plants are often seen in forest preserve savannas, where the grasses do not compete early and scattered trees provide shade. Plant divisions in late summer or fall. Existing plants may be divided and moved in fall. Set them at the same depth they were growing before. The seeds may be sown in a small nursery bed. Set the seedlings in the garden when large enough to handle. The seed may be broadcast in naturalized woodland plantings.

Growing Tips

If the plants are growing in an area that tends to dry out, apply compost to cool the soil and help maintain moisture.

Care and Maintenance

No diseases or insect pests seriously affect Virginia Bluebells. These plants will develop sizable crowns, but they usually spread by means of dropped seeds. Beds will enlarge in favorable areas. If the tops are cut down before they ripen, the plants will decline and die out. Although these plants are difficult to situate in the garden because they disappear quickly, they are so delightful while they last that it is worth the effort.

Companion Planting and Design

Combine Virginia Bluebells with other early wildflowers such as Trilliums, Jack-in-the-Pulpit, or May Apples. The foliage of these plants will cover the bare spaces left as the Bluebells disappear.

Did You Know

These plants spread by means of dropped seeds. Beds will enlarge in favorable areas and splendid naturalized plantings of Virginia Bluebells pop up in unexpected places. If out hiking in spring, don't be surprised to see some of these delightful flowers in any semi-open woodlands.

Virginia Bluebells are welcome spring visitors that add something different to the garden. They bloom at the same time as many of the spring-flowering bulbs. Virginia Bluebells are inhabitants of the moist, deciduous woods. They emerge, bloom, and dry down before the trees completely leaf out. This allows them to replenish the overwintering tubers. If grown in dark areas, they tend to thin out and may disappear. The ideal situation is a moist soil with plenty of organic matter and filtered light as they bloom. Since these plants disappear in the garden in early summer, don't plant masses of them where a void will be noticed. They work well with later-developing plants such as Ferns or Columbines that will not compete with them for light.

Bloom Period and Color
March to May blooms in blue.

Mature Height × Spread
2 feet × 2 feet

Wild Columbine

Aquilegia canadensis

Wild Columbines have distinctive flowers with small red-and-yellow petals surrounded by red sepals, each ending in an elongated spur. These flowers are borne on nodding stems in spring and early summer. They grow in the shade, for the most part, and not in clumps. It is more common to see a few of them in one place. They don't compete well with grasses and other vigorous plants. They are perfectly capable of growing in cracks in cliffs. It is unlikely that there is a cliff in your garden, but Wild Columbine can do very well in a rock garden. This plant is one of the parents of some hybrid Columbines. All Columbines are attractive to hummingbirds, butterflies, and moths, which feed on their nectar.

Bloom Period and Color
April to July blooms in red and yellow.

Mature Height × Spread
2 to 3 feet × 2 feet

When, Where, and How to Plant
Wild Columbines can be grown from seed sown in midsummer. Plants may be divided in fall after the foliage begins to ripen. Plant in dappled sun or shade, though full sun will be tolerated. Use in rock gardens, wooded areas, and shaded wild-flower gardens. Soil should be well drained, or even poor. The seeds may be sown in a small nursery bed. Set the seedlings in the garden when they are large enough to handle. The seed may be broadcast in combination with other wildflower seeds in naturalized plantings. Winter stratification is needed to break dormancy. Plants will flower the second season. Divisions may be made or plants from containers planted in fall or early spring. Once established, Wild Columbines will maintain themselves by reseeding.

Growing Tips
Wildflowers are well adapted to the natural conditions and do not need to be fertilized or watered once established. As with many native plants, moist, fertile soils result in plants becoming overly lush and tending to lodge. Columbines grow naturally in places that are wet in the spring but go dry in summer. The plants prefer the dry soil during hot weather, suffering from crown rot if soils are too wet.

Care and Maintenance
Wild Columbines require little care. Leaf miners will damage the foliage, but in naturalized plantings there is no need to control this pest. Garlic mustard, a weed, occupies the same kind of environment as does Wild Columbine; it will take over the planting if not controlled.

Companion Planting and Design
Because the flowering season ends early and the plants die back, combine Columbines with later flowering plants that will hide the vacated spaces.

Did You Know
Hybrid Columbines, if allowed to reseed, quickly deteriorate to inferior types. Introduced plantings that have reverted can be seen in old farmsteads or abandoned pastures, or wherever they were planted and abandoned.

Wild Geranium
Geranium maculatum

When, Where, and How to Plant

Wild Geraniums can be started from seed, or divisions can be made in early spring. Plant in moist woodlands, shaded wildflower gardens, or tree-lined roadside plantings in any average soil. While these are woodland plants, they are commonly seen growing along roadsides, just beyond the mowed strip, where they are in full sun much of the day. The seeds may be sown in a small nursery bed. The addition of organic matter to improve moisture retention and soil structure is beneficial. Set the seedlings in the garden when they are large enough to handle. Divisions should be planted at the same depth they were growing, and each clump should have several eyes. Set the clumps at least 3 feet apart. They will spread. In naturalized settings, the plants will reseed themselves and develop sizable beds.

Growing Tips

Wild Geraniums are well adapted to the natural conditions. As with many native plants, moist, fertile soils result in plants becoming overly lush and weak. Wild Geraniums grow naturally in places that are wet in the spring but go dry in summer. The plants prefer the dry soil during hot weather, suffering from crown rot if soils are too wet.

Care and Maintenance

Wild Geraniums are essentially trouble-free. The seeds are borne in capsules that split open, scattering the seeds some distance from the plants. This ensures the planting will spread. Garlic mustard has invaded naturalized plantings; it will squeeze these plants out unless controlled.

Companion Planting and Design

In nature, Wild Geraniums are usually found with Trilliums, May Apples, Hydrophyllums, and, most consistently, with Blue Phlox. Use them in naturalized plantings and at woodland edges.

Did You Know

The Geranium was used for medicinal purposes by Native Americans and early settlers as an astringent and for other varied treatments. The plant has a high tannin content and was used for tanning hides.

The flowers of this springtime favorite seem to pop up overnight in wooded areas and along roadsides with the first nice spring weather. The flowers are rosy to pink and have delicate darker veins and five wide, nearly crepe-like petals. The leaves are finely cut, similar to those of some of the fragrant Pelargoniums. Wild Geraniums are among the more common of the woodland spring flowers. They are often found with Blue Phlox. Wild Geraniums are much more tolerant of sites than some think. They are found in wet places and on fairly dry slopes. They grow in full shade and in full sun. In the sun, they do better if the soil has some moisture.

Other Name
Cranesbill

Bloom Period and Color
April to June blooms in rose-lavender, pink.

Mature Height × Spread
18 inches to 2 feet × 18 inches to 2 feet

Glossary

AAS: All-America Selections, awarded to plant cultivars that have given outstanding performance in trial gardens throughout the country.

AARS: All-American Rose Selections, awarded to rose cultivars that have given outstanding performance in trial gardens throughout the country.

Alkaline soil: soil with a pH greater than 7.0, the converse of acid soil, often with a high limestone content.

All-purpose fertilizer: powdered, liquid, or granular fertilizer containing nitrogen (N), phosphorus (P), and potassium (K); suitable for application to most plants.

Annual: a plant that starts from seed and grows, flowers, and produces a fruit and seeds in one season. Marigolds and Impatiens are examples.

Balled and burlapped: describes a tree or shrub grown in the field on which the soilball was wrapped with protective burlap and twine when the plant was dug for relocation.

Bare root: describes plants that have been packaged without any soil around their roots. (Often young shrubs and trees purchased through the mail arrive with their exposed roots covered with moist peat or sphagnum moss, sawdust, or similar material, and wrapped in plastic.)

Barrier plant: a plant that has intimidating thorns or spines and is sited purposely to block foot traffic or other access to a property.

Basal: Growing at the base or bottom of a plant.

Beneficial insects: insects or their larvae that prey on pest organisms and their eggs. They may be flying insects, such as ladybugs, parasitic wasps, praying mantids, and soldier bugs; or soil dwellers such as predatory nematodes, spiders, and ants.

Berm: a raised, elongated, hill-like soil mass used as a barrier or to screen out undesirable sights and sounds. Often planted with trees, shrubs, and grass.

Biennial: A plant requiring 2 seasons to produce seed-growing a rosette of foliage from seed the first year; producing flowers, fruit, and seed the second year; and dying.

Bract: a modified leaf structure usually subtending the flower, resembling a petal, and often more colorful than the flower, as in Dogwood.

Canopy: the crown of a tree, usually referring to its volume and including branches and foliage.

Chlorosis: yellowing of leaves due to a failure to develop chlorophyll; often due to high soil pH or nutrient deficiencies.

Cold hardiness: the ability of a perennial plant to survive the anticipated low temperatures in a particular geographic area.

Composite: plants characterized by flower heads consisting of petalless disk flowers surrounded by ray flowers each with a colorful petal. Sunflowers, Daisies, and Dandelions are composites.

Compost: organic matter that has undergone progressive decomposition by microbial and macrobial activity until it is reduced to a spongy, fluffy texture. Added to soil of any type, it improves the soil's ability to hold air and water and to drain well.

Corm: a swollen energy-storing bulb-like structure beneath the soil at the base of the stems of plants such as Crocus and Gladiolus.

Crown: center part of plant. The point at which the leaves and stems of a plant join the roots.

Cultivar: a cultivated variety. The correct nomenclature for a variety that is developed and persists under cultivation.

Deadhead: to remove faded flower heads from plants, improving their appearance, aborting seed production, and stimulating further flowering.

Deciduous plants: trees and shrubs that shed their leaves each fall.

Desiccation: drying out of plant tissues due to inability of roots or stem to provide sufficient water.

Dibble: a small, hand-held, pointed stick used to make holes in the soil for planting seedlings. Also, to poke a hole in the soil with a dibble.

Dioecious: plants bearing separate male and female flowers on different plants.

Division: the practice of splitting apart perennial plants to create several smaller segments, useful for controlling the plant's size and acquiring more plants; division may contribute to the health and continued flowering of some plants. Also, each divided segment is a division.

Dormancy: the rest period when perennial plants temporarily cease active growth.

Ecotype: a subspecies especially adapted to a specific environment or climate.

Established: the point at which a newly planted tree, shrub, or flower has overcome the effects of transplanting.

Evergreen: a perennial plant that does not shed its foliage with the onset of winter; the foliage persisting and functioning for two or more seasons.

Fallow: to keep soil free of all plants for a season or more, thus reducing subsequent weed problems.

Foliar: referring to the leaves of a plant.

Floret: a tiny individual flower, usually one of many, forming an inflorescence such as a panicle or head.

Fungicide: a pesticide used to control fungus diseases.

Frost-free date: average date of last frost (as compared to latest date of last frost).

Germinate: to begin growth as a plant from a seed.

Graft (union): a bud or shoot (scion) of a plant inserted into a groove or slit in another plant (stock) where it continues to grow.

Gynoecious: referring to female flowers, as in gynoecious plants (which have only female flowers).

Hardscape: the permanent, structural, nonplant parts of a landscape, such as walls, sheds, pools, patios, arbors, and walkways.

Herbaceous: plants having fleshy or soft stems that die back with frost; the opposite of woody.

Herbicide: a pesticide used to eliminate unwanted vegetation.

Hybrid: a plant that is the result of intentional or natural cross-pollination between two or more plants of the same or similar species or genus.

Latest date of last frost: the date after which frost does not occur in a locality.

Monoecious: plants bearing separate male and female flowers on the same plant.

Mulch: a covering of straw, compost, plastic sheeting, etc. spread on the ground around plants to reduce water loss, prevent weeds, and enrich the soil.

Naturalize: (a) to plant seeds, bulbs, or plants in a random, informal pattern as they would appear in their natural habitat; (b) to adapt to and spread throughout adopted habitats (a tendency of some nonnative plants).

Nectar: the sweet fluid produced by glands on flowers that attract pollinators such as hummingbirds and honeybees for whom it is a source of energy.

Organic material, organic matter: any material or debris that is derived from plants. It is carbon-based material capable of undergoing decomposition and decay.

Perennial: a plant that grows from seed, developing a plant for the first year, and flowering and producing fruit and seeds each year thereafter. Peonies, Daylilies, and Hostas are examples.

pH: soil pH is a measure of acidity or alkalinity. Soil is neutral at a pH of 7.0. Above 7.0, the soil is alkaline; below 7.0, the soil is acidic. Most garden plants prefer a pH of 6.0 to 7.0.

Pinch: to remove tender shoot tips to encourage branching, compactness, and flowering. Pinching can be used to remove aphids clustered at growing tips.

Pollen: the yellow, powdery grains in the center of a flower. A plant's male sex cells, they are transferred to the female plant parts by means of wind or animal pollinators to fertilize them and create seeds.

Pollination: fertilization of the female part of a flower by pollen from the male part of a flower.

Raceme: an arrangement of single stalked flowers along an elongated unbranched axis.

Rhizome: a root-like subterranean stem lying horizontally in the soil with roots emerging from its lower surface and shoots from growing points at or near its tip, as in Bearded Iris.

Rootbound (or potbound): the condition of a plant that has been confined in a container too long, its roots having filled the soil mass.

Root flare: the transition at the base of a tree trunk where the bark tissue begins to differentiate and roots begin to spread just before entering the soil. This area should not be covered with soil when planting a tree.

Root division: section of a root system used for propagation.

Rosette: a circular cluster of leaves on a compact, shortened stem; typical of many biennial plants during their first year of growth.

Self-seeding: refers to plants that spontaneously drop seed, thus perpetuating themselves.

Semievergreen: tending to be evergreen in a mild climate but deciduous in a rigorous one.

Shearing: the pruning technique whereby plant stems and branches are cut uniformly with long-bladed pruning shears (hedge shears) or powered hedge trimmers. It is used when creating and maintaining hedges and topiary.

Seedbed: finely tilled soil suitable for sowing seed. Also, a bed so prepared.

Side-dress: to apply fertilizer next to the rows of plants at about half the normal rate, thus avoiding damage from getting fertilizer on the growing plants. Sidedressing is usually applied about mid-season after the preplant fertilizers have begun to run out.

Slow-acting fertilizer: fertilizer that is water insoluble and therefore releases its nutrients gradually as a function of soil temperature, moisture, and related microbial activity. Typically granular, it may be organic or synthetic.

Soil types: sand, silt, clay or loam, etc., describing the coarseness or fineness of the soil.

Stolon: a horizontal stem growing along the soil surface, and producing roots and shoots at nodes. A runner.

Succulent growth: the sometimes undesirable production of fleshy, water-storing leaves or stems that results from overfertilization.

Sucker: undesirable shoots arising from the roots of a plant near the base or a short distance from the base. Some plants produce suckers as a result of pruning or wounding.

Tender perennial: a perennial plant that is unable to tolerate the winter temperatures in a particular climate.

Till: to work the soil by spading, digging, cultivating, rototilling, etc.

Tilth: physical condition of the soil.

Tuber: a short, thickened underground stem, often with small scale-like buds from which arise new plants. Dahlias develop tubers.

Variegated: having various colors or color patterns. The term usually refers to plant foliage that is streaked, edged, blotched, or mottled with a contrasting color, often green with yellow, cream, or white.

Variety: a cultivar.

Vegetative propagation: propagation by means of cuttings, divisions, or grafting.

Water sprouts: vigorous vertical sprouts growing from the base, trunk, or scaffold branches of a tree.

Wings: (*a*) the corky tissue that forms edges along the twigs of some woody plants such as Winged Euonymus; (*b*) the flat, dried extension of tissue on some seeds, such as those from Maples.

Woody plant: any plant developing stems that persist from year to year.

Zone: a region that differs significantly by climate and temperature from adjacent areas.

Extension Phone Numbers

Adams	217 223-8380
Alexander	618 745-6310
Bond	618 664-3665
Boone	815 544-3710
Brown	217 773-3013
Bureau	815 875-2878
Calhoun	618 576-2293
Carroll	815 244-9444
Cass	217 452-3211
Champaign	217 333-7672
Christian	217 287-7246
Clark	217 826-5422
Clay	618 665-3328
Clinton	618 526-4551
Coles	217 345-7034
Cook - Chicago North	773 755-2223
Cook - Chicago South	773 737-1178
Cook - North Surburban	847 818-2901
Cook - South Surburban	708 720-7500
Crawford	618 546-1549
Cumberland	217 849-3931
De Kalb	815 758-8194
De Witt	217 935-5764
Douglas	217 543-3755
DuPage	630 653-4114
Edgar	217 465-8585
Edwards	618 445-2934
Effingham	217 347-7773
Fayette	618 283-2753
Ford	815 268-4051
Franklin	618 439-3178
Fulton	309 547-3711
Gallatin	618 269-3049
Greene	217 942-6996
Grundy	815 942-0177
Hamilton	618 643-3416
Hancock	217 357-2150
Hardin	618 287-8673
Henderson	309 924-1163
Henry	309 853-1533
Iroquois	815 268-4051
Jackson	618 687-1727
Jasper	618 783-2521
Jefferson	618 242-0780
Jersey	618 498-2913
Jo Daviess	815 858-2273
Johnson	618 658-5321
Kane	630 584-6166
Kankakee	815 933-8337
Kendall	630 553-5824
Knox	309 342-5108
Lake	847 223-8627
LaSalle	815 433-0707
Lawrence	618 943-5018
Lee	815 857-3525
Livingston	815 842-1776
Logan	217 732-8289
Macon	217 877-6042
Macoupin	217 854-9604
Madison	618 692-7700
Marion	618 548-1446
Marshall	309 364-2356
Mason	309 543-3308
Massac	618 524-2270
McDonough	309 837-3939
McHenry	815 338-4747
McLean	309 663-8306
Menard	217 632-7491
Mercer	309 582-5106
Monroe	618 939-3434
Montgomery	217 532-3941
Morgan	217 243-7424
Moultrie	217 543-3755
Ogle	815 732-2191
Peoria	309 686-6033
Perry	618 357-2126
Piatt	217 762-2191
Pike	217 285-5543
Pope	618 683-8555
Pulaski	618 745-6310
Putnam	309 364-2356
Randolph	618 443-4364
Richland	618 395-2191
Rock Island	309 796-0512
Saline	618 252-8391
Sangamon	217 782-4617
Schuyler	217 322-3381
Scott	217 742-9572
Shelby	217 774-9546
St. Clair	618 236-8600
Stark	309 853-1533
Stephenson	815 235-4125
Tazewell	309 347-6614
Union	618 833-6363
Vermilion	217 442-8615
Wabash	618 262-5725
Warren	309 734-5161
Washington	618 327-8881
Wayne	618 842-3702
White	618 382-2662
Whiteside	815 772-4075
Will	815 727-9296
Williamson	618 993-3304
Winnebago	815 987-7379
Woodford	309 467-3789

Plant Societies

Garden clubs and plant societies are great places to learn more about gardening and plants. Members trade knowledge, resources, and often plants. In many cases you will need to contact the national organization to find the club nearest you. For those with access to the Internet, you may want to look up individual plant societies. Any good search engine, such as Google, will locate them for you using the society name for the keyword. An excellent site is the Iowa State University Guide to Plant Societies and Associations: www.extension.iastate.edu/Publications/PM1357.pdf. Then select the society you want.

Single Plant Societies

AZALEA
Azalea Society Of America, Inc.
Membership Chairman
PO Box 34536
West Bethesda, MD 20827-0536
301-365-0692
www.azaleas.org

Dir. of Public Info.
7613 Quintana Ct.
Bethesda, MD 20817
301-365-0692

BEGONIA
American Begonia Society
Greater Chicago Branch
6339 S. Kenneth
Chicago, IL 60629
773-582-7911

John Ingles, Jr.
157 Monument Rd.
Rio Dell, CA 95562
707-764-5407

BOXWOOD
American Boxwood Society
134 Methodist Church Lane
West Augusta, VA 24485
540-939-4646

BULBOUS PLANTS
International Bulb Society
Dave Lehmiller, Membership Director
550 IH-10 South, Suite 201
Beaumont, TX 77707
www.bulbsociety.com

CRABAPPLE
International Crabapple Society
David Allen Holden Arboretum
9500 Sperry Rd.
Kirtland, OH 44094
216-256-1655

CHRYSANTHEMUM
National Chrysanthemum Society
10107 Homar Pond Drive
Fairfax Station, VA 22039-1650
703-978-7981

CONIFER
American Conifer Society
PO Box 360
Keswick, VA 22947
804-984-3660

DAFFODIL
American Daffodil Society, Inc.
4126 Winfield Rd.
Columbus, OH 43220-4606
614-451-4747
614-451-2177

Midwest Daffodil Society at Chicago Botanic Garden
20753 N. Buffalo Run
Kildeer, IL 60047
708-438-5309

DAHLIA
American Dahlia Society, Inc.
1 Rock Falls Court
Rockville, MD 20854
202-326-3516

Central States Dahlia Society
440 N. Elizabeth St.
Lombard, IL 60148-1552

Southtown Dahlia Club
14408 Long Ave.
Midlothian, IL 60445
708-385-6155

Tri-City Dahlia Society
534 26th Ave.
Moline, IL 61265

DAYLILY
American Hemerocallis Society
1454 Rebel Drive
Jackson, MS 39211-6334
601-366-4362
www.daylilies.org/daylilies.html

Chicagoland Daylily Society
9225 S. Claremont Ave.
Chicago, IL 60620

Northshore Iris & Daylily Society
511 Seminary
Park Ridge, IL 60068-9999
847-696-0240

EPIPHYLLUM
American Fern Society, Inc.
David B. Lellinger
326 West St. NW
Vienna, VA 22180-4151
www.amerfernsoc.org

Epiphyllum Society of America
PO Box 2395
Monrovia, CA 91017-1395
310-670-8148

GERANIUM
International Geranium Society
Mid-West Association
11441 Hwy 275
Council Bluffs, IA 51503-7053
760-727-0309

GINKGO
International Golden Fossil Tree Society
2530 Atlantic
Waukegan, IL 60148

GLADIOLUS
North American Gladiolus Council
RR #1 Box 70
Belgrade, ME 04917

HOLLY
Holly Society Of North America
11318 W. Murdock
Wichita, KS 67212-6609

HOSTA
American Hosta Society
Robyn Duback
7802 NE 63rd St.
Vancouver, WA 98662
E-mail: giboshiman@aol.com

Northern Illinois Hosta Society
22W070 Stratford Ct.
Glen Ellyn, IL 60137
630-469-9091

HYDROPONIC
Hydroponic Society of America
PO Box 1183
El Cerrito, CA 94530
510-232-2323

INDOOR GARDENING
Windy City Indoor Gardeners
1603 S. Highland Ave.
Arlington Heights, IL 60005
847-439-4312

IRIS
American Iris Society
Anner M. Whitehead, Membership Secretary
PO Box 1475
Richmond, VA 23221-4750
804-358-6202

Northshore Iris & Daylily Society
1514 N. Elston, 1st Floor
Chicago, IL 60622

Society For Siberian Irises
PO Box 445
Parkdale, OR 97041
507-332-8437

Species Iris Group Of North America
18341 Paulson St. SW
Rochester, WA 98579

The Society For Japanese Irises
9823 E. Michigan Ave.
Galesburg, MI 49053
616-665-7500

IVY
American Ivy Society
PO Box 2123
Naples, FL 34106-2123

LILAC
International Lilac Society, Inc.
Robert S. Gilbert, Assistant Treasurer
PO Box 83
Hyde Park, NY 12538
216-946-4400

LILY
North American Lily Society, Inc.
Executive Secretary
PO Box 272
Owatonna, MN 55060-0272
507-451-2170

Wisconsin - Illinois Lily Society
520 Orchard Lane
Winnetka, IL 60093
847-446-2574
847-733-0074

NATIVE PLANT
Illinois Dunesland Preservation Society
PO Box 446
Zion, IL 60099
847-746-1090

Illinois Native Plant Society
Forest Glen Preserve
20301 E. 900 North Rd.
Westville, IL 61883
217-662-2142
217-662-2146

Illinois Native Plant Society
Northeastern Chapter
39W684 Caribou Trail
St. Charles, IL 60175
630-443-6126

PERENNIAL
Perennial Plant Association
3383 Schirtzinger Rd.
Hilliard, OH 43026
614-771-8431
614-876-5238

PONDS AND KOI
Midwest Pond & Koi Society
PO Box 1251
North Riverside, IL 60546
708-460-9209

RHODODENDRON
American Rhododendron Society
11 Pinecrest Dr.
Fortuna, CA 95540
707-725-3043

Midwest Chapter of American Rhododendron Society
1583 Bedlington Dr.
Barrington, IL 60010

ROCK & ALPINE GARDENING
North American Rock Garden Society
Executive Secretary
PO Box 67
Millwood, NY 10546
www.nargs.org

ROSE

American Rose Society
PO Box 30,000
Shreveport, LA 71130-5405
800-637-6534
Fax: 318-938-9405

Heritage Rose Group
W6365 Wald Rd.
Monroe, WI 53566
608-325-3695

TREE

National Arbor Day Foundation
John Rosenow, President
100 Arbor Ave.
Nebraska City, NE 68410
402-474-5655
www.arborday.org

WATER LILY

International Water Lily and Water Gardening Society
1410 Johnson Ferry Rd.
Ste. 328-G12
Marietta, GA 30062-8115
770-929-6601
Fax: 770-517-5746
E-mail: info@iwgs.org

WILDFLOWER

Lake To Prairie Wild Ones
1411 Wild Iris Lane
Grayslake, IL 60030
847-548-1649

National Wildflower Research Center
Du Page Chapter
924 E. 4th Ave.
Aurora, IL 60505-4938
630-820-1584

North Park Chapter
5801 N. Pulaski Rd.
Chicago, IL 60646
773-594-0012

Rock River Valley Chapter
3733 Freeport Rd.
Rockton, IL 61072
815-624-6076

First Fall Frost Average Dates

Median Dates

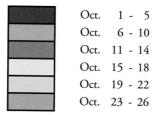

Oct.	1 - 5
Oct.	6 - 10
Oct.	11 - 14
Oct.	15 - 18
Oct.	19 - 22
Oct.	23 - 26

Illinois State
Climatologist Office,
Illinois State Water Survey

Last Spring Frost Average Dates

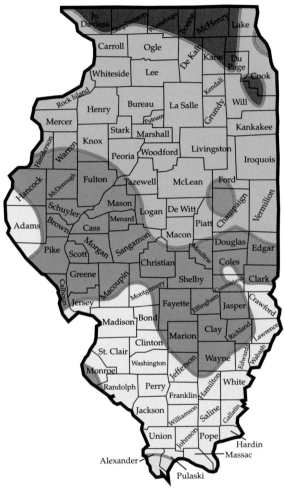

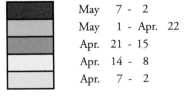

Median Dates

May 7 - 2
May 1 - Apr. 22
Apr. 21 - 15
Apr. 14 - 8
Apr. 7 - 2

Illinois State
Climatologist Office,
Illinois State Water Survey

259

Total Precipitation in Inches

January 1 to December 31
Averaged from 1961 to 1990

30   35   40   45   50

Data from the "Midwestern Regional
Climate Center, Champaign, Illinois"

Bibliography

Bailey, L Hyde: *Standard Cyclopedia of Horticulture,* The Macmillan Company, NY, 1963.

Ball, Vic: *Ball Redbook,* Geo J. Ball, Inc., West Chicago, IL 1974.

Better Homes and Gardens: *Successful Rose Gardening,* Better Homes and Gardens Books, Des Moines IA, 1993.

Brickell, Christopher (Editor): *Encyclopedia of Garden Plants,* The American Horticultural Society, Macmillan Publishing Company, NY, 1997.

Bush-Brown and Bush-Brown: *America's Garden Book,* Scribners, NY, 1953.

Chicago Botanic Garden, Glencoe IL.

DeHertogh, August: *Holland Bulb Forcer's Guide,* Michigan State University, 1977

Dirr, Michael: *Manual of Woody Landscape Plants, ed. 4* Stipes Publishing Co., Urbana IL, 1990.

Fizzell, James A: *Month-by-Month Gardening in Illinois,* Cool Springs Press, Franklin TN, 1999.

Fizzell, James A: *Month-by-Month Gardening in Indiana,* Cool Springs Press, Franklin TN, 1999.

Fizzell, James A: *Month-by-Month Gardening in Michigan,* Cool Springs Press, Franklin TN, 1999.

Hill, May B: *Grandmother's Garden: The Old-Fashioned American Garden,* Harry N Abrams , NY, 1995.

Holmes, Roger (Editor): *Taylor's Guide to Ornamental Grasses,* Houghton Mifflin Company, New York, 1997.

Loewer, Peter: *Ornamental Grasses,* Better Homes and Gardens Books, Des Moines IA, 1995.

Papworth, David: *Garden Ponds,* Salamander Books, Ltd., London, UK, 1984.

Reddell, Rayford C: *The Roses Bible,* Harmony Books, New York, NY, 1994.

Robinson, Peter: *Robinson Complete Guide to Water Gardening,* American Horticulture Society, DK Publishing Co., NY, 1997.

Robinson, Peter: *The Water Garden,* Sterling Publishing Co., NY, 1995.

Runkel S and Bull A: *Wildflowers of Illinois Woodlands,* Iowa State University Press, 1994.

Runkel S and Roosa D: *Wildflowers of the Tallgrass Prairie: The Upper Midwest, ed. 4* Iowa State University Press, 1994.

Still, Steven M: *Manual of Herbaceous Ornamental Plants, ed. 4* Stipes Publishing Co., Urbana IL, 1994.

Swink F, and Wilhelm G: *Plants of the Chicago Region, ed. 4* Indiana Academy of Science, 1994.

Wilson, Andrew: *The Creative Water Gardener,* Sterling Publishing Co., NY, 1995.

Photography Credits

Thomas Eltzroth: pages 6, 16, 19, 20, 21, 24, 26, 27, 28, 30, 31, 32, 33, 34, 35, 36, 37, 42, 43, 44, 45, 47, 50, 51, 53, 54, 57, 58, 61, 62, 63, 64, 66, 67, 69, 72, 76, 77, 78, 79, 80, 87, 88, 89, 90, 91, 94, 97, 99, 103, 104, 105, 106, 107, 108, 110, 111, 113, 114, 115, 116, 117, 119, 120, 121, 122, 124, 125, 127, 129, 132, 134, 140, 144, 145, 146, 148, 150, 151, 152, 157, 159, 165, 172, 177, 182, 184, 185, 189, 192, 193, 194, 196, 197, 198, 199, 200, 201, 203, 205, 206, 207, 209, 213, 215, 216, 218, 219, 225, 229, 231, 233, 234, 235, 240, 247, and the photos on the back cover

Liz Ball and Rick Ray: pages 10, 12, 13, 17, 18, 23, 40, 41, 48, 49, 52, 55, 56, 60, 68, 70, 75, 93, 95, 96, 101, 102, 133, 143, 147, 149, 154, 158, 164, 168, 174, 178, 179, 186, 190, 210, 211, 214, 217, 221, 222, 230, 232, 238

Pam Harper: pages 29, 38, 73, 112, 131, 137, 138, 139, 141, 142, 153, 156, 166, 167, 171, 176, 180, 187, 188, 212, 243

William Adams: pages 39, 84, 204, 226, 227, 228, 245, 248

Charles Mann: pages 46, 74; 86, 100, 130, 135, 163, 169

Dency Kane: pages 22, 81, 92, 109, 136, 242

Ralph Snodsmith: pages 9, 59, 126, 155, 160, 173

Michael Dirr: pages 128, 162, 175, 191

Jerry Pavia: pages 83, 183, 237, 239

Rob Cardillo: pages 65, 98, 244

Robert Lyons: pages 71, 82, 208

© 2002 Mark Turner: pages 236, 241, 246

Cathy Barash: pages 181, 224

Tim Boland and Laura Coit: pages 170, 249

Greg Speichert: pages 220, 223

Bruce Asakawa: page 123

Lorenzo Gunn: page 25

Dave MacKenzie: page 85

© Martien Vinkesteijn/gardenIMAGE: page 202

Index

Meet James Fizzell

Photo by Jane Fizzell

James A. Fizzell is best known as the Staff Horticulturist on Chicago's WGN radio where he has answered garden questions for more than 40 years. As President of James A. Fizzell & Associates, the author provides consulting services to the commercial horticulture industry. The author's projects include serving as a consultant on such important landmarks as Wrigley Field, Chicago's O'Hare and Midway airports, and assisting the Chicago Park District. He is often featured on television, radio and in leading trade journals and has become a celebrated guest speaker.

For nearly 30 years, the author served as horticulturist with the University of Illinois extension service in northeastern Illinois. In that capacity he wrote gardening columns for 200 newspapers in the Midwest, and hundreds of articles for commercial horticulture trade publications. He is author of many popular gardening books. Other books Fizzell has written for Cool Springs Press include the first edition of the *Illinois Gardener's Guide, Month-by-Month Gardening in Illinois, Month-by-Month Gardening in Indiana, Month-by-Month Gardening in Michigan* and *The Midwest Fruit and Vegetable Book.*

Fizzell holds degrees in horticulture from the University of Illinois. The esteemed horticulturist has received many honors including the prestigious Linnaeus Award from the Chicago Horticulture Society for lifetime service to horticulture. The author's contributions include his instrumental role in developing the Master Gardener Program in Illinois, and in forming the Illinois Landscape Contractors Association and the Illinois Arborist Association. He authored the Illinois Arborist Certification program and edited the certification exam. Fizzell has resided in many parts of the country, where he developed nursery production facilities and trained the staff to manage them.

The author and his wife, Jane, enjoy gardening at their Northern Illinois home on Garden Street.